Dante's
REBELLIOUS
ANGEL

Dante's REBELLIOUS ANGEL

Arletta Maria Wozniak

Translation: Limitless Mind Publishing
Proofreading: Karolina Kadluczka
Text Composition: InkWander
Technical Correction: Joanna Sosnowka, Karolina Kadluczka
Cover Design: Monika Zalewska

ISBN: 9788397392601

Limitless Mind Publishing Ltd
15 Carleton Road
Chichester
PO19 3NX
England
Tel. +44 7747761146
Email: office@limitlessmindpublishing.com

Dear Reader!

*Find us on **Facebook/Instagram:***
limitless mind publishing

*And visit our page on **Amazon***
by entering: limitless mind publishing into the search bar
or by scanning the QR code to see our other titles.

♥ We would greatly appreciate your opinion. It means a lot to us.

BEGGED BY THE DEVIL,
HATED BY PEOPLE,
LOVED BY HIM.

HELL

CHRISTMAS EVE IN HELL

Right after baby Jesus was born, my uncle slipped his hand into my underwear. I was about nine years old. It was Christmas Eve. But he wasn't my real uncle. He was some drifter who showed up in our house without anyone knowing when or why. He seemed to have come only to cause harm. But I learned not to feel. Because what's the point?

What a wonderful holiday atmosphere!

Christmas Eve has always been the most important day for me. It was a magical day, a special one. Don't ask why, because I don't know myself.

Something drew me to that day. I waited for it all year. *Just believe that it was so, without questioning why*, as a certain Italian poet and philosopher, whom I'll mention more than once, used to say. Anyway, Christmas Eve was and still is a symbol for me. Of what? I don't even know. It's associated with happiness, but was it always? I doubt it! As a child, I spent Christmas Eve in hell. Each one had something strange, suspicious about it, but the worst was when I was about nine years old.

I don't remember most of the Christmas Eves from my childhood. The ones that do stick in my mind aren't associated with anything good. I tried to cover them with other memories, but they keep leaking out and demanding to be remembered. Yet today, I'm an adult, and I've lived through many Christmas Eve dinners since childhood. Were they better than those from my early years? Some could compete with those distant memories. I'll talk about them later.

What do children associate Christmas Eve with? It's easy to guess. Mostly with presents. Except, I don't really remember the gifts I got as a child under the Christmas tree. I don't remember any, except one. It was a book. I devoured books passionately and received them on other occasions too. What book? I won't reveal that just yet, because I don't want to spoil the story. And other presents? I know there were some. But I don't recall the details. All those memories have evaporated from my mind, or rather, I forced them out. Only scraps remain, flashes. Nothing concrete.

"Look at this marvel!" my mother smiled in one of them.

"And are you happy?" my father looked at me with a strange expression.

Other than that, nothing. Everything has vanished into the past. Yes, in some distant memory, I see my parents bustling in the kitchen. I assume they're frying carp, which no one at home liked anyway. But such is tradition: Carp must be on the Christmas Eve table. Nonsense! And then the fish would end up in the trash.

Do I remember anything else from Christmas Eve when I was a child? Maybe some scents. Maybe the nerves while breaking the wafer. Insincere wishes. Boredom. Impatience. And always fear. That was a given. Everyone only watched my father. They tried to gauge his mood. The family tried to determine whether he was already upset or if he was about to explode. His mood marked not only Christmas Eve but every other day, our everyday life at home.

Christmas Eve. The day when you wanted to scream, like the poet mentioned earlier:

"Lasciate ogne speranza, voi ch'intrate!"

Or in English:

"Abandon all hope, ye who enter here!"

Here, into hell! Christmas Eve in hell had just begun.

Everything seemed to unfold like any other Christmas Eve, but from the morning, I knew something bad would happen. I just felt it. This anxiety filled me, pushing against every part of my body. Instead of enjoying the Christmas tree, the presents, singing carols, I was waiting for something inevitably bad. And the bad came.

The doorbell rang out in a drawn-out moan, as if lamenting its own fate. Then silence comforted it. Short but somehow very deep. And again, the doorbell groaned. This time, the complaint was clearer, more pronounced, louder. Right after the bell came knocking – insistent, impatient.

"Is someone going to open that goddamn door or not?!" my father yelled from the bathroom.

Mother looked at us as if expecting someone to rush to the door.

But none of her children moved a muscle.

"Of course, don't trouble yourselves," she sighed and shuffled off to open it.

As soon as she left the kitchen, we attacked the bowl where she had been mixing with a wooden spoon. We greedily scooped out the sweet cream, which was supposed to go into the holiday cake.

Suddenly, something struck me. I licked my finger clean and wiped it on my shirt. I peeked out of the kitchen.

In the hallway, my mother was adjusting her hair in front of the mirror. Suddenly, she remembered she was wearing an apron. She shook her head in disbelief, untied it, and threw it on the dresser.

Meanwhile, the knocking persisted.

"If I get out there, I'll...!" my father threatened from the bathroom.

I leaned out of the kitchen a bit more as my mother opened the door. She stepped back because he entered. Uncle. That's what he made us call him, but he wasn't our uncle at all. Julius Romer – about forty years old. To this day, I don't know if that was his real last name or if it referred to his origins. He was swarthy, and his eyes were always shifty. Mother claimed he was Italian, but I don't believe that. He probably hadn't seen an Italian in his life.

"Jules, isn't it a bit early?" Mother laughed, fluttering her lashes oddly.

Uncle chuckled.

"I came, I saw, I emptied!" he declared, pulling a bottle of vodka from behind his back.

That's when my siblings joined me – Ursula, Lydia, and Walter. We stood there with cream-smeared hands, staring at the scene in the hallway.

"Jules, did you bring the fuel?" my father called from the bathroom. "Because you know, I'll be here for a while."

"No worries, master. Take your time!" The Romer shouted back and placed his hand on our mother's butt.

She didn't resist at all. She just giggled. Meanwhile, the Swarthy man groped her backside with increasing enthusiasm.

"Come on, stop it," she said, but not very convincingly.

"Is that how you welcome me?" he laughed.

Then mother glanced nervously at the bathroom door.

"We're not alone," she noted.

"You're worried about him?"

She shook her head.

"I'm talking about them," she indicated us with her eyes.

Terrified, we hid back in the kitchen. We waited. Punishment was inevitable. For the cream we ate. For spying. Yes, punishment was guaranteed if the father found out. He never let punishment slide. He applied it with relish. Maybe it even aroused him.

We waited in that kitchen, trembling more and more. But my father didn't come. Nor did my mother. Instead, the Romer appeared.

"Is it nice to spy?" he asked right away.

We hung our heads.

"So, your mom and dad didn't teach you manners?" the Swarthy man shook his head. "What do you say when someone arrives?"

"Good day," we said almost in unison.

He stared at us for a moment, then suddenly smiled.

"What, aren't you going to give your uncle a hug?" he asked in disbelief, spreading his arms.

We instinctively recoiled. He didn't like that.

His smile faded. He moved. He grabbed me first.

"Merry Christmas," he said.

Then I felt his hand in my underwear. I tried to break free, but he was too strong.

Finally, he let me go. He approached my older sister. But Ursula was lucky. Mother finally came into the kitchen. I immediately noticed she had changed into an elegant floral dress.

"We're not ready yet," she announced.

"That's fine, I'm not in a hurry," Julius said, ruffling my brother's hair. Walter, not understanding much, smiled timidly.

That's when father appeared in the kitchen doorway.

The table in the room was large. It was the most important place in our home. If my father taught me anything in life, it was the importance of family meals together. It was our daily ritual. We gathered around that table almost every day. If someone was late, father would get terribly angry, and a fight would break out.

So, it's no surprise that on Christmas Eve, we also sat at our table. And we were not allowed to be late. We gathered around the table where father usually slurped his soup with delight, keeping a constant watch on us. On Christmas Eve, he slurped too. Red borscht dripped down his chin. Father wiped it off from time to time with the cuff of his white shirt and laughed at the Romer's jokes.

"Holy crap, you're killing me!" he would say occasionally, patting the guest on the shoulder.

The Swarthy man just nodded. And so, the minutes passed, hours dragged on, and we sat at that wretched table.

"Maybe we should open the presents?" Mother suddenly suggested. "The kids are getting impatient."

Father looked at us with a red face, as if he didn't quite understand what she was talking about.

Then the Romer spoke up:

"Fuck that, what is this? When we finish the bottle, then there'll be presents!

The most important thing is tradition! First the Christmas Eve dishes and drinks."

He stood up, clutching the bottle and began pouring vodka into glasses. He did it clumsily, his hand shaking. He spilled more than he poured. Finally, he shouted:

"Cheers!" Then, downed the shot in one go.

My parents just watched him, and my father even made some kind of grimace.

We watched in silence as this strange spectacle of hypocrisy and degeneracy unfolded. The clinking of glasses mixed with the Romer's drunken laughter and the occasional curses from my father. The head of our family sat at the head of the table, across from him sat the Romer, although he often left his seat to pour more alcohol. Interestingly, our mother, my father's wife, sat right next to the Swarthy man. When he wasn't running around with the bottle or slapping my father on the back, he was groping our mother under the table. We saw it clearly, and the Romer didn't even bother to hide it. At first, he kept his hand on her knee. Then he moved it higher, lifting the floral dress as he went. He fondled her thigh. And then his hand went even higher. Mother didn't resist at all. She pretended nothing was happening or that she didn't notice. Sometimes she would just jump up from the table to put something on my father's plate or to bring out a new dish. And so, this drunken Christmas Eve feast of the damned continued. How did it begin? As if traditionally.

"Listen, we're going to share the wafer now," Mom announced once everyone had finally gathered in the living room.

"Let the little ones go first," the Romer said, glancing at Dad as if seeking his approval.

When no reaction came, he waved his hand dismissively and resumed his ritual with the bottle.

How did this guy even end up at our Christmas Eve? He was lonely, so Mom and Dad invited him. I'll tell you more about him later, but not now. Why ruin Christmas Eve with such characters? Traditionally, Dad would first share the wafer with Mom. Then he looked at us, shrugged, and said,

"Let's do this together since everything's getting cold. My dear children, I wish you always obey me. Always be obedient to your father. And may everything be good!"

The Romer shared the wafer with our mom first. At the end, he pressed his lips against hers in a kiss.

"Well, well!" Dad laughed. "What a sight!"

Then the Swarthy man turned to share the wafer with us. That's when, for the second time that night, I felt his hand in my underwear.

"The first star's probably already gone to hell, but oh well." Dad rubbed his hands together. "Let's sit down for dinner."

And so, the feasting dragged on, taking its turns, hitting its peaks, but without any surprises. Time crawled by painfully until finally, Dad bellowed,

"It's time for presents, goddammit!"

What gift did I get under the tree that Christmas Eve? It was the only one I still remember to this day. I eagerly tore off the decorative paper to reveal a thick book with a hard cover. It was a truly beautiful edition. I still have it. That book marked my life in ways I never imagined. I received Dante's *The Divine Comedy*. Surprised? I was too. Who thought of buying me such a book? I had no idea. I never found out. But I was immediately engrossed in the reading. Back then, I didn't even realize what I was holding in my hands. I had no idea who this Dante was or why he wrote in such a strange way. And yet, I couldn't tear myself away from the book. It was as if I had suddenly been transported to another world. In an instant, I escaped the suffocating space of our apartment. I sat on the couch and read. And nothing else mattered anymore.

That's when the Romer sat next to me. I immediately felt uneasy.

"So, do you like your little present?" he laughed, his piggish eyes gleaming as he glanced at me.

Then I felt his hand in my underwear again. For the third time that night. I could feel it as everyone around me sang the carol:

"Today in Bethlehem, today in Bethlehem, a joyful message..."

Even Uncle was singing, without taking his hand out of my underwear.

Neither the first, second, nor third rooster crowed. The whole world couldn't care less about what was being done to me while Christ was being born. Because this was my hell.

Welcome to it!

And then they sang another carol. And another. And the whole world celebrated.

And you? Did you celebrate too?

If you're not afraid, come with me to the first circle of hell. Do you want to get to know these sinners better? Are you ready for it? I will be your guide. Because I know hell the best.

CHAPTER 1

My father was a tyrant, a mentally ill bastard! How else could I explain his behavior toward his children? I can't imagine hitting someone I love, yet he beat us at every turn for the slightest thing. He beat us for nothing, really. Apparently, the mere fact that we existed was reason enough for him. He might as well have beaten us for the sun rising or setting. The reason didn't matter. Today, I think that what was important to him was the act of beating itself. Maybe it compensated for some kind of inferiority complex? Maybe it was his way of fighting his own demons? Maybe he believed that by beating us bloody, he would raise us to be... What, exactly? Tyrants like him? Or maybe he just didn't love us? I don't recall ever hearing those words from him. He would mumble something sometimes.

"You know... I..." he tried to explain something to my sister once, then added, "Did you do your homework?"

Another time, he looked at me with what seemed like a trace of affection. He opened his mouth, and I was sure he was about to say something kind, but instead, he snapped,

"Damn it, are you slacking off again?"

And that was my father's way of expressing love.

Or maybe I just fooled myself into thinking he ever wanted to express any love. Such naive thinking. It wouldn't have been in his style anyway. I don't even know if my father ever expressed his feelings to my mother. It's hard for me to imagine that.

The worst part was the beatings. Whenever I came home, I wondered if I would get hit for something again. Often, instead of heading straight home, I would say to a friend,

"Shall we go to the meadow?"

Sometimes, such outings took hours. We would lie on the grass, counting sheep-shaped clouds. Other times, we wandered through the pastures, admiring the cows. Sometimes, we just went wherever our legs took us.

It was a way to forget about the bad things. About the inevitable sentence that had already been passed at home. Wandering around meant coming back later, which meant not being on time. Dad hated when someone was late, especially for dinner. That's when he wouldn't let it slide. "Well, now you've really done it!" he would yell furiously.

Then he would head to the old wardrobe we had at home. That's where he kept his best friend: a thick, wide leather belt. I never saw him wear it with his pants, though I knew he loved it. But Dad used his belt for entirely different purposes than it was intended for. It was his tool for administering corporal punishment. He would stand before the wardrobe for a moment, seemingly lost in thought. I don't know if he was contemplating something, pondering the meaning of what he was about to do, or just gathering his strength. Eventually, he would open the wardrobe, signaled by a loud creak. It was like a condemned man's groan or just a warning signal. I listened to it all, though I was terrified. Maybe only because I hoped I wouldn't hear any creaking. Such foolish hope. At some point, I would realize that my punishment was inevitable. I was a rebellious child, so it never occurred to me to beg Dad to spare me. Maybe also because I knew such pleas were ineffective.

"Dad, please, no!" my older sister would sometimes beg.

"I'll be better! Dad, spare me this time!" she pleaded at other times.

Yes, pleas were useless. Dad never even hesitated.

He always administered the belt punishment firmly, decisively, and mercilessly. We all knew this, but some of us couldn't take it. I never begged. Never. I was too stubborn for that.

We also knew we couldn't count on any rescue. The final word always belonged to Dad. I don't remember Mom ever defending us. I think she was afraid of him too. If I think about it deeply, I'm not surprised. Yet, I still feel some resentment. It shouldn't surprise anyone that I have few good memories from my childhood. But there are plenty of bad ones. Yes, in our family, there was no room for love, or at least for showing it. So, I keep coming back to the question of whether my father loved us. Did he love me? For years, I made it clear to everyone that I didn't care. I even tried to convince myself of that. But was that really the case? They say that hatred is close to love. And hatred pulsed between me and my father. And that's how it stayed. Some may find that shocking, but they would change their minds if they lived through what I did. Don't believe me? I can give you countless examples.

There were many smaller and larger events in my childhood that consistently destroyed my psyche and that of my siblings. Each of these events was like poison, slowly but relentlessly seeping in. It mercilessly eroded my sensitivity, distorted my dreams and plans. I could make an entire list of such events. Like the time we came home, and our parents were bustling around, watching whatever was on TV. Mom was standing by the wardrobe, getting ready for her second shift, and Dad, sitting at the table, was scribbling something on a newspaper. Nothing out of the ordinary, except for the fact that a porn movie was playing on TV. Yes, porn! And it happened repeatedly! Just an ordinary day, 1:00 PM. Everything seemed normal. Seemed! At that time, other people were watching soap operas, but in our home, it was goddamn porn! Dad thought there was nothing wrong with us kids watching it. Watch all you want!

All these childhood events drained me of any joy a young person should have when stepping into life and discovering the world. I had no joy left. Instead, I knew that even the slightest incident, especially a negative one, could end in Dad's cursing or a beating. I vividly remember, for example, when they cut off our electricity at home. Nowadays, no one can imagine life without electricity. I don't blame them; I can't imagine it either. Electrical power is as vital to us today as air. Without it, we become helpless, blind, and feeble. Its absence was already painfully felt by me years ago. I experienced it firsthand.

"A power outage?!" my older sister Ursula blurted out.

It was evening. We were sitting with our books, doing homework, when suddenly everything went dark.

"I can't see anything," I said rashly.

In response, I heard Dad curse.

"Is it a power outage?" Ursula kept asking. "It's so dark!"

"It's night; it's supposed to be dark," Dad replied philosophically, but it wasn't a deep thought at all. I immediately noticed that. But I didn't comment.

"But I have a test tomorrow," Ursula sobbed. "How am I supposed to study in the dark?"

We heard the scrape of a chair being pushed back. That could only mean one thing: a beating. That's the first thing that came to my mind. Ursula must have thought so too because I heard her whimper. She was waiting. Waiting for the inevitable: Dad's first strike. We were all waiting with her, including Mom.

Suddenly, we heard Dad's rough voice:

"You should have studied when it was light!"

Then we heard his footsteps fading away. I was sure the beating had been postponed because of the darkness. Dad never forgot about overdue punishments. I remember getting a beating a month after I got a failing grade in math because Dad suddenly remembered it. Well, Mom helped him with that. One evening, she caught me reading *The Divine Comedy* at the table. She looked at the title and shook her head, then said,

"Instead of sitting with that all the time, you could improve your math." Then she suddenly asked, "Did you fix that failing grade from a month ago?"

It seemed innocent enough: "Did you fix that failing grade from a month ago?" but it was enough. Dad, who was dozing at the table, picked up on it. The facts connected. As a result, Dad got up, panting heavily, and trudged to the wardrobe. Slowly, almost with a sense of ceremony, he took out his leather belt – his tool of punishment. He whipped me doubly hard that time. Additionally, for not reminding him of the overdue punishment. During this time, Mom left. She didn't want to watch. To this day, I don't know if her "Did you fix that failing grade from a month ago?" was said accidentally or with premeditation.

With such experiences, I knew full well that Ursula's punishment had also been postponed. Likely until it was light again.

At first, we really thought it was a power outage. But it quickly became clear that the neighbors had power. It was everywhere, except in our home. Our parents didn't say anything about it. We had to live by candlelight for a while. It wasn't a short period. We ate by candlelight, studied by candlelight, and did our homework by candlelight. It was hard to educate ourselves in such conditions. As a result, we started getting worse grades at school. For Dad, that was another excuse to beat us. And Ursula got a double beating. You know, the overdue punishment. That's how I learned that even small matters could become a pretext for a beating. It led to neurosis. No one knew anymore when the belt-tormentor would strike. It could happen at any moment.

Why did they cut off our power? It turned out that our parents hadn't paid the bill because there was no money. So, we lived by candlelight for a while. The lack of power also became an excuse for a beating. Yes, a beating was good for everything. At least in my father's opinion. I'm sure he believed his disciplinary methods were the best in the world! As a result, we, as children, were treated like little toy soldiers who had to follow orders without a word of protest. If we resisted or misbehaved, there was a beating. Again, a beating! Over and over. For many years. Maybe not every day, but certainly every week. That's what my childhood was like. Hard to believe, right? Today, I can say it was strange, even terrifying. But as a child, it seemed completely normal to me. I thought that's just how it was. I thought that all parents ruled with an iron fist and didn't tolerate dissent. After all, everyone complained about their "old folks." It was common at school, in the yard, everywhere. I didn't realize back then that something was off in our family. Well, maybe I had some suspicions because there were also completely terrifying things, but I'll tell you about them in the next chapter. Besides, I thought that family was inherently oppressive and that there was nothing I could change. That doesn't mean, of course, that I liked it. But I didn't have the strength to change anything. I didn't have other, better role models. So, I was stuck in this whole mess, not even fully aware that it was a mess. I was sinking into it, getting more and more bogged down, as year after year passed. All of this affected my psyche because it had to. Every day, my father's oppressive disciplinary methods hung over me and my siblings like an ax that would inevitably fall one day, but no one knew when. Such anticipation made it impossible to live fully, to find joy in life. Everything was replaced by punishment – inevitable, painful, humiliating. Only sometimes was the beating replaced by other "disciplinary" methods.

"Get to the corner!" Dad would shout, and to emphasize his words, he would point to the corner of the room.

What did we do in such a corner? We had to kneel in silence, without a word, with our hands raised and our backs straight. Once, I knelt like that for several hours. During that time, my father relaxed on the couch, taking a nap. I couldn't take it anymore, but I was too afraid to move. Paradoxically, fear gave me strength then.

When Dad woke up, all I heard was:

"And what about you? Still slacking off in that corner?"

Yes, my childhood was at least strange. I was raised by a strict father whose names were Discipline and Obedience. There was no room for spontaneity or play in my family home, at least as far as I remember.

I didn't see the pathology of my family home as a child; I thought it was all normal. After all, it was my world, and I knew nothing else. That's how the '80s were.

No showing of affection. Frequent beatings. No, that's not the end of my father's sins and faults. In fact, this list is just beginning.

Next on the list would undoubtedly be the constant hard labor that my parents, especially Dad, subjected us to during our childhood.

"What, you don't want to work?" he would yell at us when we were already exhausted after one task or another.

"You are damn lazy brats!"

So, on the brink of despair, completely worn out and devoid of any hope, we would return to the grind. You could say that our lives revolved around school and work. There was always something to do, no time for boredom or laziness. No time to rest. Everything had to be done quickly and efficiently, regardless of the conditions outside. Woe to anyone who messed something up! You could immediately hear from Dad:

"We'll settle this when we get home!"

That essentially meant one thing: a beating until the leather belt in the wardrobe was soaked with blood. Less often, the punishment was replaced with kneeling in the corner.

Throughout our childhood, we constantly had to work on the farm, in the field, or during renovations. Our lives were hard, monotonous, and very tiring. Everything around us revolved around work. And Dad would only laugh heartily and repeat:

"Good! Very good! Hard work teaches discipline! Discipline gives a person value! Hard work never hurt anyone!"

Really? And what about the millions of poor souls who die every year around the world because they toil in terrible conditions in African mines, on Arab construction sites, at Siberian oil rigs? Did they all die out of boredom? My father didn't care. He had his prayer that he recited to his god of Hard Work:

"Give us more toil, O Lord!"

But it was mostly us children who were toiling.

Today, I can say that the only thing my father taught me was to work physically! And that's what my entire life looks like: Eternal physical toil! Why do I have to labor my entire life? Why can't I just live and enjoy life like other people do? Maybe I can't do anything else because no one taught me? They say hard physical work teaches perseverance, self-discipline, and determination. Bullshit! It mostly teaches you to hate the whole world, to envy, to scorn those who don't have to toil physically.

That's the truth about the work ethic!

What I've written so far isn't even the whole story. Surprised? If you had the misfortune of knowing my father, there would be no room for surprise.

He could come into my room and stare at me for several minutes without saying a word. I would be dying of fear because I had no idea what he wanted. Maybe I had done something wrong again? Maybe he came to announce that I would be punished? Or maybe I would just hear that I had disappointed him again? That uncertainty was the worst. It was like being suspended between one minute and the next, somewhere in between. In a place where you're not needed.

Finally, Dad would sigh, shake his head, and say in a voice full of disappointment:

"My God, why are you such an ugly child?"

Then he would leave, still shaking his head.

Jesus Christ! How can you say something like that to a child? Even as a joke, you don't make such remarks. You can imagine how I felt afterward. There were many such malicious comments and jabs, covering various aspects.

I've already mentioned that as a child, I was controlled. Dad directed me like a toy with a remote. I had to do what he commanded and be the way he wanted me to be. Throughout my childhood, I tried to live up to the version of "me" that Dad had imagined. I had to be the best, the smartest, the hardest working, to do everything better than others, better than my siblings, better than the children of our acquaintances. I had to learn better than the teacher's daughter, work harder than the neighbor's son, and so on. When I failed, there was a beating. No one ever asked me what I wanted.

No wonder that in the difficult situations I faced in childhood, rebellion became my weapon. It was my form of defense. I didn't know how else to stand up to Dad. I rebelled against everyone and everything. As a result, more and more complaints about me reached my parents. Dad reacted traditionally, by beating me with the belt until he was exhausted. Yes, I'll admit it. During such beatings, I often hoped he would have a heart attack from the exertion, that the devil would take him. At that time, I didn't know that devils don't take the wicked. So, my father just fainted from exhaustion, cursed, and beat me senselessly.

"I'll show you, you little brat!" he would hiss through clenched teeth. "I'll show you! You'll regret your antics!"

And just to be sure, he would hit even harder.

As I grew up, my rebellious nature deepened. I was constantly dissatisfied with life, with people, with myself. I often felt that no one really understood me. My rebellion caused me more and more problems. I started having trouble at school, couldn't find common ground with my peers, and increasingly tried to stand up to my parents.

I was a rebellious child, then a rebellious teenager, and later, I became a rebellious adult woman.

My defiant nature was still with me and probably still is. As a result, I never felt at home on earth. This supports the idea of the soul's plan, which suggests that we come to earth to fulfill what we've planned, to learn, to experience... and then return "home"...

I longed for that "home"...

I would always look up at the stars as if they were the place I came from. Often, as a child, I would lie on the grass in the evenings and just stare at the sky. Just like that. I would clear my mind of all thoughts and just look. I don't know, maybe I was trying to connect spiritually with the entire cosmos in some way. Or maybe I was simply trying to calm myself, to reset, to erase everything bad from my brain? I don't know, but I do know that those were happy moments. And they were mine alone.

Another sanctuary, a haven for me, was the world of fantasy. I escaped there from my troubled childhood. I read a lot, especially fairy tales. It helped me survive. Later, when I received my Dante, I devoured his *The Divine Comedy*. I understood very little of it, but I consumed it hungrily, nonetheless. Interestingly, the part closest to me was *Inferno*. It felt so familiar. Like the protagonist of the book, I found myself deep in a dark forest with no way out. I was stuck in that dark forest, which, for some reason, took the shape of my horrific childhood.

"The banners of the king of hell approach!" I would mutter under my breath at the sight of my father.

It even amused me. For a moment.

"What's so funny?" my father would immediately snap me back to reality.

So, I kept escaping into Dante's world. It wasn't always joyful reading. It made me think, and sometimes it even brought me down. Just reading something like this was enough:

> *And he who, on earth, without a crown of laurels,*
> *Lies down in the grave*
> *Will leave behind as much trace*
> *As smoke in the air, as bubbles on water.*

It really depressed me. Even though I was still a child, I worried that I hadn't achieved anything and would leave nothing behind. Luckily, I don't feel that pressure anymore. I know that at least this book will be left behind, one that someone will one day discover in a library. In any case, both Dante and other books were an escape from the grim reality. I still use such a refuge because I still love to read. And I still love to look at the stars, but now I do it with greater humility and awareness that I'm part of something bigger. Adult life isn't exactly what I imagined, but I've learned to appreciate what I have and to find beauty in everyday things. It may not be easy, but now I know that I always have a choice and that each day I can become a better version of myself.

My father was there throughout my entire childhood. I thought he would always be there… that he would be an eternal specter haunting me. It wasn't until one event that I realized my father might not always be there. I'll admit, it was a happy moment and a joyful thought. It might scare you, but as I mentioned before, if you had to deal with him, you wouldn't be surprised.

I still remember that night perfectly. I don't know what time it was exactly. It could have been around 2:00 or 3:00 in the morning. That's the least important part of this story. We were woken up by a terrible scream from our mother. It wasn't words, more like a howl. You can imagine the fear that gripped us. We were just children and had no idea what was happening. The fear was so great that instead of checking what was going on, we pulled the covers tighter over ourselves. It wasn't until my mother's next scream that we got out of bed.

We met in the hallway.

"Should we go?" I looked at my older sister.

Ursula shrugged. She didn't seem eager. But she turned to our younger sister, Lydia, and then glanced at our brother, Walter, who was shifting nervously from foot to foot.

"Are we going?" I repeated the question.

Then our mother screamed for the third time, and I understood that something bad had happened.

We rushed to the bathroom. The sight wasn't pleasant. Dad was lying on the floor, and beside him, our tearful mother was kneeling.

"Don't leave me," she begged.

The four of us sat down next to her.

"Don't leave me, please," she continued talking to our unconscious father. To me, it was some kind of incomprehensible performance. At least at first.

"Don't go!" Mom kept pleading. "Not now! I won't be able to manage without you..."

She was trying clumsily to resuscitate Dad, but she had no idea how to do it. To his luck, and our misfortune, the ambulance arrived.

"We've got a heart attack here," one of the medics said to the other.

And then they took Dad away.

Until recently, when I thought back to that event, I felt that I could have "helped" him die back then. I would have personally finished him off! Or at least I would have covered his face with a pillow until he started suffocating, until he was gasping for every breath. He would have died there on that floor, in his underwear. Without any pathos, without any mercy. He would have died just as he deserved. I would have finished him off without batting an eye. It's strange that Mom didn't do it. She suffered with him for almost thirty years! Maybe she stayed with him because she never had her own opinion. Our father dictated what she should think and say. He even turned us against her, pitting the children against their own mother. What kind of father does that? Does such a person even deserve to live?

But for that little girl from years ago, that night was a traumatic experience. I wasn't thinking about revenge then. I didn't even know that I could be free from the tyrant, from my tormentor.

Of course, they saved him at the hospital. I told you; the devil doesn't take the wicked!

Dad weighed on us not only at home. He didn't just poison our lives there. He was over twenty years older than our young, beautiful mom, which already seemed strange to my schoolmates. Additionally, Dad was overweight and had gray hair, which only fueled their mockery. His appearance became the subject of jokes and ridicule, and I felt guilty, as if I were responsible for how my father looked.

"The fat man's daughter!" I had to hear behind my back in the school hallway.

"Is that your dad or your granddad?" some smartass from an older class would sneer.

"Did your mom marry her dad?" someone else would laugh.

However, our mom was generally not the subject of those crude jokes and taunts. On the contrary, she was admired by my peers. She made an impression, especially on the boys. Mom was always nicely dressed, made up, and well-groomed. But that only intensified my sense of guilt. I felt that Dad didn't deserve her, that he wasn't her equal, that he should change something about his appearance to deserve that beautiful woman and to earn the respect of my peers. But he clearly didn't care at all about his appearance. Or maybe he was unaware of the taunts thrown behind his back?

My mom was different. She not only took care of herself but also took great care of us. We were always clean, our clothes washed and ironed. Dad didn't bother with such details. The only good thing you could say about him was that he never denied us food. We never went hungry, unlike in some families. But none of that seemed to matter to my schoolmates.

As a child, I didn't know how to deal with all of this. I felt unfairly treated by others and didn't know how to fix it. It was a difficult time for me, but no one was teaching me then that you shouldn't judge people by their appearance.

Instead, I heard behind my back:

"Old man dad! Old man dad!"

And it made me want to cry. Not because I felt sorry for my tyrant father. But because I had something in common with that man. What else was I supposed to think when at home, my siblings and I mostly heard tirades from Dad like:

"You whores! You bastards!"

A very instructive and educational way to talk to children. In those few words, fatherly love poured out like hot lava. Ha, ha!

Were there any good moments with Dad? Throughout my childhood, he had a few good moods. Then, suddenly, he became someone else. I remember how he organized a water fight for us, even though it was July. How we played soccer together in the yard. He played with us as if trying to erase everything that was bad. Once, we sat in the kitchen by the table and read *Nostradamus' Prophecies* for half the night. Well, I read them out loud because Dad's eyesight was already poor. He handed me a glass of water because my mouth was getting dry from the reading. And in the morning, I got a beating because I was late for school...

Those were the "nice" moments with Dad.

All the crap I went through in childhood ruined half my life! Even now, as an adult, all that evil still sits inside me. Thoughts about my childhood still swirl in my head every day, forcing me to think about it constantly. They're intrusive, disturbing. They seem almost immortal. And Dad still laughs at me in those thoughts! And seems to shout mockingly with Dante's words:

Through me, the way to the city of woe...!

Yes, he's right. Because of him.

CHAPTER 2

Here, you enter the second circle of my personal hell with me. You step into another circle of my life. It's cramped here, filled with screams and groans of pain. Well, who said hell is pleasant? Probably someone who has never been there. This is how I look: a soul burdened with the stain of sin. I'm not ashamed of it. Are your souls any better? No. Each of us has our dark spots that we try to scrub away so that, even for a moment, we can shine with the light of innocence. But these stains can never be completely removed. At best, they may fade a little over time. But they will never disappear entirely. Everyone has them. We cover ourselves with these stains throughout our lives, and sometimes others smear us with the dirt of their existence.

As a child, I sometimes had a strange dream. I would wander through some wasteland, covered in mud, not understanding at all how I ended up in that place and time. And suddenly, out of nowhere, animals would appear. Wild, ruthless, ready for anything. Doesn't that description fit some people too? But let's get back to the dream. These animals that appeared in my dream were terrifying. They always behaved the same way. A panther would come down from somewhere up high, its spots menacing. A lion would approach with its head held high and roar terrifyingly. I could feel the air trembling because of it. Behind the lion walked a wolf. The wolf seemed the most frightening to me. It had sunken sides, as if it hadn't eaten anything in a long time. And it was the wolf that scared me the most. It was the fear of compassion. I knew it could tear me apart with its teeth at any moment, yet I felt terribly sorry for it. And that pity paralyzed me. However, the animals thought there was some great pride in me that kept me from running. But I just pitied them so much. And it was all strangely sensual. I still don't understand it. I don't understand my own greed for being close to those beasts. Unfortunately, I don't know how it ended, because whenever they got close to me, I would wake up drenched in sweat. Eventually, I read about the panther, lion, and wolf in Dante's work. But I began dreaming of these animals before I even read *The Divine Comedy*. Was it some kind of premonition? Prophecy? Only when I got older did I find somewhere that animals in dreams symbolize the biological side of human nature, expressing the primal instinct. But could that apply to me? Or maybe it was about something entirely different? Maybe it was just about those animals... about some kind of revenge?

I am increasingly convinced that my subconscious felt guilty. Guilty because I was too weak. I couldn't save the animals sentenced by my father.

And so, in this hellish circle, we have come full circle and returned to my father, who didn't leave the pages of the previous chapter. Unfortunately, he won't disappear into oblivion here either...

Animals. Magnificent. Majestic. Beloved. Every single one. Dad always had something against animals. Not against animals in general, but against our household pets, which he wouldn't let live in peace. He was cruel to them, especially to the dogs. Whenever something happened that he thought was wrong, the animal had to pay for it. It didn't matter whether it understood it had done wrong or was completely unaware. Dogs were always treated as objects that could be ruthlessly used and destroyed.

"Did you see that dog? It killed our chicken!" Dad would yell, storming into the house with a hysterical look in his eyes.

"Oh God, what will you do?" Mom would ask, though she knew the answer was obvious.

"Under the hammer!" Dad would scream, and his words, as always, left no doubt.

By now you've figured out that Dad was incredibly strict, almost sadistic. He treated not only us harshly but also our animals. I had the feeling that he even took pleasure in inflicting pain on these defenseless creatures. And so, one by one, our pets died at Dad's hands. For example, when our dog Barry killed the neighbor's duck, Dad, almost gleefully, killed him with a metal pipe. I still remember the sight: the poor dog hung on a chain, tied to a ladder, and Dad proudly bustled around, explaining how he had done it.

"Do you know where you have to hit to kill a dog?" he would ask calmly, as if he were talking about planting flowers.

What the hell! Seriously? Who says that to children?

Unfortunately, I remember everything. I will never forget it. I wanted to scream as loudly as I could. I wanted to shout so that everyone could hear me. I even opened my mouth...

"Quiet!" Dad cut me off before any sound could escape my lips.

In his eyes, I noticed something strange. As if he subconsciously knew he was evil.

Then he explained, step by step, how he had finished off poor Barry, our wonderful, trusting, young shepherd dog who loved everyone with all his canine heart.

I remember that suddenly Mom rushed in. She was furious. She grabbed our brother by the hand and dragged him into the house. He was only five years old. And she was too late. He had already seen the worst of it. I'm sure he'll remember it for the rest of his life because I do too. God! We were just children! That was not something for our eyes! Not for anyone's eyes! Even now, as an adult, I cannot come to terms with the harm done to animals. I just can't stand it!

And at night, I dreamed again of the panther, lion, and wolf. They looked at me with even more reproach, and I felt even guiltier.

Unfortunately, there were other terrifying events in our family life. Those poor, innocent animals, murdered in cold blood, were just the tip of the mountain of evil that had risen in our family. It's hard to comprehend it all, but that's how it was. Even I find it hard to believe, and I lived through it. I was right in the middle of that hell. This devilish circle had many demons stirring up our lives. The demon wasn't just my father.

As you already had a chance to find out, at some point in our family's life, *he* appeared – a figure of extraordinary diabolical nature. Like Dante's Satan with three heads: cunning, calculation, and unbridled lust. In those triple jaws, he held our family, mercilessly tearing apart our peace and normality, and he didn't cry with all six eyes like in Dante's work. Of course, I'm talking about the Swarthy Man – a guy who should rot in prison for the rest of his days. I doubt he ended up there. I can only hope so. But as they say, hope is the mother of Fools.

This mysterious scoundrel, who was called Julius Romer (I doubt that was his real name), suddenly became friends with our parents, even though I had never seen him before. He appeared as if he had come out of nowhere. I don't know where he came from. I don't know where Dad found him. But I do know how he won Dad over. It was one of his devilish heads: cunning. He managed to charm Dad so much that he praised him in every possible way.

"Kids, do you see?" he would point to Romer. "This is a truly intelligent man. We need more people like him in this country!"

Yeah, as if there's a shortage of such scoundrels in Poland. What we really lack are decent people!

"If you ask him anything, he always gives you an answer. And it makes sense," Dad would tell Mom with admiration, as if he were advertising a product he wanted to sell her.

Later, it turned out that it wasn't accidental. Dad did trade something, but it wasn't Julius Romer; it was our mom.

But let's go step by step.

According to our parents' stories, Romer was lonely, and Dad decided to take him in. Did he think he was going to be some damn foster family for this scoundrel? I don't know if he was even thinking. But he often laughed heartily in the company of dark-skinned Julius. Dad clearly enjoyed his company.

One day, Romer asked us:

"From now on, call me Uncle."

My mother quickly picked up on this during one of our dinners, delighted:

"Yes, call him that!"

My father added his part as well:

"He's the best uncle you could have!"

Seriously?! From the perspective of years and everything I know now, it's mind-boggling!

Julius Romer quickly became friends with our parents, but there was something unsettling about him. I knew it from the start. I felt it the moment I saw his nasty face! Subsequent events only confirmed this.

I soon realized that this dark-skinned creep had taken a liking to our mother. It paralyzed me. I began to frantically wonder how I could protect her from this guy. It seemed I was on my own (my older sister just shrugged it off), because it appeared that our father didn't notice. Then I realized it was quite the opposite. The situation made our father thrilled. He was pleased with what Romer was doing.

The most disgusting part was yet to be discovered.

One evening, when we had all gone to bed, I heard quiet whispers and laughter coming from my parents' room. As quietly as I could, I shuffled into the hallway. I saw that my father, mother, and Julius Romer were sitting together on the bed. I watched the scene for a moment until I understood what was happening.

Everyone was giggling.

Suddenly, my father stopped grinning, grabbed the bottle of vodka standing on the nightstand and tilted it, forcing my mother to drink it, then said a bit nervously:

"Catch her here! Should I teach you like a kid?" Then he put Romer's hand on my mother's chest. The dark-haired boy liked it, because he started smacking his lips in a strange way. I don't know if my mother was happy, though.

"Now, put your hand under her dress!" my father commanded, grabbing the camera lying on the shelf.

I was sinking into increasing terror. Sweat began to pour down my body. I was shaking more and more, as if I had suddenly fallen into the lowest circle of hell. But that wasn't the lowest circle. I was about to get there.

"Come on, show me how you fuck her!" my father said to the Romer, laughing and pointing the camera at them.

I ran back to my room. I sat in the corner for a few hours, crying. I felt like everything had collapsed. Like my childhood innocence had been shattered. Like all sense of security had been ripped from me. I desperately covered my ears to free myself from the noise coming from my parents' room. To no avail.

Years later I found those photos. My father had put them in the shelf with my books, knowing full well that I would find them there. Whole piles of degrading, humiliating photos of women. Fucking pervert!

I burned them all!

Unfortunately, that wasn't the only meanness that Julius the Romer committed in our house.

As his "friendship" with our parents developed, the Romer began to get closer to me and my sisters – older and younger. For some time now, I had the impression that he was watching me. I could almost feel his piercing gaze on me. At first, I tried to explain it to myself as simple phobias, hallucinations, or even my oversensitivity. However, I quickly realized that it was not a figment of my terrified imagination.

The devil in the next circle of hell began to act!

One day, when I was alone in the room, the Romer came in. For a moment, he looked at me strangely. Immediately, my heart began to pound with terror. I gripped the pen I was holding tightly until my knuckles turned white.

Meanwhile, the Romer kept looking. Finally, he started licking his lips strangely, as if he had just eaten some delicious dessert.

It turned out that I was supposed to be that dessert.

He approached me and crouched down. He slowly brushed my curls away from my forehead. I knew there was nothing innocent about it. He was lurking. He had set himself up for a victim. I realized that I was the victim.

Suddenly he started groping me. His lousy, disgusting hand greedily roamed my body. I clenched my teeth so as not to cry. I didn't want to give him the satisfaction!

"Uncle, what are you doing?!" I finally shouted, trying to free myself from his intrusive touches.

"Nothing, nothing, I'm just cuddling," he replied with a smile that sent shivers of fear through me.

I don't know what could have happened if my father's voice hadn't suddenly echoed from the room:

"Julius, how long are you going to be in this toilet? You must see this!" The Romer smiled lasciviously at me and straightened up. "We'll come back to this," he threatened, leaving.

As soon as he disappeared behind the door, I buried my face in the pillow.

I gave her a sob of helplessness and I couldn't hold it back for long.

That's how I started to slide into lower and lower circles of hell, and it wasn't just Dante's reading anymore. It was reality. Ours. Mine. When Romer stayed with us for the night, he always slept in the same bed with one of us - with his older or younger sister or with me. I don't understand how my parents could allow it! How?!

Those nights were terrible. They were terrifying. It was like looking into the deepest corners of that hell. It could be even worse than hell!

Those nights always looked the same. Julius Romer would come laughing, as if he wanted to announce that he had everything under control. It was like a warning: don't jump, because you have no chance! Don't defend yourself! Don't oppose what awaits you! This is your reality. I added all this to myself when I saw his delighted face. His bloody, fucking smile! The fucking Romer had smiles on his face, as Dante wrote. But he had nothing of the poet. He was pure, pure evil. There was also a strange coldness in him, which I could still feel in his touch. That Romer smile appeared for a second in a flash of light from the corridor, when that bastard opened the door to my room. But that second was enough for me to see the expression on his face. He had everything written there. The smile was just the punch line to his vile intentions.

He always closed the door behind him. And then I realized I was trapped. My own room became a terrible place from which I had no chance of escape. I didn't have the slightest chance! What, was I supposed to sneak between that bastard's legs? Slip out sideways? That bastard always stood in such a way that there was no chance of escape. He must have had it all planned out to perfection. Maybe he had been hurting children like this for years? Maybe he had everything rehearsed down to the smallest detail? As soon as he closed the door behind him, he always took off his pants. And everything else. Why didn't I scream? It was simple - out of fear, out of shame... I wanted to roar a terrifying scream many times. How many times had I opened my mouth to call for help! And nothing! No sound would come out of my mouth. Even though I wanted to scream, I was enveloped only by deep, impenetrable silence, accompanied by the panting of a pedophile undressing. A true symphony of evil!

Then came the worst. The fucking pervert pushed himself into my bed. I always tried to resist him, but I had no chance.

He was too strong. How could a little girl who was only 9 years old resist him? So, he pushed me against the wall without much effort.

Then he took my hand. I held it tightly to my body, but one tug was enough for him. Sometimes he just said:

"Be a good girl!"

And then he pushed his protruding, disgusting cock into my hand. I remember it clearly to this day! I feel like puking just thinking about it. He rubbed himself against me and turned me on. He panted louder and louder. He writhed on my bed like a worm that had crawled out of the darkest, stinking abyss.

After all, I was a child! Such things should not happen to a defenseless child!

I never told my parents about it. They probably wouldn't believe me anyway...

The incident I described here was not a one-time event.

At one point I had the impression that Julius Romer was staying with us more and more often. I don't know if that was really the case or if it was just my fear telling me so, but this pedophile committed his disgusting acts many times.

"I hate the bastard!" I screamed in the bathroom when no one could hear.

I didn't have the courage to shout it in the face of the scoundrel. No, I wasn't afraid of him. I was more afraid of my father's potential reaction. I'm sure he wouldn't have taken my side. Although I wouldn't call Romer my father's friend. He was more of his plaything. Everyone was a plaything to him - my mother, us, the neighbors, everyone...

In this situation, it shouldn't surprise anyone that my anger, or rather hatred, was growing towards the dark-skinned pedophile. I was afraid of every next meeting with him.

I remember that once I was alone at home. It was the middle of the day. Suddenly I heard a knock on the door. It was insistent. Very insistent. I don't know how, but I knew it was the Romer who had come. I just knew. Maybe it was my subconscious that was how it worked, or maybe he had a specific way of knocking that allowed me to recognize him without difficulty. I don't know. I was just sure that my persecutor had just appeared.

At first, I thought that I should sit as quietly as I could, and the Romer would go away. But anger was boiling inside me. I was shaking with both fear and rage. All of this was mixed inside me. Then madness took hold of me.

I knew perfectly well where my father kept the axe. I ran for it. I grabbed it without thinking, somehow instinctively. I reached the door.

The knocking became even louder. I shouted something furiously. I opened the door.

The Romer was really surprised. If he had even expected to see me, it certainly wasn't with what I was clutching in my hands. I raised the axe and shouted:

"Get out! Leave the door!"

The Romer looked at me searchingly for a moment.

"Is your father or mother here?" he finally asked, confused.

"Get out!" I shouted again in response.

"You'll cut yourself," the louse tried to laugh.

He quickly became serious when I raised the axe even higher.

I guess he understood that I wasn't joking. He took a few steps back. He stopped. He looked again, and I gripped the axe tighter and tighter. Finally, the Romer left. As soon as he disappeared, I fell to the floor and burst into tears. The fear that I had been suppressing with great effort for those few minutes suddenly exploded. I burst into tears, not letting go of the axe from my hands. Today, I would know how to use this tool. Back then, however, I was only about eleven or twelve years old.

Then, suddenly, Romer disappeared. One day, he just stopped coming over. He left, and we finally breathed a sigh of relief. Although there was always a lingering uncertainty, a tiny fragment of fear that he might come back one day. But he never returned. Maybe he died in some gutter? Or perhaps he ended up in prison? I don't know, and I don't want to know! Let hell consume him! The same hell he dragged me and my sisters into!

Let me return to my father for a moment. I couldn't count on him in the matter of Romer for yet another reason. I only learned this reason years later when I overheard a conversation between Ursula and our mother, and it still shakes me to this day.

It turned out that the damned pedophile Romer had an accomplice in his actions. Our cursed father did the same thing as him.

He had no qualms about her since she was a little girl, about 5 years old. And who knows, maybe even earlier, and she simply doesn't remember it.

He probably thought in his sick mind that since he fathered someone, he had every right to him. A fucking psycho and a pervert!

I have no excuse for anyone who hurts their own child so much. None!

It was even worse with Ursula than it was with me. She was a victim who turned into a perpetrator herself. Maybe this was how she reacted to her hurt and suffering? Her father molested her, and she did the same to her younger siblings. She was both a victim and a perpetrator.

At that time, I was about twelve, and she was fifteen. At night she would sneak into my bed. First, I would hear the door creak. If there was no Romer in the house, I would know who was approaching.

My older sister would climb on me. She would climb on me without a word.

Everything was enveloped in absolute silence. Then Ursula would pretend to do it.

She would rub herself against me while lying on top of me. Finally, she would grab my small, childish hands and touch her private parts with them. I was disgusted by her. But I didn't say anything. As usual, I lay there quietly. As usual.

After that, I was always repulsed by her. We never talked about it, and I don't think I want to bring up the topic with her. I'm not sure if it's because of shame or the reluctance to revisit what happened back then. I just don't want to.

Years later, my sister confessed to our mother. She told her that she had been molested. And what did she hear from the person who should have offered her comfort, support, and a sense of safety at that moment? Can you guess?

She heard:

"Forget about it. Learn to live with it." Unbelievable!

This is what my next circle of hell looked like. Unfortunately, it wasn't the last one.

Are you ready for another dose of cruelty?

CHAPTER 3

Here, dear readers, you are now entering the third circle of hell. If your courage hasn't abandoned you yet, I invite you in. As is customary with me, there will be no peaceful sightseeing here, no mindless staring at paintings on the walls whose meaning no one understands. There will be no aimless wandering. A guide like me won't allow that.

Do you still have the courage to set off with me? In Dante's third circle, there were drunkards and gluttons. In the third circle of my world, it will be me and my best friend from high school!

One gloomy day, I suddenly realized, to my astonishment, that I was already a teenager. The childhood phase was gone. No, it's not about the first menstruation or anything like that. It was a mental thing. Apparently, I just had to mature psychologically to be a teenager. And that gloomy day, I matured.

"Now I'll show you all!" I shouted out the window.

No one heard me because there was no one around. It didn't matter. My manifesto was shouted out. I had fulfilled my duty. Now it was time for action.

Reality, of course, quickly brought me back down to earth. And, naturally, my father did too.

I thought that as a teenager, I would have more freedom. Nothing could be further from the truth. I didn't have time to enjoy my youth. Everything was overseen by a demon whose name was "Renovation!" This renovation dragged on for years, and for years I had to slave away at it, losing what was most precious youth! Who will give it back to me when the renovation finally ends? I knew deep down that it would never end. My father made sure the renovation would drag on forever. I don't know if he did it because he loved hammering and troweling, or if he simply wanted to make our lives, his children's lives, miserable.

It didn't really matter!

Even as young children, I remember us with masonry hammers and little axes, cleaning reclaimed bricks. But that's what happens when you're the child of a bricklayer-psychopath.

As a teenager, I didn't escape this nightmare. And where was that freedom?

I remember those days, those endless afternoons when my friends were walking in the park, and I had to go home to continue the slave labor on the renovation that seemed to go on and on. I don't understand where my father got so much energy to torture us with that renovation.

As you already know, my father was a tyrant and couldn't stand any form of opposition. To make matters worse, he had a keen sense of hearing and would catch any murmurs of discontent. All the children in the neighborhood were afraid of him, but none had the bad luck that I did – they didn't have to live with him. Sometimes I wondered if his appetite for work stemmed from some hidden resentment, but I couldn't say because I was too afraid to talk to him. After all, he was my father, right?

So, instead of enjoying the privileges that come with youth and being a teenager (at least according to my stereotypes at the time), I was toiling away on a construction site as the least respected cog in the masonry machine. If it had been someone else's construction site,

I might have at least been able to throw the hammer to the ground and walk away into the setting sun, like a cowboy running away before the end credits of a western. But it wasn't someone else's. It was the worst construction site that could exist. It was my father's construction site. His private renovation and construction work on our house and outbuildings. In that situation, all I could do was grit my teeth in anger. When I started another round of work on the renovation, Dante's words often came to mind: *Through me, you enter the city of woe*. Well, my life seemed to be that city of woe, and the renovation was its seething hell. Well, a piece of hell.

A slice of it, but a terribly annoying one!

Despite my fear, one day I decided to muster the courage to confront him. I couldn't take the endless work that was consuming my youth any longer. So, I gathered what little courage I had left and issued a challenge. Although today, in hindsight, I think that might be too strong a word.

"Dad, can I go for a walk in the park with my friends today?" I asked, trembling at the thought of his reaction.

My father stopped hammering and looked at me like I was some kind of annoying fly.

"What the hell?" he said disapprovingly. "Do you think you're in some damn spa in Palm Springs that you want to go for a stroll? Is our home some kind of guesthouse for bored vacationers? You want to stroll in the park like some tramp when there's so much work to be done?"

He began to bombard me with more and more words, throwing absurd arguments at me, bombarding me with a stream of curses, and pressing down with a complete lack of logic in his statements. He was effective at this. With each word he spoke, I felt myself shrinking more and more. My fear was so overwhelming that I couldn't even respond. I looked at my father, trying to remember what it was like to have a moment of freedom. The thought crossed my mind that this must be what it would be like if someone tried to take a tiger's meal right out of its mouth. Meanwhile, I was trying to take my own self away from my father's grasp. But he wanted to tear me apart just as a tiger would.

Finally, my father straightened up and looked me directly in the eyes. A shiver of terror ran through me.

"This is not the time for damn laziness!" my father growled, and I began to tremble with fear.

"If you go for a walk now, then you'll come back and won't leave this house until the renovation is finished. Understood?"

"Yes, I understand."

That meant I would never leave this house because that renovation would never end.

Resigned, I went back to my spot by the wall and grabbed the hammer. I kept hammering away!

The truth is, I learned a lot during that never-ending renovation. But what am I supposed to do with that knowledge and those skills now? Am I supposed to work in construction? I'm a woman! Isn't a woman supposed to be delicate and graceful like spring?

Those were the beginnings of my teenage years. I was about fourteen or fifteen then. Luckily, high school came along, and everything changed.

High school was a completely new experience and brought completely new people, especially one person. Madeline. My Maddie. We met in high school and quickly became friends. We spent every possible moment together.

Many years later, we had a strange conversation. I remember it clearly. The sun was just about to set as we sat on a bench in the park, waiting for our friends. Suddenly, without thinking, I blurted out:

"You know, Madeline, sometimes I really regret meeting you. Because of you, I met most of the people who made me suffer: the jerk from my first time, my first husband and his whole crew, and everything in between. If I hadn't befriended you in high school, my life would probably look completely different. But would it be better?" I added after a moment's thought.

Madeline looked at me with a mischievous smile.

"Oh, come on, don't tell me you really regret meeting me? After all, I was the one who introduced you to this whole world of adventures and emotions," she replied, brushing her long, dark hair, which always made her stand out in a crowd.

I shook my head, slightly annoyed by her nonchalance.

"But were those adventures and emotions really worth it? Didn't they bring me more pain than joy?" I asked, trying to keep my voice calm.

Maddie shrugged.

"Well, it's hard to say. We can only speculate about what kind of life you might have had if we hadn't met. But would you really want that? Would you rather live a life full of unknowns and uncertainties instead of the one you lived with me?"

I looked at her, surprised.

"Didn't we already live a life full of unknowns and uncertainties?" I asked, somewhat uncertainly.

"Well, yeah, actually!" Madeline laughed. "Besides, while we might regret some decisions we made, we can't turn back time and change what happened. We can only learn from our mistakes and try to live a better life, keeping in mind the lessons those experiences taught us."

She suddenly leaned closer to me.

"Do you really regret the crazy stuff we did in high school?" she laughed.

I wanted to say something, but then our friends joined us, and the conversation with Maddie had to wait for another time.

Did I really regret meeting her? If I hadn't met Madeline, I wouldn't have had so many incredible moments that, though sometimes painful, shaped who I became as a person.

And we never returned to that conversation.

I met that little troublemaker, Madeline, when I was about 14 years old. We met during the entrance exams for high school. Interestingly, out of all the people there, I only remembered her – a small, feisty, and beautiful girl with long, dark hair. She looked much younger than she really was. It's strange that on that day, I noticed Maddie, even though I didn't yet know her name. It must have been fate... or maybe a decree from the heavens...? Maybe...

Dante wrote about a person's destiny being tied to eternity, and I had my own destiny – madness. Sometimes that madness bordered on the edge of evil.

After the summer, when Madeline and I ended up in the same high school class, our shared adventure began. No, it was more than just an adventure. It was a significant part of our lives.

High school is a time when the bitterness of growing up mixes with the fever of discovering a new world, and the taste of caviar and champagne is replaced only by the sadness of ingratitude. You start searching for your place in the world, and every encounter with peers becomes either a fascinating experiment or an unimaginable trauma. It's not uncommon that in this colorful mosaic, we find people who will accompany us throughout our lives, whether we want them to or not.

Well, as you already know, Madeline was that person for me. An unassuming girl with beautiful brown eyes who captivated me with her soul, where waves of rebellion and discontent with reality were constantly brewing.

We were like two opposites that irresistibly attracted each other.

I would escape to Madeline's place whenever the days in high school drowned in grayness. I spent practically all those four years with her, which should have been full of joy but were marked by sadness and a sense of being unappreciated.

She had such wonderful parents! A lovely mother who prepared us delicious dinners with a smile, and a fantastic father who would puff on his cigarette with satisfaction, blowing out clouds of smoke as if he wanted to surround us with an aura of mystery.

"Well, girls, how's high school life?" Maddie's dad would ask during those moments, feigning interest in our daily concerns.

Madeline usually shrugged then, as she wasn't keen on confiding in her parents.

"Well, it's great, of course," I would respond with irony. "It's always wonderful during that magical time when life becomes one big experiment," I added, repeating lines I had heard in some TV show.

"Ha! How true!" Maddie's dad would laugh, while her mother shook her head with indulgence.

I was an outsider in their home, but I never felt that way. Madeline's parents treated me like their own child, sometimes even better, though I didn't deserve it. I felt their support whenever I needed it. They were the refuge that protected me from the storms of my restless mind.

Of course, Madeline didn't appreciate what she had. In her eyes, her parents were a burdensome obligation that couldn't be avoided. She complained about them as if they were a whip that fate used to lash her.

"My parents are so annoying," she would say with a certain ease or nonchalance, as if testing whether the bathwater was warm enough for a comfortable soak.

Meanwhile, I envied her those parents. If only Maddie could have lived with my father for just one day!

Ah, those were the days! Long hours spent reading and talking by the window overlooking a tousled linden tree, its branches seemingly gathering the world into its green arms. Sometimes, when the grayness of the days seemed unbearable, we would lock ourselves in Madeline's room, listening to music that wove a magical story about the life that awaited us.

Those were the high school days – full of irony and ingratitude. At that time, we didn't realize how much those feelings poisoned our lives. Only years later did I understand that those moments were like golden strings on which fate played, and we were just marionettes who had not yet learned to appreciate our happy moments.

Today, I smile at the memory of those times... Now that each of us has our own family, I realize how valuable those moments we spent together were, full of the support and kindness of Madeline's parents. And despite our indifference, they continuously showed us love and care, teaching us how important it is to appreciate what we have.

Maddie, if you're reading these words, remember that I will never stop being grateful for those moments spent in your family home.

I wish that in your heart, you always find room for love, support, and the same understanding we found in your parents during high school.

Yes, I know, those are big words, but I owe them to my friend and, above all, to her parents.

There were many great times with Madeline. Some were terrifying, and some were just funny, like the time we fried bacon on... No, I won't reveal that right away. The whole situation went something like this:

I remember one late afternoon after school when, as usual, Madeline and I went to her place. It was a time when friendship meant spending every moment together, and the daily troubles seemed insignificant compared to our youthful antics. Simply: we had a great time together!

"Maddie, do you have something to snack on?" I asked, inhaling the cozy scent of her home.

"Of course, my dear lady!" she replied with amusement. "I'll get you something to eat quickly, don't worry. I'm hungry too. All that droning at school really makes you hungry!"

Madeline, that scatterbrain, grabbed whatever was at hand: large, juicy pieces of bacon and a mysterious jar with yellow liquid, which she assumed was oil. She poured the "oil" into the pan, tossed in the beautiful pieces of bacon, and we waited. As it began to sizzle, it also started to smoke and stink. Maddie, seemingly oblivious to the strange smell, flipped the bacon over.

"Does something seem off to you?" I asked, feeling uneasy.

"What? Not enough bacon? Should I add more slices?" she laughed. "I'm making delicious bacon!"

Having grown up in the midst of endless renovations, I knew a thing or two about certain things, so I took a closer look at that jar of supposed oil. I quickly realized it wasn't oil at all – it was contact adhesive!

"Madeline!" I shouted, trying to stifle my laughter. "That's not oil, it's glue!"

This nutcase was frying bacon in glue!

It took a moment for the realization to dawn on her, and then she burst into uncontrollable laughter.

"Oh my God!" she whispered through tears. "How could I have messed that up?"

I'll never forget that moment – the smoke, the stench, and the laughter! That was when I realized that our friendship was about more than just shared moments over fried bacon. It was about the ability to laugh at our own mistakes, to find joy in the most unexpected situations, and to support each other through everyday adventures. But somehow, there was always a lingering doubt. Later, that bacon fried in glue became our private joke, something we always returned to whenever we met up. Our friendship, though tested many times by the passage of time and distance, remained consistently strong and authentic. Within each of us lay not just the memory of our shared past, but also of the many crazy things, like frying bacon in glue. That's why I know it's true friendship. Not the kind that runs away like a cowardly, lying politician being pelted with eggs at a rally. It's a friendship for life. A forever kind!

"Memories instead of an education," I sometimes say to myself when I reflect on how my friendship with Madeline unfolded and how it all began. That clever saying seems to be the most fitting description of all the adventures we shared long ago.

In my first year of high school, I was a good, dutiful student. I carried a backpack full of books, dreams, and plans for the future. Everything was fine until my friend from class, none other than Madeline, started showing me how city folks have fun. I, a poor girl from a small town, was fascinated by the life in the big city. Everything was so new, unfamiliar, and unattainable.

When I was 13, my family moved from a tiny village to a nearby town, where I finished the last grade of primary school. Most of the teachers there were old, leftover remnants from the communist era. In their eyes, I was a loser simply because I was a newcomer, poor, and from the countryside. I was set up for failure right from the start. I ended up in a class with the Elite, the children of wealthy parents. I stood out among the others – I was poorly dressed, a bit rough around the edges, introverted, alienated. Not only did I have to fight with myself to fit in, but also with a system that seemed determined to crush me. I was bullied, singled out, my grades were lowered, mainly because my ambitions reached higher than those of the other students. I dreamed of attending a high school with an administrative-office profile, which, of course, didn't sit well with some teachers. After all, how could a peasant girl aspire to a better school than the children whose fathers earned Deutsche marks in the West? According to them, the place for someone like me was a vocational school for bakers or plumbers. But despite everything and everyone, I had no intention of giving up. A well-passed entrance exam opened the door to my dream high school, and I was accepted despite my social status.

The school building was less than 20 km from my home. Of course, my parents couldn't afford a bus ticket, so for the entire four years, I hitchhiked to and from school. I never complained, never whined, I stood there like an idiot on the side of the road, patiently waiting for someone to stop and give me a ride to school or back home. It was fine in the spring, but in autumn and winter, it was much harder. Sometimes hours passed, and dark clouds of night loomed overhead; sometimes it rained, other times the ground was covered with snow that froze my feet... Often, Madeline would invite me to stay over at her place, knowing that I still hadn't made it home. Eventually, I started going to her place more often, and more often... until I no longer even bothered to stand on the road and ask random drivers for a lift home... I would just call my parents and tell them I was at Madeline's. My dad stopped giving me a hard time; he got used to the idea that I was spending the night at my friend's place, knowing that I was safe there and that we were studying hard together. Hahhh, now I know where I got my naivety from. Besides, he was very proud of me for being the first in the family to attend a good school. He bragged about me to friends and family, and my siblings had a rough time, especially Lydia, because he had high hopes for her too. For years, he compared her to me, saying she didn't study like I did, didn't work like I did, wasn't like me... because I had to be the best, I had to be daddy's pride. I had to be the person he had imagined me to be. That's why my escapes to Madeline's felt like a breath of freedom, a chance to take a break from the miserable reality that awaited me at home. Unfortunately, my stays at my friend's place came with something else...

You already know that Maddie had something irresistible about her, something that made me want to be a part of her world, even though I instinctively knew it was a world full of temptations. And yet, somehow, she was a magnet that effectively drew my attention.

We started skipping school, slacking off, going to parties, midweek discos, meeting boys, and taking spontaneous trips. We were quite the duo! I thought we were invincible together, that the world was ours for the taking, and that we, two girls united, could achieve the impossible.

We had a lot of fun together, but sometimes I regret all of it because if I had studied properly, I might have finished college and had a cozy, comfortable job in a bank. In fact, I have memories instead of an education. And you can't feed children with memories. And again, I return to the point of that unfinished conversation with Maddie in the park. There's still some lingering resentment.

Time passed, and our friendship endured. My relationship with Madeline continues to this day, and we've known each other for almost 30 years! We were like two sides of the same coin, seemingly inseparable, yet internally so different.

I realize now that over all these years, she hasn't changed a bit, while I've changed a lot. I understood that this friendship, though full of unforgettable adventures, cost me a great deal. I looked at my life and saw the gap between what I desired and where I am now.

And again, I return to that unfortunate conversation in the park. I find myself wondering more and more often if I would have become a different person if I hadn't met Madeline. Would my life, dreams, and aspirations have turned out differently? But then I quickly realize that this friendship, despite all its imperfections, gave me something no education or prestigious job could have – it taught me the importance of values and the choices we make.

Now, when I sometimes meet Madeline and observe her life, full of carefree adventures, I realize that sometimes it takes distance to understand what is truly important. No, I don't regret our friendship, but I do regret not having the strength to choose differently when those choices were shaping my future.

I'm trying now to make up for lost time, to understand how I can use these experiences and learn from them. Maybe it's too late for school, but it's not too late to understand that life is a series of choices whose consequences we feel for years.

I hope that my children will have the strength and wisdom to make better choices than I did. That they won't fall for the temptations that so effectively led me astray, and that they will find a balance between a life full of memories and one that gives them a chance to fulfill their dreams.

In the meantime, I'm learning from my mistakes, and though our meetings with Maddie are less frequent than before, they still allow me to remember who I was, who I am, and who I want to be. Isn't that what true, mature friendship looks like?

So, despite the regret that lingers somewhere deep in my heart, I appreciate what I experienced with Madeline. She taught me that life has many faces and that the values we hold onto shape our future paths.

Memories, though they're not the same as an education, give us lessons worth remembering. And those lessons, though painful, are invaluable when the time comes to pass them on. In this context, my "memories instead of an education" have value after all. That thought comforts me. Or maybe I'm just fooling myself to keep my life from being overwhelmed by regret?

During high school, we passionately attended discos where La Bouche's "Be My Lover" reigned supreme. Those were my nightly adventures with Maddie. We spent so much time at parties that they felt like our second home (in my case, the third, because my second home was at Madeline's). There was no other place in the world where we could lose ourselves like that. We immersed ourselves in the darkness, the music, and the atmosphere of freedom that hung in the air.

We had various adventures there. For example, at one of those discos, while we were dancing to the pulsing music, a guy with indistinct features and a flirtatious smile approached us. He was definitely interested in Maddie, but he had trouble breaking through the barrier that our duo presented.

"Hey, girls, I haven't seen you here before, and I'd definitely remember such beauties. How are you doing?" he said casually, trying to catch our attention.

Madeline, always quick with a retort, replied with amusement, "As for us, we're doing just fine, but I can see you need some tips on how to talk to girls."

The guy, clearly flustered, tried to regain his confidence. "Okay, maybe I messed up a little, but I can do better. How about a drink?"

That's when I added cheekily, "Why not? But only if you drink it alone and not in our company."

We burst out laughing like complete idiots. I still feel sorry for that guy. He was judged by us in an instant, and the sentence was the highest level of humiliation. I'm not proud of it now, but back then we loved to torment desperate boys like that.

We had many strange adventures at those discos.

One time, when everyone was already quite drunk, we decided to participate in a karaoke contest being held at the club. Everyone was annoyed by our presence because neither of us could sing for the life of us – we howled like drunk wolves at the moon – but we managed to captivate the audience so much that we triumphantly won first place. In retrospect, it even has its charm. But what else?

When Madeline and I reminisce about those high school parties, it's impossible not to smile at the thought of those crazy, emotional nights full of unexpected twists and turns that happened to us suspiciously often. It was as if we were some kind of chosen ones from a godforsaken place! We definitely didn't make wise decisions back then. Today, these memories are like colorful snapshots from a time when life seemed limitless and infinite. And today, life seems full of limitations, not to mention its finite and fragile nature.

Do you want more strange adventures from the disco? Here you go!

Even Dante couldn't have made this up!

One night, during another party, something happened that I can't really boast about, and definitely not in front of my own children. We came up with the brilliant idea of climbing onto the roof of the building during the ongoing disco, knowing that it offered a beautiful view of the city.

Struggling up the ladder and carrying a bottle of champagne, we suddenly heard a shout:

"What are you doing?! Are you crazy?!"

We barely recognized the guy. He had been hanging around the dance floor, mostly leaning against the wall. That exhausting piece of information convinced us that he wasn't worth worrying about. We kept going with that cursed champagne. But the guy must have wanted to promote himself to Guardian Angel Gabriel because he interrupted again:

"One of you is going to fall any second!"

A real prophet!

"Relax, we're totally sober," Maddie retorted cheekily.

I added with a smile, "Well, maybe not entirely, but definitely not so drunk that we don't know what we're doing. Yeah, right!"

The guy, clearly nervous but also fascinated by our recklessness, decided to join us in this unusual adventure. Together with him, sharing the bottle of champagne, we admired the night city spreading out below us. Although we didn't even like him!

Everything seemed perfect (except for the not-so-handsome guy) until we noticed the club's security guard. He was shouting at us from below to get off the roof immediately. Or at least that's what we thought because it was hard to hear. Maddie shouted in her usual style:

"What? We're just admiring the view! Surely that's not against the rules?"

Apparently, the security guard had a different opinion because, furious beyond belief, he started climbing up the roof as well. The guy with us, like a real man, immediately panicked and was on the verge of tears. Surely nothing would have saved us from being dragged off the roof if the security guard hadn't suddenly screamed and fallen like a rag doll. The rusty ladder couldn't bear the weight of his bulked-up muscles.

Another security guard appeared by the unlucky one.

That's when the guy with us suddenly remembered that there was an entrance to the disco building's hallway on the roof. We escaped at the last moment. I admit, I felt uneasy the next day. After all, we didn't know what had happened to the security guard. Eventually, we found out by chance.

"Hey, do you know what happened at the disco last night?" a classmate asked us. "Apparently, a security guard was fighting terrorists on the roof. His buddy confirms that he was bravely beating up the bastards."

"And?" Madeline yawned, not particularly interested.

"He was overwhelmed by superior forces."

"Did he die?!" I almost screamed in horror.

"No, he broke his leg," our classmate clarified.

Unfortunately, we had to change discos. Apparently, the police even started looking for those terrorists.

That's how Maddie and I knew how to have fun.

We kept coming up with crazier and crazier ideas. Once, we pretended to be Red Cross volunteers, going door-to-door collecting money for a noble cause, which unfortunately turned out to be clothes and mint cigarettes. I'm still ashamed of that stunt. Another time, we switched price tags in stores, swapping the cheaper ones onto more expensive items to buy them at a discount.

Madeline even managed to open a jar of spaghetti sauce in a store, lick it to taste it, claiming she wouldn't buy something without trying it first. Of course, if it didn't suit her taste buds, she'd screw the lid back on and put it back on the shelf. Gross.

We were young, crazy bitches, little devils. But we felt alive!

We often skipped classes and were always on the move. It's a miracle that we always returned safe and sound from those escapades. God must have had a special watch over us.

One of our next ideas was to go to Poznan for my cousin's military oath ceremony. It was a spontaneous trip, planned just a few days before the event. During this journey, Madeline, as usual, couldn't resist approaching passersby, asking them for directions to the nearest bar:

"Excuse me, where can we get a drink around here? My friend and I are here for a military oath, and we can't go without a toast to our hero!"

Some passersby found it amusing; others were annoyed. But Madeline and I laughed ourselves silly. We finally managed to reach the military base. Standing with me in the main square, Maddie suddenly noticed:

"We need to change into our flowy dresses because I'm going to roast in these jeans!"

"And we don't look sexy enough," I added.

We burst out laughing, so much so that the soldiers' parents started shushing us. But the idea of changing seemed good enough that we decided it was worth doing. However, there was one serious problem: finding a suitable place for such an operation in a military base full of people wasn't easy.

"There!" Maddie grabbed my arm.

I looked in the direction she was pointing. It was a bunker, guarded by two heavily armed sentries.

"Are you crazy? They're guarding it!" I glanced at my friend.

"That's even better; no one will bother us," she said, then grabbed my hand and pulled me toward the bunker.

To this day, I don't know how we managed to get inside. Madeline did everything she could to charm the guards. I'm not sure if it was our charm or if those guys were just fed up with us, but they finally allowed us to change in the bunker. Of course, we didn't hurry. We put on our flowy, alluring dresses and even had time for makeup. Finally, we were ready. As quietly as we could, we began to leave the bunker, sure that the ceremony was about to begin. Outside, we were stunned. We saw, to our horror, entire rows of soldiers marching straight toward us.

"Eyes front! Forward march! Eyes front!" their commander shouted.

But at the sight of us, those poor guys started losing their rhythm, mixing up their steps, tripping over their own feet. It was a total disaster. Madeline and I still laugh ourselves to tears whenever we remember that situation. And the oath ceremony for my cousin? We missed the whole event while we were getting dolled up in the bunker. But it was still fun!

Another crazy trip was our pilgrimage to Czestochowa to see Pope John Paul II. There, standing among the crowd of believers, we wondered how to get the Pope's blessing. Of course, Maddie had her idea. She suddenly announced:

"We need to climb up somewhere so we're visible! Then the Pope will definitely notice us and bless us!"

Eventually, we managed to get up on a railing, and the Pope smiled at us and blessed us. At least, that's what we believed at the time. And faith can work wonders. What really happened? I'll leave that veiled in silence, as Dante might say. In any case, after that pilgrimage, we believed even more that we had some divine connections in Heaven. So, we felt we could afford even more. After all, we felt invincible, maybe even chosen.

But the most unforgettable were our visits to the "Nutters from the Capital," as everyone called them, including themselves. It was all about good marketing! This was the crew of my future first husband. A motley bunch, to say the least – his brothers, friends, neighbors, and the rest. As a teenager, I was fascinated by this world full of adventures, parties, craziness, and the constant presence of the police. Madeline, as usual, took everything in stride, laughing even during a police raid on the house during one of the parties.

"Listen, this is the best! The cops asked if we organized this party, and I said, 'No, we just came here for the Pope's blessing!'" She laughed for a good few minutes, and I laughed with her.

Back then, the antics of the "Nutters from the Capital" seemed awesome. I was in love with the whole chaotic scene – their craziness, parties, nonchalance, the police constantly on their tail, and more! I was so impressed! But now, looking back as an adult woman,

I realize it was all messed up. The amount of stupidity and crime I witnessed was unbelievable!

Of course, Maddie had her response to that as well:

"You know what, girl? In a few years, we'll be telling our kids how to have fun!"

A crappy idea!

There's really nothing to brag about. What was I thinking back then?

Probably nothing at all!

Sometimes I wish I could forget all of it. When I analyze all our escapades and foolishness, I get more and more horrified. Sometimes I pretend to myself that they were just childish pranks. The problem is, they weren't as innocent as I'd like to believe. They weren't!

Today, I know all too well that every choice we make, however small, impacts who we'll become tomorrow. Denying reality won't help because hell doesn't easily let go of those who enter its welcoming gates.

But my life goes on, and every day of my fate is woven. Still. And the words from that unfinished conversation in the park keep coming back to me:

"Madeline, sometimes I really regret meeting you... Is this still Hell, or is it something else?"

CHAPTER 4

Ah, those wild years of youth! Especially the ones when I turned sixteen. That's when I fell in love. My first, true, teenage love. It all began at a disco, a place that both Maddie and I still considered very important.

Somewhere on the outskirts of the city, far from the hustle and bustle of daily life and routine, there was a small club where the discos took place. It was well-known in high school circles, a sort of place where we would meet on weekends. It might have seemed like nothing special, but for me, it became a sort of... Dantean Forest. Yes, you read that right. A Dantean Forest, where we emerged in the middle of the night, half-conscious from dancing and alcohol, entangled in a whirlwind of romantic entanglements. A Dantean Forest, something mysterious, unknown, sometimes dark and not always welcoming. That's how I understood it back then.

And in that forest, something happened that changed my life. At least, that's what I thought at the time. For the first time, I walked in there alone, a bit shy and full of anxiety. I saw Him in that small club on the outskirts of the city. He, as tough as steel, freshly released from the embrace of the military, stood there with that confident look in his eyes. I, a sixteen-year-old with a head full of dreams and romantic fantasies, looked at him as if he were the hero of my disturbingly vivid dreams. I noticed him immediately, standing on the edge of the dance floor, like a lonely wanderer on the brink of a Dantean Forest.

When our eyes met, something sparked. At first, I thought it was just a spotlight, but it turned out to be something more. Something that made my heart beat faster, and my hands become sweaty.

He approached me with a smile on his face. I knew he was going to say something clever. Something that would shake me to my core, bring me to my knees.

"Care to dance, beautiful?" he asked.

And you know what? It really did shake me. Not the words themselves, but the timbre of his voice – low, almost mesmerizing.

"So, what do you say?" he pressed, growing more impatient.

Despite my heart pounding wildly, I managed to stammer out something I thought was witty at the time:

"If you can keep rhythm better than a rifle, then I guess I can risk it."

The laughter that burst from his lips gave me confidence. Oh yes! We danced together for the next few months. Sometimes to disco music, sometimes to rock, and sometimes to tango, which turned out to be our favorite dance. Yes, tango! Surprised? If so, then you've probably never danced a true tango. How did we come across such a dance? In that steamy club, they played all sorts of interesting tracks.

So, tango. Every step, every turn was a new page in the story of our first love. It was a dance full of emotions and mysteries, dripping with passion that often left reason behind.

One evening, when ABBA's hit was playing on the dance floor, I tripped over my own feet. Well, even the best dancers stumble sometimes. That's when he made the sweetest comment I've ever heard:

"Don't worry, beautiful. I'll catch you every time your legs fail you."

That moment has stayed with me to this day, a reminder that love, like dancing, isn't perfect, but it's those little stumbles, those small imperfections, that make it truly beautiful.

Even after all these years, when I think of Eric, warmth spreads through my heart. Eric... He was a tall, well-built guy with dark, almost chocolate eyes. He had that unique charisma that you could feel even when he was barely within sight. He worked as a bouncer at the discos. I'm not sure if it was because of that job or if he just had it in his genes, but he danced like a young god. We danced through our entire relationship. And while I don't remember much from those years, I'll never forget dancing with him. Every step, every turn, every look... it was all magical. And his sense of humor! Indescribable! He had this knack for goofing around that could make me laugh even on the worst days.

He was always surrounded by a group of friends. They were like brothers to him, and to me, they were like family. Each one was different, but together they formed a unique group.

This journey with Eric was full of unexpected twists, just like in Dante's stories. There were moments when we got lost, tangled in our own emotions, but we always found our way back. We always ended up in the same place – on the dance floor, in the heart of our Dantean Forest.

And yes, just like Dante in his *The Divine Comedy*, I too learned something about myself. That I'm capable of loving and being loved, and that love can be complicated and full of twists and turns, just like a Dantean Forest. But most importantly, I realized that every love, even the most painful and complicated one, is a journey worth taking.

Our love was like a dancing wind – sometimes gentle and soothing, other times wild and unpredictable. It was a romance full of euphoria, sadness, joy, and pain, and because of that, it was incredibly real. But just like everything beautiful, it couldn't last forever...

At the end of our Dantean journey, Eric, my love, my hell, and my heaven, left. He left me and our dance. What remained was only a shadow and emptiness that filled my heart. Despite that loss, despite the painful loneliness I experienced, I knew that this journey was worth every step, every word, every look. After all, there's no *Divine Comedy* without hell, no love without pain, and a true journey requires courage and a willingness to face challenges. And although my journey with Eric had come to an end, I understood that it wasn't the end of my own Dantean Forest. I knew that many more times, I would have to enter its depths, traverse more circles, to find love and happiness again.

Sometimes I think of him, of all the good times we spent together. There were years when I regretted that it was over...

Eric was my first teenage love. The first man who caught my eye. The first who taught me to dance with emotions I hadn't known before. The first who showed me what it feels like to love. But nothing ever happened between us in the sexual realm. Maybe that's why he left... Maybe I was too young, too unsure, too naive... If I had been ready for more, would everything have turned out differently? If I had been braver, more confident, could we have been together? These questions, these "what ifs," haunted me for years. But I always come back to the same thought: it was love. It was true, uncomplicated, teenage love. And even though we're not together, even though Eric is now just a memory, I'll never forget him. I'll always remember our dance.

After Eric, as if fate had something against my happiness, He appeared. I met him through Madeline, something I still can't forgive her for. I knew right away that he was a complete jerk. But still, that "bad boy" aura fascinated me, just like it fascinates every naive teenager who thinks that bad boys love the most.

"This is Sebastian," Maddie introduced him, and I, as if hypnotized, stared into his gray eyes.

"Welcome to my kingdom," he said with a smile that could melt Siberia.

Sebastian. A character worthy of being described by Dante. He had something about him that both attracted and repelled. On one hand, he commanded respect, and on the other, fear. Yes, he could have been one of those monsters that Dante placed at the bottom of his hell, as the personification of sin and evil. There was nothing endearing about him, yet he was handsome in his crude way. His face was sculpted like that of a marble hero, his eyes always cold and defiant. Could you love him? No. Could you desire him? Oh yes, definitely! He was like a walking, breathing paradox.

As Schopenhauer said, *people are like hedgehogs that try to get close to each other for warmth, but always end up getting pricked by their own quills.*

Sebastian had quills, indeed, but quills so sharp that they always hurt. So why was he so attractive? Is human nature so cruel that it seeks out those who can hurt us? Since I'm diving into philosophy, Nietzsche also wondered if man is willing to destroy himself for his desires. Is desire stronger than fear? Nietzsche might be surprised, but Sebastian was the answer to those questions. Yes, man is capable of self-destruction for his desires. Yes, desire can be stronger than fear. Maybe that's why Sebastian was the king of the city. Despite his crude nature, despite his menacing appearance, despite being the walking personification of sin, people desired him. They craved the corrupted beauty he represented. Maybe that's the true image of our hell – the desire for what we know as evil yet being unable to turn away.

Yes, Sebastian was like Dante's hell: terrifying but fascinating. He was like that dark circle that Dante described so vividly – a place full of pain and suffering, yet simultaneously alluring with its mysterious power. Isn't this an image of our human nature? Aren't we all, like Dante, travelers through our own hells, drawn to what we know as evil?

Sebastian was that reminder – a symbol of the cursed magnet that attracts, even though we know the consequences. And like Dante's hell, it was impossible to take your eyes off him. He pulled us all in, and I was no exception. I looked at him like a lost soul, knowing I was heading in the wrong direction but too weak to turn back. His presence was like a swirling black hole in the city's center, swallowing everything and everyone. He was like a fatal flaw in the moral compass that always pointed you in the wrong direction, no matter how hard you tried to go the right way.

Even now, as I write about him, I feel that strange attraction, that dark desire he awakened. Was it connected to our human nature? Is the desire for what is forbidden, what we know as evil, embedded in our biological makeup? Are we programmed for self-destruction?

And yes, looking at Sebastian, at his rude beauty, I felt something inside me break. I saw my understanding of the world start to crumble. I realized then that hell is not a place you go to after death. Hell is here, on earth, in our daily choices, in our desires and fears. This is the true hell of Dante; this is the true *Divine Comedy* – the tragedy of our own desires that lead us to self-destruction.

Sebastian was like hell within arm's reach. He was like sin you could touch, like a cursed fruit that could be tasted. But just as in Dante's hell, the consequences were always painful.

It was with that bastard that I experienced my first time. I had always thought it would be a wonderful moment, but now I know it was rape. Unfortunately, I didn't realize it at the time. I just lay there quietly, praying in my mind for it to be over. I didn't have the courage to say it out loud. I didn't know I could. I lay there with my eyes squeezed shut, tears streaming down my face... and he used me...

It was horrible! After it was over, I quickly dressed and ran away. The feeling of shame and disgust stayed with me forever. I still feel it today, as if it happened only yesterday. Seb – damned rapist!

What did I expect from someone who had slapped me across the face in public? That he would love, adore, and respect me? Was I naive? Well, yes, I was. Who knows, maybe it was the contrast between Eric and Sebastian? Maybe that's what attracted me?

Maybe it was what made me agree to that wild ride?

But it ended. And it's good that it did. In fact, I don't want to remember him at all. Apparently, he died somewhere in a gutter. A fitting death for such a bastard, as if his inner demon finally consumed him. As if that rude, handsome face finally saw itself in the mirror.

"Have you heard about Sebastian?" Madeline asked one day, sitting on the couch in my apartment.

"No, and I don't want to," I replied, not looking at her.

"Apparently..."

"Madeline, I really don't want to know," I interrupted her.

But she told me. She told me how he died. A part of me wanted to rejoice, but another part... another part was devastated. Not because I loved him. No, that was long ago. But because, despite everything, he was a part of my life. He was my mistake, my lesson. And now, with him gone, I could only look back and wonder how I could have been so foolish.

After that bastard, I was alone for months; I didn't want to see anyone, didn't want anything at all... The disgust and anger remain to this day.

All that was left for me was to escape into the world of dreams and the world of love hidden in the pages of books. That love was somehow safer. It didn't carry the same risks as the one in the real world. I didn't have to fear rejection, pain, broken promises, or disappointed expectations.

What intrigued me most was the love between Dante and Beatrice. It was something that always fascinated me and gave me the sense that love could be pure, untainted by human flaws. I wondered if what I felt was even love at all, or rather a desire to possess something that seemed unattainable? Was it infatuation, or was it self-destruction?

And so, diving into these thoughts, I realized that perhaps, like Dante, I had idealized love too much. Perhaps I was searching for something that didn't exist? Perhaps what I called love for Sebastian was more of a desire, an obsession?

Or maybe love doesn't exist at all? Maybe it's all just an illusion we create to give ourselves a sense of meaning?

As I continued to escape into the world of dreams and the world of literary love, I began to see my own mistakes, my own delusions. I began to realize that what I called love was something entirely different.

Shortly after graduating, I decided to redo my first time, but this time with someone who deserved it and for whom I had real feelings. It was a boy who would stay in my heart for years. Boris. He was part of the "Nutters from the Capital".

Boris was out of this world! He started by charming me with his looks, and then I couldn't let go. His sense of humor, personality, and tenderness brought me to my knees. God, how I fell in love with him!

Boris had something that made me forget about the whole world. His gaze made me feel like the only woman on earth. And there was that wild magnetism that drew me to him with an inexplicable force. We danced, we laughed, we talked about everything and nothing. Our dates were magical. Boris was a true gentleman. He always opened doors for me, took off his jacket to cover me when I was cold, and his smile was the most beautiful thing I could see. We had our special place – a small ice cream shop where he always ordered two pink sorbets for us. Sometimes we would walk along the Vistula boulevards, sipping cheap wine in silence, savoring our closeness. Those were moments that belonged only to us.

But love is not just those sweet, magical moments. It's also desire, the craving for another person, the craving for touch. Boris and I reveled in all of it. Every meeting ended at his apartment, where we weren't constrained by social conventions. There were moments when desire overwhelmed us, when our bodies longed for each other. There were moments when I felt his touch on my skin, his kisses on my lips. Moments were born that were only ours, filled with passion and desire. There was something incredibly exhilarating in those moments, something that made me feel more alive than ever. With Boris, sex was like a beautiful dance, full of passion, tenderness, and desire. He knew how to touch me, how to kiss me, how to make me feel beautiful and desired.

Boris was the kind of guy every girl dream of.

I knew then that he was the one I wanted to spend my life with. He was handsome, funny, tender, and passionate. He was the one who made my heart beat faster, who made my mind dream of the future, who made my body crave his closeness. But not everything was as perfect as it seemed.

With Boris, I had the chance to experience more than just physical thrills. He showed me what it meant to be understood, loved, and respected. He made me realize how beautiful it can feel when instead of emptiness, you feel warmth spreading inside you. He showed me what it means when someone looks at you like you're the most beautiful thing in the world, even when you're disheveled and sleepy.

What surprised me the most, however, was how easy it was to cross the boundaries of decency, how easy it was to forget the rules that once seemed so obvious. For Boris, there were no barriers. When we were together, the world outside of us simply didn't exist. Everything else didn't matter. It was a time full of passionate kisses, long talks by candlelight, a time when I could feel truly happy. But it was also a time when I had to face the truth. The truth that not everything is as beautiful as it seems. And that love isn't always easy and trouble-free.

"I'm engaged," he said one day, as if it were the most normal thing in the world.

It was like a bolt from the blue. Yes, it's a cliché. But it captures the essence. In one moment, I lost everything that mattered to me.

"Oh, really?" I replied, trying to stay calm, though inside, I felt something break.

He knew my feelings; knew I was madly in love with him. He confessed that he had fallen in love too. I remember sitting on a park bench with him when he asked:

"It would be best if I stayed with you, right?"

"You know that..." I replied, trying to hide the tremor in my voice.

But I knew it was impossible. I wanted it more than anything in the world! But since he already had a settled, mature relationship, why would he want to play with a teenager?

And he left me.

I was left alone with my pain, with my disappointment.

"I shouldn't care," I told myself, trying to convince my heart that it was true.

But the heart isn't easily fooled.

I couldn't forget him. For the next few years, my heart was like a wounded animal – desperate to escape but unable to.

Still, I regret nothing because what I experienced with him was beautiful.

To this day, when I hear Alphaville's "Forever Young," I get chills. Because that was our song. Every time I heard the first notes, my heart would start beating faster. That song reminded me of Boris, of our love, of the times that were beautiful and innocent for us. The catchy synth-pop rhythm, the nostalgic melody, and the soft, un-forced vocals of the singer – all of it created the backdrop for our love story. The first sounds of the song, those subtle, almost ethereal notes that flowed calmly and gently, reminded me of the beginnings of our love. Of how our feelings slowly and shyly began. How, with each passing day, they became stronger, more intense. This part of the song, full of subtle anticipation, reminded me of our first kisses, the first looks full of passion.

Then came the moment when the melody picked up tempo. This was the stage of our love full of excitement and desire. These were the moments when I realized that Boris was more than just an acquaintance. It was a time when every touch of his made my heart beat faster and my knees go weak.

The chorus of the song was the apotheosis of our love. The singer's voice resonated with a message full of passion about eternal youth. In those moments, singing together "Forever young, I want to be forever young," we felt that our love was eternal, that time had no power over us. These were the moments when we forgot about the world when it was just the two of us.

When the song came to an end, when the sounds slowly faded, it reminded me of the end of our love. Of the moments when we had to part. When my heart was broken. Despite everything, despite the tears that flowed down my cheeks, despite the pain I felt in my heart, there was always hope at the end of that song. Hope that maybe one day we would be together again.

"That's your and Boris's song, isn't it?" Madeline asked one day when that melody played on the radio.

"Yes, it was our song," I confirmed, then looked out the window at the crowded streets of the city. "It always will be," I added quietly.

It's hard enough to go through your own personal hell, but it's even harder when you're a lovestruck teenager, literally experiencing a Dantean hell, descending slowly, unknowingly, into your own romantic circles.

It all started innocently, just like the First Circle of Dante's *Inferno* – limbo. There was some uncertainty, a constant questioning of whether it was worth it. But I was curious, wondering if this was the love I had read so much about.

"I'm in limbo," I confessed to Madeline during one of our late-night talks.

"Limbo? Like from Dante's Hell?" She looked at me with surprise.

"Yes, exactly. I still don't know where I am or where I'm going."

When I met Boris, I found myself in the Second Circle – on the very edge of hell, full of desire. But then, when I learned about his engagement, I fell straight into the Third Circle – hunger and cold.

"Madeline, I feel like something inside me has frozen," I confessed to my friend. That's when I started reading about the Fourth Circle – anger and jealousy. I realized that this was exactly what I felt. Anger at Boris, jealousy of his fiancée. But then I realized that it wasn't the end.

I kept descending lower, into the Fifth Circle – laziness and tears, then the Sixth – heresy, the Seventh – violence, the Eighth – lies, and the Ninth – betrayal. Each circle was like a new phase of my relationship, like a new wound on my heart.

"This is like some kind of nightmare journey," I finally told Maddie when we reached the end of the journey through Dante's hell.

"Well, Dante had to go through hell before he reached paradise. Maybe now you will too," my friend pondered, quite seriously.

Maybe Madeline was right. Maybe I had to go through all of this to learn something about myself, about love, about what really matters. Maybe I had to go through these Dantean circles to understand how important my dignity is to me and how precious my body is.

Unfortunately, I didn't learn anything back then.

When Pandora's Box is opened, everything really does escape from it, and we become helpless. That's a fact, and I experienced it firsthand. When I lost my most precious treasure, my virginity, I felt that it was a pivotal moment, something unique, something that defined my next years. It was the moment after which I felt I had become someone else. I felt that I had lost something incredibly valuable, something that was only mine, something I would never get back.

So, I opened my Pandora's Box wide, not thinking about the consequences. My naivety makes me cry over spilled milk now. Once I lost what was most precious, I felt that it didn't matter who else looked inside. My body, which was once hidden away, suddenly became an object of interest to others. After all, there was nothing left to protect, nothing left to hide.

"It doesn't matter anymore," I repeated to my reflection in the mirror, trying to convince myself of my own words. "Now, anyone can look into my Pandora's Box."

I wanted to believe it was true, I wanted to believe that my worth didn't depend on what had happened in the past.

I didn't know back then that I should still protect both myself and my body. I didn't realize that my body wasn't just a treasure that could be lost but also a temple that needed to be respected and cared for. That was something no one had ever told me, something no one had ever taught me. Because who would have done that?

"Mom, can I talk to you?" I asked one day.

She looked at me, surprised.

"Should I... Should I protect myself?" I continued down this absurd path.

In her eyes, I saw surprise, then sadness. She knew what I meant. She knew I had lost something valuable, and now I had no idea how to deal with it.

At home, I had a rather poor example. That's why there were occasional one-night stands. But honestly, I never felt anything – no pleasure, no closeness.

"Is this all there is?" I asked Madeline one day when I was telling her about my latest fling.

"What do you mean?" she replied with a worried look.

"Is this what it's supposed to be like? Is this how it's supposed to be?" I kept asking.

And so, both my dignity and I kept spiraling down to the bottom.

"You have to deal with it," Madeline told me one day when I had fallen into another spiral of self-destruction. "You can't just give up like this."

"But what am I supposed to do? " I responded, looking at her with despair. "I've already lost everything."

And then Maddie unexpectedly said, "You still have yourself. That's the most important thing."

Finally, the end of my crazy journey through the valley of high school tears came. Like a modern Beatrice, staring at Dante's unattainable star, I felt lost. It was an endless road through my personal labyrinth of emotions, my own hell.

"Why did Dante have to write it so damn accurately?" I asked Madeline one day, clutching my copy of *The Divine Comedy*. "Couldn't he have been a bit less dramatic?"

"Well, it's Dante, you idiot!" Maddie pointed out, frowning.

And just as Dante wandered through the nine circles of hell, so I wandered through the nine stages of a relationship that rekindled my heart. Each phase was like a new circle of my personal hell: from innocent fascination, through passion, to disappointment, jealousy, heartbreak, betrayal, separation, despair, and finally – a sense of wasted time.

You only had to look at my life, and you'd have a ready-made script for a modern adaptation of Dante's *Inferno*. I even had my own Virgil – Madeline, who guided me through those infernal circles, though I wasn't always sure I wanted to enter them.

"Is this the end of our journey, Madeline?" I asked when we reached the last circle of my hell, the one where I broke up with Boris.

She again pointed out wisely, "Remember, Dante went through hell to reach paradise. So, who knows? Maybe this is just the beginning of your journey."

To be honest, I wasn't sure if I wanted to go further. But I knew I had to. And just like Dante, I had to keep moving forward... hopefully to my own paradise.

Because even though hell was terrifying, without it, we would never truly appreciate the beauty of love.

So, I went through these relationships with men, always with the same hope and always with the same result. Like Sisyphus, who took a step up only to fall back down to the bottom again.

With each failure, with each failed relationship, my sense of shame and helplessness grew.

And yet, I continued to beg for love, to plead for attention and acceptance. I asked for all those feelings I had never experienced in my childhood.

I began to doubt whether I would ever find the love I dreamed of. Whether I would ever know true closeness, genuine tenderness, and complete understanding.

My heart became a veritable cemetery of love. It was full of graves... full of the past... full of sorrow...

"All that's left for me is to escape into the world of dreams and the world of love hidden in the pages of books," I repeated to myself, burying my face in a pillow and trying to drown out the sobs that filled me.

I felt my dignity slowly fade away, crushed by the weight of my mistakes, my imperfections, and my wounds.

I closed my eyes, trying for a moment to detach myself from the reality in which I felt so powerless. Powerless in the face of all those relationships that turned out to be mistakes. Powerless in the face of those men who promised love but gave only pain. Desperately, I searched for something that could replace the growing shame, the unspeakable regret. But what could replace the sense of loss? Could I replace it with something else that would make me not feel so help-less, so alone?

I felt my soul scream, and my body tremble. I wanted to run away; I wanted to disappear. But I couldn't. The shame and helpless-ness were with me, accompanying me, reminding me of my past. In the midst of it all, I found a small ray of hope. I read Dante's *Divine Comedy* and realized that my situation wasn't unique. Dante, despite going through hell, always believed he would see Beatrice again. And me? Could I have that kind of faith? Could I have hope that des-pite all these mistakes, despite the shame, despite the helplessness, I could find true love? Could I have hope that I would see my Dante, my own hero who would lead me through my own hell?

I read Dante's words. Those words became my guidepost, my light at the end of the tunnel. *In the midst of the dark valley of life, where the true path was lost...* The true path, my path, seemed lost. I had lost it somewhere amidst broken promises, betrayed feelings, and a heart torn to shreds. Could I find it again? Could I return to the right path, just like Dante?

Helplessness seemed to crush me; each failed relationship only added to the weight. Shame was like a blade cutting into my soul, wounding me with every move, with every reminder of the past.

CHAPTER 5

Those were the days of teenage oblivion, when immaturity and recklessness mixed with hope and faith in a better tomorrow.

A breeze blew through my memories, carrying with it the scents of youth, carefree moments, and audacity. Back in those days, when we were seventeen or eighteen, everything seemed simpler. Those years felt like a dance on a tightrope, on the edge of awareness and ignorance. At times, balancing on the thin line of life was difficult, but it was also incredibly exciting.

Madeline and I flitted like butterflies from one flower to another, from one city to another, always in search of something new and thrilling.

I had just finished high school, and the world lay at my feet when Maddie, her eyes shining with love, desire, and longing, declared:

"We're going to Warsaw, to see my boyfriend, Rafael. We must!"

"Of course, we're going," I replied, needing no persuasion. We packed a few things into a backpack, and thus began a new chapter in our pursuit of adventure.

Warsaw, along with Rafael and the rest of the Crew, welcomed us with open arms, and Boris, whom I had fallen in love with, ignited feelings in me that I had never experienced before. He was like lightning on a summer night – surprising, beautiful, and fleeting. But you already know that.

After he left me, the world seemed gray and cold once more.

Then he appeared, Anthony. He was also part of the "Nutters from the Capital" from the capital. And it was he who took care of me when everyone else had used and discarded me, leaving me sad and alone, with a torn heart.

"Don't cry," he begged, holding me tenderly. "That's not the solution."

He was like warm sunshine after a storm, gentle and kind. Whenever I needed support, he was there. Whenever I feared loneliness, he stayed with me late into the night, talking about life, dreams, and the future.

And so, for the next few months, he was always by my side.

A wonderful person, a marvelous friend.

"You're a special person," Anthony whispered to me once, looking deeply into my eyes.

Even then, I suspected where this might lead. I suspected it, but I didn't believe it. Boris – he was everywhere! But it wasn't as simple as it might have seemed to someone else.

I thought Anthony was just taking care of a poor, abandoned lamb out of the goodness of his heart. It was much later that I learned from Madeline that he had set his sights on me. He had decided that I would be his! Only me – no one else! He took advantage of my moments of weakness and quietly slipped into my life under the guise of friendship.

In any case, during that time, he cared for me like no one else ever had. He was good to me. Just plain good. And I suppose that's what I needed back then. There was some feeling between us, but it wasn't love, because I still carried someone else in my heart.

Eventually, Anthony fell deeply in love with me. He often looked at me with that mixture of admiration and wonder that only his eyes knew. Honestly, I don't know what he loved about me.

"You're the love of my life," he would say, smiling charmingly.

The words sounded so sincere that I couldn't resist them.

"How could this end?" I asked Madeline, worry evident in my voice.

"It's love," she answered, full of hope and naivety, madly in love with Rafael, Anthony's brother.

One night, after a party, Anthony and I came up with the crazy idea of visiting a fortune teller. She was an older woman, known for her accurate predictions. She looked wise and experienced, with deep wrinkles and eyes full of mystery.

"Oh, I see you're truly in love," she said, gazing into the cards. "A wedding and a child await you."

I must admit, we were actually pleased by this news. I thought that I would get married, escape from home, start a family, and begin to live a normal life.

"Will it really come true?" I kept asking the fortune teller.

"The cards don't lie," she replied calmly. "But remember, fate gives and takes. You must be careful."

Anthony squeezed my hand, and I looked into his eyes as if to assure him that we would make it, just us.

A few months later, on a magical, cool evening, Anthony knelt before me, and something extraordinary sparkled in his eyes.

"Will you marry me?" he asked, pulling out a beautiful ring with a red stone.

"Yes," I nodded, though I don't think I fully understood what I was saying.

That was the beginning of something beautiful, or so I thought at the time. Everything seemed so perfect. The meeting of our parents took place in a warm and friendly atmosphere. He brought a stunning basket of velvet-red roses, and everyone was charmed by his gesture.

"He's a true gentleman," my mother said, looking at Anthony with approval.

"We're very happy that our daughter has found such a man," my father added, smiling broadly at my future in-laws.

My parents liked my fiancé, and a sense of harmony and optimism settled over us. It seemed that nothing could go wrong.

At the same time, we confessed to our parents that I was pregnant. This was another wonderful, though surprising, piece of news for the family. I felt fulfilled and happy, as if everything was falling into place exactly as it should. It was a wonderful time, one that nourished my heart with joy and hope. The pregnancy enveloped me in an aura of love and care that I had never experienced before. I loved this child from the first moment I knew of its existence, and each day brought a new dimension to that love.

I cared for Adam from the very beginning, whispering sweetly to him, singing lullabies, letting him know he was loved. I felt his movements, the pulsing life, and our hearts beat in perfect harmony.

Everyone said it would be a girl. And I wanted a son! But regardless of the gender, I promised my little miracle that they would be loved unconditionally. And then, in that magical moment when the child was born, and the world held its breath, the midwife announced it was a boy. I wept with joy. It was a cry of fulfillment, of absolute, unblemished love.

Our wedding was beautiful – on the surface. The church was adorned with delicate flowers, and the orchestra played romantic melodies. Everyone seemed happy. Everyone, except me. Today, I consider that decision the most senseless one of my life. I wouldn't repeat it if I had the chance. Anthony was radiant, eagerly awaiting the wedding. His hands trembled with emotion as he held mine. When I looked into his eyes, I saw love, hope, and the future. But my heart was elsewhere. With the best man. And who was the best man? Boris. Yes! Boris was Anthony's best man! We stood at the altar, and I looked at Boris, standing right next to him. After all, he was Anthony's friend. He seemed somewhat absent, his gaze cold and distant. His eyes – the same ones that had once looked at me with love – now appeared completely empty.

The altar, the priest, the vows – all of it became insignificant. My words were directed at Boris, not my future husband! I was making vows, but not to Anthony. And so I stood before the altar, bound to a man who seemed to have ended up there by chance. Who stood between me and Boris like some anonymous passerby.

After the ceremony, during the wedding reception, Boris approached me, clearly unsure of himself.

"Congratulations," he said, trying to smile.

But his smile wasn't genuine. In his voice, I heard something that seemed like sadness. Or maybe I just wanted to find it there.

"Thank you," I replied, but deep down, I knew those weren't words of gratitude for the congratulations. They were thanks for being there. For letting me look into his eyes one more time. There were no tears of joy that day. Only the whispers of the heart, the longing for what could have been but never was.

It was the beginning of the end. I already knew that. I just didn't have the courage to admit it.

Marriage to Anthony was like a beautiful dream that turned into a nightmare. I felt something for him, but probably not what I should have. Boris was always there, in the corner of my heart – immortal, impossible to ignore. Anthony was tender, he cared for me, but he knew. He felt it throughout our marriage. Sometimes he would look at me with that piercing gaze, full of sadness and pain, asking:

"Will I ever be more to you than he is?"

My heart broke when I heard those words, but I couldn't promise him anything more. I knew that answering that question would be a lie.

"I'm trying, Antosh," I once replied, tears streaming down my face. "I'm really trying."

Days passed, and the invisible wall between us grew. Boris was like a shadow that wouldn't leave. Sometimes I would see him on the street; we would bump into each other at friends' parties. Every glance, every word was like a dagger in my heart. Anthony watched us from a distance, saw how my heart raced, how my hands trembled. He suffered, but he never showed it. He was too proud, too honorable. Until one evening, as we sat in front of the television, Anthony asked me directly:

"Will you ever love me the way you love him?"

I wanted to scream yes. I wanted to give him hope, but the truth was too cruel.

"No," I whispered. "I'm sorry."

There was nothing left to say. Anthony left, and I was alone with my thoughts, my memories, and a love that had no right to exist.

This was another stage of destruction. The erosion of our marriage accelerated. Everything began to fall apart with increasing noise. Anthony knew from the beginning that I loved Boris, but he deluded himself. In the end, those illusions dissipated like morning mist in the wind. Later, he always said that our marriage fell apart because I still loved him. Well, there was a lot of truth in that.

Unfortunately, that was the truth! Boris was still in my heart. It was a sadness that accompanied me for years. It was a shadow that wouldn't disappear. It was a pain that couldn't pass.

At the beginning of this marriage, there was hope. *Okay, I'm a married woman now, I thought, things will get better. I have a husband who will take me away from this madhouse, my family home. He will take care of me and our child, give me the sense of security that I had lacked so much throughout my life.*

Keep dreaming, girl!

From one mess, I ended up in another!

At the beginning of my pregnancy and during the first few months of my child's life, I lived with my parents, and Anthony would visit every weekend, then every two weeks... every five weeks... gradually less and less. Eventually, I noticed he felt uncomfortable in my family home. I understood him perfectly. He stopped getting along with my father because he had his own opinions. And he shouldn't have had any! He was supposed to agree with his father-in-law in everything, always.

One evening, when Anthony visited us again after a few weeks of absence, my father couldn't hold back.

"I don't understand," he said, looking at him sternly. "Why do you visit so rarely? Is your family not important to you?"

Anthony looked at him with surprise and then pressed his lips together. "I don't think I visit rarely," he replied calmly, though his face clearly showed his dissatisfaction.

The atmosphere in the room grew tense. My father glared at him angrily.

"Is that how clever you are? Remember, I'm your father-in-law, and I deserve respect!" he shouted.

Anthony stood up from his chair. "I won't do what you tell me!" he declared firmly. "I'm a grown man, and I have the right to my own opinions."

My father was furious, but Anthony didn't back down. He was no longer the obedient son-in-law who did everything he was told.

Later, when Anthony lost his job, the situation worsened. He had to stay at my parents' house, which led to even more frequent arguments. Ultimately, these misunderstandings, differences of opinion, and conflicts made our life unbearable. So, my hope for a peaceful, happy life with a husband who was supposed to take care of me and our child turned out to be nothing but an illusion. I felt lost and isolated again, without a shred of the security I so desperately longed for.

Anthony was a rebel, so eventually, my father couldn't take it anymore. The bitterness and misunderstanding built up in him until he had to explode.

"Get the hell out of here!" he shouted at his son-in-law one day.

Anthony didn't say a word, but his look said it all. It wasn't the look of a submissive man. Finally, he left, slamming the door behind him. As a good wife, I packed myself and our few-month-old child and followed him.

It was early March. Winter. Snow up to our knees. We stood by the roadside with our little baby, trying to hitch a ride. The wind lashed at our faces with icy gusts, the cold seeping into our bones. The tiny fingers of our child trembled with cold, and his quiet cries tore at my heart. I felt helpless. We stood there for too long, far too long. Finally, I couldn't take it anymore.

"What now?" I asked, tears in my eyes. "What about our child? What about us?"

Anthony shrugged. "What do you expect?" he muttered, lighting another cigarette. "We're going to my parents' house."

Time passed, and we still stood on that cold, snowy roadside. Every car that passed us without stopping sent waves of despair through me. The baby cried louder and louder, and my own heart cried along with him as I tried to soothe him. Anthony stared off into the distance, barely blinking, as if his thoughts were far away.

Finally, when we had almost lost hope, a car stopped. The man behind the wheel looked at us with pity and agreed to take us. We were more grateful to him than to anyone before. After many hardships, we finally arrived at Anthony's parents' house. I was tired, frozen, but full of hope. My thoughts revolved around the promise of a new life, far away from my despotic father.

Oh no, not so fast! Soon I realized that I had stepped into even deeper shit than the one I had left behind. My in-laws turned out to be just as difficult, if not worse, than my father. Without money, without a job, without a place of our own, we became a burden no one wanted to bear.

This was not the life I had dreamed of. It was another nightmare. Not only were the conditions in Anthony's parents' house literally Spartan, but the complete backwardness of their minds made it even worse! The décor of the house and the way of thinking seemed to come from a distant era. I tried to adapt to the conditions there, but sometimes I cried in helplessness. Secretly.

No bathroom, no toilet, no hot water in the tap, no heating. Total failure! But I didn't complain! I was glad I had escaped my father!

I washed clothes in cold water that I had to draw from the well myself. My hands cracked from the cold, and my back ached from bending over. I rinsed the clothes in plastic buckets used for paint, placed outside near the well. The wind mercilessly lashed at my face, and the clothes, soaked in cold water, became as heavy as stones.

Fortunately, Adam gave me strength. His smile, his innocence in the face of daily struggles, his warmth and sweetness were like balm on open wounds. If it weren't for him, I probably would have broken down. But I couldn't let that happen. I had to believe that somewhere, beyond this harsh, frozen period of our lives, there was sunshine and warmth waiting for us. But the Spartan conditions, the backwardness, this daily battle with reality became harder and harder to bear. I felt like I was trapped, with no way out. And even though I had escaped one nightmare, I had fallen into another, one that seemed even more cruel and relentless. But whenever I felt like losing hope, I looked at my little boy, into his innocent eyes, and knew I had to keep going. His smile was my beacon in the tunnel, my compass in this storm of life.

Doing laundry by hand without a bathroom took me all day, and even then, my mother-in-law would show up in the evening and scold me for not hanging the clothes by color! Are you kidding me?! Lady, don't you have more serious problems in life?!

Gertrude, my mentioned mother-in-law, was the epitome of everything conservative and old-fashioned. She became my daily test of patience. Every day spent in her presence was like a heavy exam in endurance, where her dogmas and rules became her weapons. One day, when Anthony took care of the baby, which was rare, Gertrude went into a rage.

"What's this supposed to be?!" she shouted, looking at her son rocking the baby. "A father has no obligation to care for the child! That's a woman's job!"

I stared at her, utterly amazed by her backwardness. Did she really live in such a world?

"Are you freaking serious?!" I replied, unable to hold back. "Did I make this baby by myself, or what?! I thought it was a shared responsibility, but I see I've got the wrong era!"

Gertrude looked at me as if I were insane, her face immediately turning red with anger.

"You have no right to tell me what's proper!" she screamed. "I've lived like this for years, and I don't need your modern nonsense to know what's right! In my house, we live by my rules!" she declared finally, and I felt that my words had fallen into the void of her prejudices.

That's when I realized that this battle was lost. I couldn't convince a woman who had spent her whole life in her small-mindedness and didn't want to peek out of it. For her, the world hadn't changed. At least, she didn't want to hear about it. Once again, I felt like Sisyphus, who kept trying to push a huge boulder up a hill, only to see it roll back down again. But I was also angry and disappointed that I had to fight for something that seemed so obvious to me. It was like shouting the truth into an empty cave, where only my own words echoed back, and the walls remained impenetrable and unmoved. I felt crushed and isolated, lost in a world that had no place for me.

The days passed like a slow funeral march, each day filled with struggle and humiliation. It seemed to me that I could endure every ugliness of this place, every inhuman rule, and every bitter comment. But eventually, I started to doubt it.

One day, as I was returning home, I overheard my mother-in-law whispering something to my little Adam, holding a bottle with a strange liquid.

"A few drops in your tea, and you won't be so fussy," she said with a smile, looking at the baby.

I froze in the doorway, stunned by what I heard. The old woman was holding a bottle of Nervosol. My heart stopped, and my mind screamed.

"WHAT THE HELL?!" I exploded, bursting into the room. "What are you doing?!"

My mother-in-law turned, surprised by my presence.

"It's just a few drops... it's nothing bad," she began to explain, but all I could hear in her voice was lies and manipulation.

"Nothing bad?!" I shouted again. "Enough! No more! I won't let you poison my child!"

I quickly packed up myself and the baby. I don't even remember exactly when and how I did it, I was so furious. There was no longer a place for me in this house, in this family. I'd rather have my father's yelling! At least there, my child's health and life weren't at risk!

For the rest of the night, I sat holding Adam in my arms, listening to his breathing. In those moments, between shadow and light, between fear and hope, I found something I thought was lost.

I found myself. And in the morning, I got on a bus.

As I returned to my family home, I felt that I had left behind more than just a bad house.

I had left behind a piece of myself, a piece of faith in humanity, a piece of hope for a better tomorrow.

CHAPTER 6

I was awakened by shouting and crashing noises coming from behind the wall... just the usual, everyday chaos I had grown accustomed to. I rubbed my eyes and looked around to make sure I was where I wanted to be at that moment... that I really wanted to be in this place. I took a deep breath, as if trying to fill my soul with everything surrounding me in that single moment. I buried my face in the sleeping Adam next to me. *Finally, back home. It won't be easy... but... in my own backyard*, I thought.

To support myself and my child, I quickly decided to look for a job.

I received an interesting offer, good pay, and even the possibility of advancement, but unfortunately, it involved travel. I will never forget the day when I had to leave for a business trip to Gdynia. It was a big event for me, a chance for promotion and new experience. Adam was supposed to stay with Ulla, as usual, but this time my father decided that as a pensioner who spent all his days at home, he would take care of his grandson himself. I was glad I could count on his help, but I knew that when this man offered help, it was still something to fear.

Unfortunately, the trip got extended. During the journey, my cell phone suddenly started vibrating in my pocket. I answered because I recognized my father's number. His voice was angry, full of fury and hatred.

"How could you leave the child for so long?!" he yelled into the phone. "Come back immediately, or not even God Himself will be able to help you!"

He started threatening me with death, saying I deserved the worst. Hearing those words, I began to panic. My son was with him. My child was with that monster!

I returned. I returned to the city, but I didn't dare go back home. Instead, I hid in a small shed on someone's allotment. For several days, I stayed there, trembling from the cold, fear, and hunger, but I was too scared to return. Each night was colder than the last, and the fear growing inside me was even more paralyzing.

I lay there, curled up in the shed, listening to the night sounds and wondering what my son was doing. Was he safe? Was his grandfather hurting him? Should I return and face my worst nightmare?

I had no choice.

I had to go back and get my child. Filled with fear but with a determination that came from my love for my son, I finally decided to confront my father. Enough! I shouted into the darkness, and the echo only confirmed my words. Enough! How much longer do you want to live like this?! How much longer do you want to be afraid of him?! I asked myself.

And that was the turning point. At that moment, I decided never again to feel fear at the thought of my father. And with that resolve, I returned for my child.

It was the beginning of the end!

My relationship with my father was more strained than ever before. Just looking at each other created a cascade of sparks fueled by hatred. Living under the same roof caused constant tension, leading to sharp arguments.

This was the time when I openly and fully rebelled against him and his methods of upbringing.

My father couldn't understand that his time was over, that I would no longer allow him to continue what he had been feeding me throughout my childhood.

I started setting boundaries, which drove him into a rage. Unfortunately, his body, weakened and worn out by this eternal battle, gave up. My father fell ill and was taken to the hospital.

"I don't want to see her, do you understand?! Don't let her come here!" he shouted at my mother when she visited him.

Everyone could come, but not me.

He didn't want to see me.

And he didn't!

Never again. The law of attraction worked!

He died a few days later. He suffocated due to a pulmonary embolism.

What a paradox – he died unable to catch his breath, just as we couldn't breathe around him for all those years.

His last breath was our first.

My father's days in the hospital were filled with tension and anger. My heart beat faster with pure rage that I could no longer suppress. I couldn't forget all those years when he crushed me with his methodical, harsh parenting methods when he shaped my childhood with his iron fist.

My mother would return from visiting him in the hospital with red eyes and a pained expression. In her gaze, I could sense something that fueled my anger even more. I almost felt like she wanted to blame me for my father's suffering. "I don't want to see her!" he had told her. Those words struck me with unexpected force. Did he want to erase me from his life just as I wanted to erase his presence from mine? It happened as he wished. He didn't see me again. He died. But my heart, beating with anger, did not feel relief. Instead, the anger intensified tenfold. Anger at him for his weakness, anger at myself for my helplessness. Did the law of attraction really work? Had my dreams of being free from him come true in the worst possible way? Despite all the anger, despite the hatred I could no longer hide, I felt no sorrow. I didn't allow myself to. Anger and hatred dominated my heart, leaving no room for grief. I couldn't let myself feel such an emotion for my father, even after his death. He remained for me the same man I had hated. He remained a man who did not deserve my sorrow.

My father's death was like a blinding flash in the darkness. Impossible to ignore, unimaginably intense.

I sat in the warm, homely surroundings of Madeline and her parents, not in the hospital. After all, my father didn't want to see me. My thoughts revolved around one fact – he was dead. He was no longer in this world. It seemed impossible. "This will all pass," Madeline said, her voice as gentle as the touch of a butterfly's wings. She sat next to me, holding my hand with a caring grip. My friend's parents, always kind to me, looked on with unspoken sympathy. I don't know if they understood what was churning inside me. I don't even know if I fully understood it. It was my mother who told me the news of my father's death. In the first moments, I didn't know what to do next. My father had always dictated how I should live, what I should do, what I should fear. His words, sharp as a razor, carved my world and my fear. Who would control my terror now? Who would set the direction I would follow?

"He always told me what to do," I suddenly blurted out. "What now?"

Madeline looked at me with concern.

"You'll know," she said. "You'll know what to do."

But those questions, those doubts quickly faded. The relief that began to fill me was indescribable. I felt the tension, the burden that had been inside me since childhood, suddenly shrink, crumble. My father was dead. And he was no more. That monster who had twisted my childhood no longer had power over me. Afterward, there were no tears. None. Only relief. Did that mean I was a monster, just like him? My father was now only a shadow that had disappeared. Without him, my life was now like a blank parchment, ready for a new story. The overwhelming relief and impossible sense of freedom filled the space he had previously occupied with his domination. My heart beat like a bell of freedom. And I could finally begin to live. One less bastard in the world!

My father's funeral took place on my twenty-first birthday. Thanks for the party! I had a great time! Damn him! Even after death, he decided to hit me where it hurt.

I felt strange that day – not sad, not happy. My entire family came to my "celebration," though not for the birthday. It was the most unusual birthday of my life. There was no cake, no presents, but there was a funeral. My father's funeral. A day that should have been filled with celebration and joy was bizarrely intertwined with sorrow and relief.

"You have such nice skin," my cousin suddenly commented, leaning toward me as we stood by the freshly dug grave.

"Self-tanner," I replied automatically.

"Really? It looks great. Did you apply it evenly?" she asked, as if death, the funeral, and the whole situation weren't happening.

"I hope so. I need to look good for this ceremony, right?" I remarked and then pulled out a mirror from my purse. I looked at myself in it for a long time.

These were definitely the strangest birthdays I had ever had.

The first few months after my father's death were complicated and uncertain. Even though I hated him, his absence filled me with a strange emptiness. I wondered what would happen now, how I would manage without his constant supervision and tyranny. But over time, I began to discover new possibilities and build my identity anew, free from his influence. I realized that I had to learn to live for myself, not for his expectations. It was difficult but also incredibly liberating. Every day became a new opportunity to understand myself and my true desires. My father was no longer my censor, and I could start living by my own rules.

But the days without my father were hard, though I never admitted it to anyone. After all, I'm tough, and it wouldn't be proper to complain! When my father was alive, I knew what to do, how to do it, what to say, how to think. And after? Afterward, I was completely lost. No one told me what to do, how to do it. No one gave me orders on where to go and how to get there. My mind and life were in total chaos!

After his death, I slowly began to shape my personality and character. But it wasn't easy. Such a delay comes at a price. I don't know if it's really possible to make up for it. I still don't fully know who I am, who I'm supposed to be... Unfortunately, the need for constant competition and proving myself, which my tyrant father instilled in me, remains with me to this day. What he ingrained in me during my childhood still lingers within me. Even now, I sometimes feel the need to be the best, to prove that I am worthy of love and respect. It's a thought that has haunted me for a long time. I'm just now learning that I don't have to be perfect to be loved and respected. I'm slowly discovering that people love me for who I am, not for what I've achieved. So, I'm just beginning to learn to accept myself and my imperfections. But I'm still lost... The mess in my head remains...

The worst was at home. My father, for all his faults, kept everything under control. There was one leader, and there was order! And after his death, everyone suddenly wanted to take his place; everyone was vying for the throne to rule! And each one was more foolish than the last! Total chaos!

My father was a bastard in every way, except one – he never skimped on food for us. On the contrary, he always made sure the fridge was full, and we never lacked anything. He was obsessed when one of us refused to eat out of spite. Sometimes I think he was so eager to feed us so that one day he could devour us, like in the fairy tale of Hansel and Gretel. And yet, he was the only one who could gather the whole family at the table. After his death, we never sat together again... Everything fell apart.

I remember how my father used to prepare colorful sandwiches and make coffee or tea for everyone. Each of us received our portion on a plate, served just the way we liked it. He often cooked dinner too, and he did it very well. The taste of his sauce still lingers in my memory...

From time to time, the image of my father standing by the kit-chen counter preparing dinner comes back to me. It's certainly not the typical image you might imagine when you think of your fathers cooking for the family. But it was my image. Mine!

There he stood in the kitchen, wearing an old flannel shirt and worn-out jeans, his hands covered in tattoos. He stood with his tongue slightly sticking out, focused on what he was doing. In one hand, he held a knife, and in the other, an onion. He didn't look at what he was doing – he just did it. As if it was something natural, something he had always done. And he did it really well. In the kitchen, everything in his hands became magical. The sauce he prepared had an extraordinary taste – it was spicy, but not too much, sweet, but just right. It was simply perfect.

I remember watching him with admiration as he put everything together. Every piece of onion, every basil leaf, every slice of meat – it was all meticulously prepared, with care and precision.

But this image was not entirely idyllic. It wasn't the picture of a father cooking for his family out of love. No, it was the image of a father cooking with cold precision, with a determination that reminded me of who he really was. It was a scene straight out of Dante's *Inferno* – a scene filled with tension and unease. Yet, it was one of the most authentic images of my father that I know.

Finally, after many minutes of work, my father would put down the knife. His hands were covered in sauce, and a smug smile spread across his face. He knew he had done something well. He knew he had created something exceptional. And then, breaking the silence around him, his loud, menacing voice would ring out:

"Get your asses to the table, you brats!"

And always, no matter what we were doing, no matter how much we hated him, we would rush to the table obediently. Because even though my father was a monster, when it came to cooking, he was a true master. And besides, he was terrifying when we disobeyed.

As we entered the kitchen, the smell of the food he had prepared would immediately hit us. A recognizable, comforting smell that was connected to one of the few happy memories from childhood. We would sit at the table, looking at the dish my father had made for us. We were still filled with fragments of fear, but also with a certain sense of excitement.

My father's dinners were always delicious. The sauce he so carefully prepared often covered everything on the plate, giving the dish unique and exceptional qualities.

We never talked during meals. My father didn't say anything either. It was a moment of silence. A moment when each of us focused solely on the food. I still remember that silence.

Despite everything my father did to us, despite all the painful memories I carried in my heart, those moments at dinner were like balm to me. They were moments when I could forget who he was and focus only on what he was doing. They were moments when I could forget the hell at home.

The dishes my father prepared were as ambiguous as he was. They were intense, full of contrasts, delicate yet laced with sharpness, seemingly sweet but always with a hint of bitterness. And despite everything, despite the hatred I felt for my father, I will always remember those moments at the table. Because then, he wasn't a monster – he was a master.

To this day, I can perfectly remember his command:

"Get your asses to the table, you brats!"

It seemed that the tone of his voice changed at that moment. It was stern, but somehow, in his hurtful sarcasm, he seemed a little less scary, a little less unpleasant.

So, we would sit at our table, eating quietly, not speaking to him or to each other. Everything that could have been said had already been shouted out earlier. Now, only eating mattered; it was our momentary salvation, our small paradise in the midst of daily hell.

Those were the moments when I could look at my father and see something more than just the man I hated so much. I could see him as a master who passionately and skillfully created all these dishes for us.

In those moments, watching my father, the maestro of cooking, I wondered if there was a place down below, in Dante's *Inferno*, for people like him. Is there a place where he could continue to cook, to create? Could he be who he might have wanted to become? Is there a place where he could find a moment of relief, just as we did during his dinners?

My father was a man full of paradoxes. He was both a cruel tyrant and a kind-hearted dad who sometimes managed to forget his role as a strict disciplinarian, if only for a short moment.

I remember one day when he came home drunk. My mother was at work, and he was supposed to buy a new car. Although he didn't drink often, getting a new car required a celebration, so it wouldn't break down – a tradition in this part of Europe. So, my father celebrated his new automotive acquisition. He came home in the new car, swerving slightly. A rare smile was plastered across his face, one we seldom had the chance to see. He was so cheerful, so unreal. He talked to us, made jokes that seemed the funniest in the world.

I remember him grabbing me and my younger sister by the hands, then spinning us around. Laughter filled the room. Our walls witnessed something unusual – spontaneous, genuine joy. At that moment, I thought of him as... dad...

"Get in the car!" he suddenly called out, and we jumped into the front seats like obedient puppies.

We pretended to steer the car, while my father imitated the sounds of the engine and screeching brakes. The entire evening was filled with incredible euphoria. Every moment of that night was like a drop of golden honey falling onto the bitter bread of our everyday lives. That evening was like a star in the dark sky, like a shining stone on a rocky shore. It was a time that reminded me that my father, despite everything, was still human. He was a man who could find joy in simple things, even if only for brief moments. Those were some of the few times when my father allowed us, and himself, a bit of freedom and carefree joy.

It was the same during family outings. He seemed to forget his dominance again, though only for a while, allowing us to breathe.

He would tell jokes and laugh at ours. He could be a dad again... A dad I longed to have.

"All aboard!" he would shout as we got into the car, and we, except for my mother, would respond with giggles. I always looked forward to those moments. Outings to Aunt Zoe's, my father's sister, were full of such moments. During one of those trips, when we were laughing hysterically at some absurd joke I don't even remember, I saw something in my father's eyes that surprised me. Laughter. Genuine, authentic laughter. It seemed that, for a moment, he had bared his soul, and I saw something more in him than just the man I hated. It was like looking at him through the prism of a different reality. Like understanding that even he, my oppressor, had something human within him.

But those moments were like fleeting rays of sunshine on a winter's sky – short-lived and surprising, yet always passing too quickly.

On All Saints' Day, November 1st, we would visit the cemeteries. It was a time full of melancholy and reflection, but it was always beautiful. After sunset, the cemeteries transformed into lands of light. Thousands of flickering candles illuminated the darkness, creating an atmosphere of unearthly peace and beauty. Sitting in the back seat of the car, I watched those shimmering lights, like stars that had fallen to the earth.

Those were the moments when my feelings toward my father became more complicated. Could I hate him for what he had done and at the same time enjoy these moments of peace and joy? Could I hate him and yet long for those rare moments when he seemed to be human?

That's what our family outings were like – full of contradictions, emotions, moments of temporary solace, and the ever-present underlying fear. And although these moments were ambiguous, they undeniably shaped my feelings toward my father.

Sometimes, during those trips, when my father drove with an unusual sense of confidence, it seemed to me that I could observe something different, something almost imperceptible. For a moment, his eyes seemed less harsh, his posture less tense. It looked as if, for a moment, he allowed himself to detach from his usual role – as the ruthless dictator who constantly controlled our lives. In those moments, there appeared something resembling real emotions – joy, amusement, and even something akin to care.

All these conflicting moments and memories that my father left behind, those few moments of laughter and joy, showed me a different side of him. They showed someone who, despite his cruelty, could find traces of sensitivity. It was those moments that made me realize how complicated understanding a person can be.

Sometimes I had the feeling that my father believed in me more than I did... That he saw in me someone who would achieve something in life. Unfortunately, his behavior helped ensure that I achieved nothing. His way of raising us wasn't supportive. He taught us how to scheme, how to steal, instead of teaching us how to cope so that we wouldn't have to do those things.

But despite everything, there were times when I felt that he was proud of me, that he believed I would achieve what I wanted in life and fulfill my dreams – or maybe his dreams. He often engaged in conversations with me on difficult, complex topics. We would read books together... He didn't do that with the other three siblings. I felt that he treated me differently than the others... or maybe I just wanted to feel that way...? Because I got beaten just the same as the rest of them.

My father was authoritative; it always had to be his way! Unfortunately, I inherited that trait from him. How can you be a good person when you have the genes of the devil? Or maybe I wasn't a good person at all? Maybe all those other people were good, and I was the bad one? If I am the spawn of Satan, that could very well be the case. The anxiety about my genes and heritage was utterly overwhelming. Living under the weight of such a legacy was, to put it mildly, exhausting. It was like carrying a giant stone on my back, a stone that seemed to get heavier with each passing day. Yet, it couldn't be thrown away, it couldn't be ignored. It was always there, constantly pulling me down.

"Your father is a pedophile!" These words echoed in my head like a boomerang, thrown once and returning endlessly. I was terrified that this horrible tendency could be in my genes. I was haunted by the fear that my father might have passed it on. This wasn't just a thought that crossed my mind occasionally. It was something that tormented me every day, from the moment I woke up until the moment I fell asleep. I was scared that maybe this shit was genetic.

The fear that I might have inherited it from my father made me avoid children. I was afraid to change their clothes, to bathe them, to even help them. Anything to avoid the possibility that I might hurt them. What if it turned out that this cursed "gift" from my father was inside me? What then? I wondered if I would be able to deal with it on my own and blow my brains out, or if I would have to ask someone to help me do it before I hurt anyone. This fear didn't let me rest. It became my worst nightmare. Fear. It was always tied to my father.

Maybe if he had gone to therapy, he would have been a good father, because overall, he probably wasn't a terrible person.

No kid in the neighborhood dared to touch us; everyone was afraid of "Gremlin." And it went like this. The nearby street and the sounds of children playing in the yard were a constant backdrop to my childhood. There, on the border between our home and the outside world, my father became an indestructible wall, the guardian of our innocent years.

"Gremlin's coming! Run!" shouted little Chris one day when he saw our father driving onto the property in his old Volkswagen.

The nickname quickly caught on among the local kids. I once asked my father if it bothered him. He just laughed, looking at me with his piercing eyes.

"Let them be afraid," he said. "It's good they know who to avoid. Like wolves on the steppe. A wolf doesn't attack unless it feels threatened, but the other animals know it's better to keep their distance."

At the time, I didn't fully understand what he meant. Now I know that my father was like that wolf, and we were his pack, protected from predators, who were sometimes the kids in the yard, and sometimes the larger outside world. No matter how much I feared him, I couldn't deny one thing – he protected us in his own way, as best he could. He defended us from all sorts of people, even from the neighbor. The angry banging on the door often meant one thing – a confrontation with our neighbor, Mrs. Johnson. Each visit followed a similar pattern: she would appear with a concerned look, clutching her son, usually with tears in her eyes and a dramatic story on her lips. My father always stood in the doorway with an expression of barely concealed irritation.

"What is it now?" he asked one day when he saw her at the door again.

"Your daughters hit my Michael again! This time with a shovel to the head!" she said, showing my father the bruise on her son's forehead.

"And what was your Michael doing?" my father asked, narrowing his eyes.

"Nothing!" she replied, looking at him indignantly. "My child is innocent!"

My father laughed in response.

"Well, that's clear," he muttered. "Your kid's a wimp, letting himself get beat up by girls with a shovel!"

The neighbor wasn't listening anymore. She was fleeing, dragging the crying Michael behind her. She probably wanted to protect him from the truth.

Yes, my father always took our side. That knowledge, despite everything, gave us a certain sense of security.

Yes, he protected us from all sorts of people.

But not from the worst ones, like that fucking Julius Romer.

And he didn't protect us from himself.

CHAPTER 7

A lot had changed in my family home. After my father's death, the shouting stopped, but so did any semblance of order that had once existed. Everything had, in essence, ended. The day came when the house lost its guardian, and the world lost its tyrant. My father was gone forever, leaving behind a silence that was just as loud as his shouting.

The following months were awful. It was a time of chaos and emptiness. Trying to comprehend my father's passing, trying to reconcile with a new life without him, was harder than I had imagined. I had hoped for support from my mother, but it was like searching for shelter in a wasteland. It was as if the devil himself had taken possession of her. Was it my father's spirit? Or was this his way of continuing to torment me from beyond the grave? I couldn't understand it.

"Mom, why are you acting like this?" I asked one day, seeing that another argument was about to erupt. "You're different."

"It's you who has changed; it's you who is different!" she screamed, pointing a finger at me. "Your father would have set you straight!"

Was it his voice speaking through her? Was it his will imposing itself on our lives again? I didn't know what to think. I didn't know what to feel. I found myself trapped in some sort of paradox. Everything had ended, yet nothing had finished. Everything was different, yet nothing had changed. I was caught in an endless loop of contradictions, moving to a rhythm I couldn't understand.

Nights were spent alone, staring at the empty walls, listening to the silence that was louder than any words. I thought about my father, I thought about my mother, I thought about who they were before and who my mother had become. Was this part of my father's plan? Was this his way of maintaining control even after death? Was this his final revenge? I had no answers. I only knew that it was a battle I could not win, a puzzle I could not solve.

For nearly a year after my father's death, I was trapped in the family home that had once been a refuge (albeit a poor one) and had now become a prison. The mother who should have been my anchor had become my tormentor. Words that had once been a sweet song had turned into blows. Hands that had once been a warm touch had become a whip.

I had a husband, but he was absent. Anthony was a shadow, a figure in the background, an image without form. Each of us lived our own lives, each of us walked our own path. A marriage that had once been a promise had become a meaningless smear.

My mother, whom I had once thought of with love, had now become nothing but anger and fury. She tied me to her with an iron chain of greed, mercilessly exploiting my skills in home renovations. Yes, those skills! Renovation, which had once been a necessity, had now become the price of shelter.

"You have hands, so use them!" she shouted one day, throwing a brush and work gloves at me. "At least your father had the sense to teach you how to use tools. Finally, you're useful for something!" I looked at her with a mix of anger and despair. This was the woman who had given birth to me, but she had become a stranger driven by hatred and rage.

"Thank you," I replied with a bitter laugh. "Thank you for reminding me of that damn renovation. Not only do I have to endure your insults, but now you want me to slave away with a hammer too!"

"If you don't like it, you can leave!" she snarled, almost like a dog, pointing to the door. "No one is forcing you to stay."

I grabbed the brush. What else could I do? My son needed a roof over his head.

Renovation became my daily routine and my nightmare once more. The walls, which had once been just a backdrop, now became my companion, my friend, and at the same time, my enemy. In those walls, I saw my father, I saw my husband, I saw myself...

I renovated the house, but I couldn't "renovate" my life. Those walls held my history, my soul, and my heart. They contained my love, my hatred, my hope, and my despair.

Thanks, Dad, for teaching me the tough art of renovation! Thanks for giving me those damn skills that are now both my curse and my blessing!

The atmosphere in the house was grim, filled with hatred. The air was thick with bitterness and despair. My husband had become distant, unreachable, as if he wasn't even there. His lack of support was like a knife twisting in my heart. My mother and older sister had become my greatest enemies. Anger, frustration, and humiliation were their language, and I was their victim.

Every day I heard their shouts, accusations, and insults. My mother, once full of love and care, had become consumed by anger and aggression. My sister, with whom I used to laugh, now laughed at me.

"You're nothing!" my mother screamed one day when the renovation wasn't progressing as quickly as she wanted. "Even your husband doesn't want you! What have you done with your life, daughter?"

Her words were like a spear that finished me off in my humiliation. I fell to my knees, tears streaming down my face like a river of pain and despair. I wanted to say something. I wanted to scream something. I even opened my mouth, but only helpless silence escaped from it. Meanwhile, my mother continued to scream:

"You've failed! You've failed us all!"

Then, as if nothing had happened, she slapped me across the face. In my rage, I probably didn't even feel it. I just looked at her in despair. I couldn't believe that the woman who had given birth to me could hurt me like this.

"Mom, why?" I stammered finally. "Why are you treating me like this? Can't you see that I need your help, not your anger?"

She only laughed in response. And it was a sinister laugh, sending chills of fear down my spine.

Where was my husband? Almost three years had passed since our wedding day, and he still wasn't with me. Why hadn't he taken me away from here? Why hadn't he saved me from this hatred, from this humiliation?

Because our marriage never really existed! That's why!

I was tough, but there was a limit to my endurance. I was strong, but there was a limit to my perseverance.

Early December brought the first snow, and with it, my mother's cold gaze and icy words.

"I don't think you should be here for Christmas Eve," she said, looking at me sideways as if even her eyes couldn't bear the sight of me. "It would probably be better if you spent it elsewhere."

And how to comment on that? This was my mother! My own mother!

"I understand," I replied, trying to hide the pain in my voice. "If you don't want me and Adam here for Christmas Eve, you'll never see us at the holiday table again!"

On Christmas Eve, I found myself at Madeline's place. It was a strange, almost surreal situation. Anthony was there too, invited by his brother Raphael. And once again, we played the role of a married couple, though we both knew it was just an act. Once again, we sat at the table together, yet apart. Once again, we looked into each other's eyes but didn't see each other. We held hands but didn't feel each other's warmth. And so, we remained in this strange, silent play, pretending to be someone we weren't, pretending to feel something we didn't feel.

Throughout the dinner, I thought of Boris, of his eyes, his smile, his touch. In my heart, he still remained, unchanged for years. And even then.

"You seem to be missing someone?" Maddie noticed, looking at me with concern.

"Yes," I admitted, unable to hide the truth. "I miss someone I can't have. Someone who is far from me, yet close because they dwell in my dreams."

"Maybe one day that will change," she said, trying to comfort me.

"Maybe," I replied, but I knew it wouldn't happen. Boris was now just a shadow of my life, the twilight of my love, the echo of my heart.

Yes, that Christmas Eve was strange, but it was also real. It was real in its absurdity.

Eventually, I ended up living with my child in a rented house, right in the neighborhood of the "family nest." I had nothing. We slept on a mattress, and I did laundry in a borrowed Frania washing machine, which my mother later took back, along with the mattress, after some argument.

I was left with nothing – no money, no prospects, and a small child. Still married, but only on paper.

To afford the rent for the house, I worked for the owner of the building where I lived. I labored in the fields, in the barn, always with my little boy by my side, always together. Sometimes, when we had nothing to eat, I could count on the help of my younger sister and brother.

Lydia and Walter would sneak sandwiches from the table and bring them to us. Sometimes we'd go together to someone's field to dig up potatoes, and then I'd cook them for Adam's meal.

The question is, where was my husband then? Where was the father of my child? He was somewhere. That was my marriage. If my father had been alive, I think he would have put an end to this mockery of a marriage! I know he would have protected me if he had known how bad things were. After all, he did protect us from the evils of the world in his own way.

One day, Anthony showed up at my door.

"Please! Give us one last chance!" he begged, his face full of pain.

I was surprised by the situation. I didn't want this. I felt nothing for him anymore. But seeing the happiness in my child's eyes at the sight of his father, I softened... I agreed.

But I knew deep down that our relationship had no chance of surviving.

We moved back to Warsaw to try to save something that had long been reduced to ashes, buried under a pile of rubble.

My life with Anthony was like a song whose melody I could no longer bear. At first, it was harmonious, filled with notes of hope. But with each passing day, it became more and more discordant, like an instrument out of tune. How could I have let our marriage turn into a series of worsening repetitions of the same false melody? Over the years, our relationship faded, losing color and clarity, like an old photograph. Each day became another lost puzzle piece in the complicated picture of our marriage.

I wondered why I kept trying to fit these incomplete pieces together when I knew deep down that the picture would never be whole. Why did I agree to this last attempt, knowing how it would end?

Eventually, I said enough! Like in a song. Except this wasn't a song.

"I'm going home for New Year's Eve," I announced to Anthony one day, even though I knew it was just an excuse to break away from this discordant melody, to seek silence in my family home. "I'm just going for New Year's Eve," I lied, even though I had no intention of returning to Warsaw or to Anthony.

Yes, I went to seek silence in my family home! But that silence was just an illusion, just like my belief that I could fix something that had already been irreparably lost.

With the farewell to the capital, I also said goodbye to Anthony.

Anthony – such a multi-layered character, yet so predictable in his unpredictable approach to life. He was a soul full of joy.

Just like Dante, who traveled through Hell on his way to God, Anthony and I traversed the ups and downs of our marriage. Except there were far more downs than ups. Too many. But don't get me wrong. I have no intention of spitting on him or cursing him. Anthony was, in fact, a very good man. The problem was that he was also too amusing, perhaps too much so. Everything was like an open book with scrambled letters to him. Unfortunately, Anthony always took everything lightly. He treated everything with a lack of seriousness, even our marriage, fatherhood, and being a husband. In retrospect, I think both he and I were unlucky. If we had started building our relationship now, we would surely have created something beautiful, something lasting. I am sure of it. Maybe then our marital Hell would have had a different tone. Maybe... Unfortunately, we met too early.

Our marriage was like a broken clock that started too soon and stopped at the wrong moment.

A few wasted years – without learning, without lessons, without joy.

Time spent in the wrong environment, with the wrong people, in the wrong place.

Sometimes, looking back, I regret those lost years, but then I remind myself of my beloved son, who wouldn't exist without Anthony. Adam – the only good that came out of that relationship. His laughter was like a melody that filled my world when everything else fell silent.

It was always the two of us, my little boy and me, as Anthony, truth be told, didn't even live with us. He just stayed occasionally, like a migratory bird passing through, leaving no trace.

And so, despite the pain, disappointments, and broken promises, my heart found solace in my love for my child. For it was an authentic love – unwavering and indestructible.

This was my destiny, my true path, my life's lesson.

Our marriage was doomed from the start. Life with Anthony, instead of being a joyful adventure, became a daily struggle. We weren't ready for what was to come. We didn't understand that true love requires time, patience, and understanding. That it's not enough just to love, you also must know how to live together.

And so, our story, which began so beautifully, ended in disappointment and sadness. What remained were memories, moments of happiness, and the pain of lost dreams. We weren't meant to be together.

Our relationship was like a beautiful melody played at the wrong time.

We met at the wrong time... in the wrong life...

PURGATORY

CHRISTMAS EVE IN PURGATORY

Right after baby Jesus was born, my second husband slapped me hard across the face. It happened in the kitchen. Oscar was essentially a good man, but sometimes he had his bad moments. I know this is how every victim of domestic violence, especially a wife, explains things, but I'm not straying from the truth. After all, I had escaped the Hell of my life a few years earlier, and I had to realize that I wouldn't immediately reach Heaven. Even Dante had to traverse Purgatory to reach his Beatrice.

Yes, I remembered clearly how Dante walked through Purgatory, among rows of tormented souls shedding the sins that had clung to them throughout their lives. Or maybe the souls had clung to the sins themselves? On each level, he encountered those cleansing themselves of pride, envy, and anger. Each of those souls reminded me of what I had gone through with my father, what I had experienced later, and what I was enduring now with Oscar.

I, too, had to fight against various sins. My pride was the attempt to maintain a "happy home" for my children at all costs, even at the expense of my own pain. I felt envy when I looked at happy, normal families. And anger flared up in me every time I uncovered the hypocrisy of my mother-in-law and the deceit of Oscar's family.

And my husband couldn't protect me or our children from this stinking cesspool. Yet, I had to endure all of this to cleanse myself, to earn my own Heaven. At least that's how I felt at the time. I didn't even consider whether I was right. Whether such an attitude made any sense at all.

But even in the worst moments, there was always a spark of hope. When I sometimes sat in the kitchen at night, wallowing in my misery, I remembered my children sleeping in the next room. I knew I had to endure, not for myself, but for them. For our little piece of Heaven that we were creating together.

Today, I'm horrified by the attitude I displayed back then. It was sheer stupidity! I should have left that mess immediately and marched in another direction!

At that time, however, it seemed to me that I was only temporarily in that misery, that it was a temporary place and state. I was convinced that it was my Purgatory, my journey to Heaven. A stop on the way to unending happiness. Like Dante, I had to go through this period of purification before reaching a place where I could truly live. That place was a bright future – for my children, for me. And although I knew the road ahead would be long and difficult, I was determined to walk it.

"Even Dante had to traverse Purgatory," I kept repeating to myself, trying to find meaning in surviving another difficult hour.

I kept telling myself that on that day too. It was Christmas Eve. Christmas Eve in Purgatory – my personal holy night, full of pain and promise. And it was still better than all those Christmas Eves in Hell that I had spent as a child.

As Dante said, *let not evil prevail over us, but good.* That's what I was waiting for. For myself, for my children, for our future. At first, even for my marriage. My Heaven was waiting. I knew that and was ready to reach it.

This wasn't my first Christmas Eve with Oscar's family. I pretty much knew what to expect. I never felt like I belonged there. However, I knew I was doing the right, sensible thing by building a family atmosphere with them for Christmas. But that building was a struggle and was actually an illusion. Nothing more.

It was a Polish Christmas Eve in Germany, where I lived with my second husband, our children, and... his family. The Christmas tree twinkled with colorful lights in the corner of the living room, and the table was laden with traditional Christmas dishes. Just like in Poland. No one could eat all of it, but it had to be there, and it had to create an impression of abundance.

I felt like an outsider, watching them celebrate this Christmas Eve. They looked content and happy. Don't be fooled! I knew that behind the smiles and warm words, their true intentions, grudges, and years of animosity were hiding.

"Thank you, Lord, for this beautiful evening," Oscar began, looking at me as if to confirm that everything was alright. But I knew better.

"It's a blessing that we can all be together," added his mother, my then mother-in-law, Irene, glancing at me as I served fish onto my plate. I could clearly hear the note of sarcasm in her voice.

Everyone at the table pretended that everything was normal, that this was a loving family gathering where no one was excluded. My sister-in-law Veronica boasted about her designer outfit. My mother-in-law claimed she was wearing her favorite white blouse and didn't need anything else. My brother-in-law Mark devoured the dumplings with visible satisfaction, while the uncle and aunt sat quietly, observing everything closely.

But I knew better. I knew what was hiding beneath it all.

"Oh, these dumplings are fantastic, Mom!" Mark guffawed. "You make the best dumplings in the world. No one can match you! That's probably why they're afraid to try!" He glanced at me meaningfully.

They all laughed. And I laughed too, even though I knew it was a direct attack on me. A few days earlier, Oscar had wondered if this year I should be the one to make the dumplings. But it never came to that. Irene would never have allowed it! I knew the subject would come up sooner or later. So, at the Christmas Eve table, I felt a sharp sting. All these little jabs, the mockery, the scheming were like a test of strength, and somehow, they usually targeted me.

The dumplings were just the beginning. After them came other snide remarks, not even worth mentioning here. Some were more, some less veiled. Their target was clear: me! Normally, it would have been hard for me to survive there. But I assumed that it wasn't easy in Purgatory. I had a way to cope. A wall. I had built it around myself long ago. It had separated me from this hostile environment for years. I was beginning to appreciate it more and more. No one was allowed behind that wall! No one, except my children. Inside, we were safe, though isolated. Well, everyone pays a price in life.

As the years went by, my wall grew thicker, taller. Although on the outside, I was seen as a happy woman, inside I felt empty. At least that wall of indifference gave me some protection. In the house where I lived with my second husband, I was alone. Even when surrounded by people, I was always alone. But that loneliness, instead of weakening me, gave me strength. I didn't need anyone. I had my children, I had my work. And I had my solitude.

But deep down, anger grew in me – anger at my husband, at his family, at this whole false, hypocritical world. Anger at myself for not being able to change it. For not being able to find another way out. For allowing my life to become so complicated. That anger turned into resentment, and resentment into hatred. Hatred for that family that was now gorging themselves on Polish dishes at the Christmas Eve table in this German town. I knew that hatred would destroy me. Yet I wanted to move on. For myself, for my children. I wanted to lead us to our Heaven. So, I had to find a way out of my current cage. During that Christmas Eve, I was still trapped in it. That was what crushed me the most. However, those Christmas Eves in Germany were still better than the hellish holidays of my childhood, which still loomed somewhere in my memory. I felt safer here, despite all the hypocrisy that hovered over the Christmas table.

"I don't know about you, but I'm going to have more of my borscht with dumplings," my mother-in-law suddenly announced, even though she had already eaten her second, even third, serving. "Does anyone else want some?"

I jumped up from the table.

"Don't bother, Mom," I shouted. "I'll get it. No need to trouble yourself."

I almost added "at your age," but bit my tongue. Why did I volunteer so eagerly? I really don't know. It was some kind of impulse.

I think my subconscious kicked in.

I rushed to the kitchen and, waiting for the borscht to heat up, wondered what had gotten into me. I even swore under my breath. That old hen should be carrying her own soup! I finally calmed down. Maybe God, up there somewhere, would count this as a good deed and let me out of this damned Purgatory faster?

I laughed at the thought. OK, let the old woman have a little satisfaction! I exhaled. I decided not to think about it, not to get upset. I watched the small bubbles slowly begin to appear on the surface of the borscht. The soup's aroma gradually filled the kitchen. I covered the pot and sat down on a chair, waiting.

Yes, this was it. The moment when I could be alone, in silence, with my thoughts. Unfortunately, it didn't last long. Eventually, I had to leave that peaceful space. I walked carefully. Very slowly.

"Finally! It took so long! I thought you were cooking that borscht!" Irene laughed as I finally appeared in the room.

Everyone gathered around the table burst into laughter. Meanwhile, I was getting closer to my mother-in-law. I won't lie – my hands started to tremble a bit. I tried with all my might to control it.

"Oscar, maybe it's time for your wife to finally dare to cook some borscht?" Irene continued. "She should learn to make it just like her mother-in-law does!"

The room filled with laughter again.

I reached her. I smiled. Then, suddenly, I tilted the bowl. The red borscht joyfully splashed onto my mother-in-law's favorite blouse, instantly ruining the white fabric.

"Oh dear, what a klutz I am!" I groaned, making doe eyes.

Irene jumped up from her chair, erupting in a mix of sobs and perhaps a wail of despair.

Now you know why I got slapped in the face by my husband in the kitchen as the Christ Child was being born.

"You clumsy fool!" he yelled at me. "You did that on purpose!"

"Not true!" I lied, rubbing my cheek where he had struck me. "I can even swear to it." I crossed my fingers behind my back just in case.

That was my Christmas Eve in Purgatory.

One of many I lived through there. If you want to know how I ended up in that place, we'll need to go back a few years.

CHAPTER 8

I was fortunate enough to finally escape the Hell in which I had been trapped for years. But it wasn't easy. I went through a lot to claw my way out of that devilish world. The journey was long and thorny, marked by doubt, tears, harsh curses, and lips bitten until they bled.

When did my arduous climb toward life's Purgatory begin? I believe it started when I realized that what I called my life was a complete failure, that I couldn't go on like that any longer. That was the moment I left everything behind – the shadows of my past that cast darkness over my life... when I left... But let's go back a bit.

The sky looked like a canvas painted by a shaken artist. Golden rays of the sun danced with each other, trying to resist the looming clouds, heavy with the promise of a storm, pressing down on the horizon. It felt as if those clouds were woven from my fears, doubts, and uncertainties. But was I ready for the rain they were about to bring?

Standing on the threshold of my family home, I began to question why I had even come here. It was sheer madness! My thoughts swirled like leaves caught in an autumn storm. I knew better than to expect any sympathy from my mother. When I knocked, she opened the door and looked at me as if she hadn't expected me at all. Well, I hadn't expected to come here either... Not after how I'd been treated before. Yet I came because I had no other ideas. I simply ran away. I had no intention of returning to Warsaw, where every corner reminded me of what had been. I had no intention of returning to Anthony, no matter what. I was too exhausted for that. Unfortunately, I couldn't escape from myself, from my heart, torn to shreds by the decisions I made and those I didn't make. But could running away ever bring relief?

Nothing had changed in the family home. The atmosphere was still just as nasty and tense as ever. Luckily, my brother-in-law – my older sister Ursula's husband – arrived soon after me, and the attention shifted to him. Our relationship hadn't been good lately. He had treated me coldly and condescendingly. But now, he suddenly became strangely friendly.

"Hi," he said, trying to smile. "How are you?" he asked in a kind voice.

We exchanged a few meaningless words, and it seemed like it might not be so bad. My brother-in-law managed to surprise me.

"I have a proposition for you," he suddenly said.

I admit, at first, I was scared.

"I'm heading back to Holland soon, and I can take you with me," he explained. "As you know, I've been working there for a long time. They're looking for someone at a horse farm, and I know you like those animals. They need someone for two weeks. Interested?"

Immediately, I envisioned it in my mind. Images of majestic beauties, magnificent wild pastures where horses lazily grazed far from the hustle and bustle of everyday life, flashed before my eyes. It would smell of freedom, of open spaces. I admit, a shiver of excitement ran through me. And then reality brought me back to earth.

"But... what about my son?" The words escaped my lips almost automatically. The shield of maternal instincts stood guard over my actions, tempering my dreams. "Who will take care of Adam while I'm in Holland?"

My thoughts began to swirl in a dance of doubts. Could I allow myself a moment of respite, leaving my son in someone else's care, even if it was family? Inside me, a battle raged between the desire for freedom and motherly concerns. I knew this decision could bring many changes to my life. But why risk the greatest treasure I had?

My brother-in-law suddenly stood up and gestured toward my mother, who was sitting across the room, holding a cup of coffee. Their eyes met, and a thick atmosphere of anticipation hung in the air.

"Mom, will you help?" he finally asked. "You'll finally get to spend more time with your grandson."

Clever! He struck right at the softest spot. Now she had to balance her dislike for me with her love for Adam.

Mother pondered for a moment, lost in thought. In her eyes, there was something more than just curiosity or concern for her grandson. It was a glint of greed. Richard had been working in Holland for years and often brought back gifts, not to mention money. He had always been generous to Mom. I'm sure she remembered that.

"I agree," she finally said. "Since you're asking..." She looked at me pointedly, as if she resented that I hadn't knelt before her. My brother-in-law smiled, walked over to her, and kissed her on the forehead. There was something theatrical about it.

"Thank you," he muttered, then turned to me and gave me a thumbs up.

I could feel emotions surging inside me, mixing with uncertainty. Was I ready to leave my son, even for such a short time? But then I remembered the horses, the wind in my hair, and the sense of freedom. Maybe this trip would be my chance for a fresh start. A start without Anthony.

The night wrapped the room in a silky darkness like a curtain hiding secrets and unfulfilled dreams. It was a horrible night. I lay down to sleep, though I knew I wouldn't sleep. Not with what was swirling in my head. So, I lay still, staring at the ceiling hidden in darkness. In one corner of my mind, the golden Dutch guilders shimmered, dancing in the rays of desire, tempting and promising a better tomorrow. I imagined myself in elegant clothes, taking the first steps on the path to independence. But then, like a boomerang thrown by fate, the thought of my son, my little pearl, whose shine outshone all that Dutch gold, returned. I pictured his uncertain smile at breakfast as he asked when his mommy would be back. My heart tightened as if someone were squeezing it in their hands, trying to drive me to madness.

Somewhere deep inside me, an inner bell rang, sounding the alarm. On one hand, it called for escape from problems, for a brief respite in a foreign land. On the other hand, it urged me to stay, to be the mother who would never leave her child. These two melodies intertwined, creating dissonance in my heart.

I turned on my side, trying to escape these thoughts. In desperation, I pressed my head into the pillow, hoping to find a moment of peace. But my mind was in chaos, a storm of emotions tossing me between terror and euphoria. I felt my heart racing, as if it wanted to leap out of my chest and flee from these dilemmas. The night passed, and I continued to wrestle with myself, wondering what price I was willing to pay for independence. Finally, I made my decision.

The time for departure arrived, coinciding with my 23rd birthday. Perhaps this coincidence was some sign from fate? I don't know, but I must admit, it was a strange coincidence.

We left in the evening, so I had time to eat a piece of cake at the family home and wash it down with another drink. Then we drove off into the dark night, where the uncertainty of tomorrow lay hidden.

Holland awaited me; the world awaited me. Was I ready? *Time will tell*, I thought.

When I took my first step on Dutch soil, it felt as if I had stepped into a painting drawn with pastel crayons. The sky seemed bigger, bluer, stretching over the flat, green meadows that ended somewhere on the horizon, embraced by the silvery mirror of the canals.

Holland was like a beautiful melody – calm, harmonious, yet full of life. I felt as if I had become part of this picturesque symphony – of green, water, sky, and people. The Dutch countryside was like a soothing lullaby I had longed for my whole life, without even knowing of its existence. In this country, among these people, I found myself again, discovering the simplicity, beauty, and harmony of everyday life.

In the morning, when the first rays of the sun gleamed on the dewdrops, I entered the world of horses. Among the golden ears of wheat and green meadows, the stable rose majestically like a palace for these magnificent creatures.

It started with a greeting. The horse's nostrils flared in a delicate whisper, exploring my scent, while its large, trusting eyes looked at me with deep curiosity. I could feel all the emotions these horses bestowed upon me.

The work at the stable wasn't easy. Cleaning their coats of the previous day's smells, tangled in branches and grass, required patience.

But every stroke of the comb, every glide of my hand over their soft skin, resulted in a bond of trust. As a result, the horses quickly became my friends. They became an essential part of my day. And though my hands swelled from the effort, and my back was massaged by pain, there was joy in my heart.

When night spread its velvet wings over the Dutch landscape, my body screamed with exhaustion. But when I looked at the horses, their silhouettes outlined against the setting sun, I felt that the fatigue didn't matter. They stood there like dancing shadows, lowering their heads as if to thank me for taking care of them during the day.

"Take care, beautiful ones," I whispered to them as I left the stable. And they, these magnificent creatures, responded in silence with their calmness, which was like a balm for my wounds.

As the days passed on the calendar, they felt like notes in a favorite melody that eventually came to an end. I was supposed to return, to leave behind this country that had become a place full of magic for me. But like the princesses in fairy tales who lose track of time in enchanted forests, I too lost myself in the Dutch landscape. Somehow, my two weeks there had quietly stretched into months. Was it the magic of this place? Or was there something deeper at play?

The hardest part was explaining it all to my mother. Don't get me wrong; I'm not ungrateful. I truly appreciated everything she was doing for me and my son. But I must add that she wasn't doing it for free. I sent her money not only for Adam's upkeep but also paid her for taking care of my little boy.

I recalled all her complaints, every grievance, every sarcastic joke about how I was living like a lady while she had to work hard. She complained and took the money I sent.

"When are you coming back?" my brother asked when I called home once again. His voice was full of worry and longing.

"Soon," I promised, though I wasn't sure when exactly "soon" would be. "I miss you all so much. I know leaving Adam for so long is a big ask. Thank you for your help," I added, tears welling up in my eyes. My brother laughed in response.

And so went our phone conversations.

With each day I spent in Holland, I grew more appreciative of my family. I knew that despite the difficulties and tensions that sometimes arose between us, they were there for me when I needed them the most.

With each passing day, with each new contract, I found more strength and determination within myself. Yet, I couldn't return to Poland. Eventually, Anthony took care of Adam. Well, after all, he was his father! I learned that his older sister helped him. She always filled me with a strange sense of fear and unease! She never liked me... It turned out that she was Boris's fiancée. Yes, my Boris!

I never would have imagined that our paths would cross in such an unusual way. It's ironic that she, the fiancée of my former love, became the guardian angel of my son during my absence. I never had the chance to thank her for it. And that's a shame. Will time, that most ruthless of judges, ever give me another opportunity? Will there ever be a chance to do so? Who knows? I feel that I owe her that much.

I was young, so I didn't confine my life solely to work. After all, that's the prerogative of youth. At least, that's what people say, and I won't argue with that. After all, youth must have its wild moments. In Holland, I followed that maxim as well. When evening fell, my second life began to awaken. The night streets of the Dutch city, full of vibrant bars and clubs, became a new realm for me to explore reality. Neon lights outlined the buildings, and diverse music poured out of the open doors of venues. I was like a moth drawn to the bright lights.

In one of the clubs, I danced until I couldn't anymore, surrounded by people from all over the world. The bass pulsed through the air, and the rhythm pulled me into a whirl where fatigue didn't exist.

"You're amazing!" shouted a tall, blond Dutchman, whose name I don't even remember. I laughed, floating on waves of euphoria, feeling as if all my worries had been left at the club's door.

In other places, I met wonderful people who showed me that life could be celebrated in many ways. There were picnics by the canals, evenings in jazz bars where you could feel the spirit of old, romantic Europe. Different people came and went in my life. Take Ludwig, for example, a German artist who painted nighttime cityscapes.

"I see longing in your eyes, but also wildness and untamed passion," he whispered to me one night as we gazed at the stars. Then he got slapped because he started reaching where his eyes shouldn't go.

There were also other innocent wild moments. Adventures that, even now, years later, I can't recount without blushing. At some point, I realized I was walking a fine line – between freedom and self-destruction. But it was part of my journey, part of my search for myself. Holland not only gave me freedom but also taught me how important it is to find balance.

Amid the nightly dances and wild parties, I found myself – a young woman who, despite everything, knew that at some point she would have to return to reality. But until that moment came, I was ready to take life by the horns. After all, I hadn't had a chance to let loose before. I got married quickly, had a child at 19. The daily responsibilities weighed me down, and in Holland, I felt free.

Then came the day that changed my life once again. The sun reflected off the windows, and rays of light filtered through the curtains, fading in the shadow of the hallway. As I descended the stairs, each step seemed heavier, as if every inch of space was saturated with magic and anticipation. And indeed, the place turned out to be magical.

I saw him from afar, standing right next to my brother-in-law. He was perfection carved into the shape of a man. Clearly, he must have been sculpted by a genius, guided by goddesses themselves. He was tall, slim, with dark hair and dark eyes. And he looked at me with clear embarrassment, with a strange awkwardness.

This can't be happening! I thought. *Could it be that an angel had fallen straight from heaven to stand in this hallway?* I quickly recalled the scene from the movie "Titanic" where Rose appears on the grand staircase, and Jack looks at her with his mouth agape. Oh, yes! That's exactly how I felt!

With every step I took, I felt my heart beat faster. Those trembling notes of emotion that filled the air between us were almost tangible. Our eyes met, and the world around us suddenly ceased to exist. Everything else faded, and we were like two magnets drawn to each other by an irresistible force.

"This is Rolando," my brother-in-law introduced him with a slight smile, seeing what a treasure he had given me.

"Hi," I whispered with difficulty, trying to hide the emotions that were bursting inside me.

Rolando, without breaking eye contact, nodded and smiled slightly.

"Nice to meet you," he said with joy.

At that moment, we didn't know what else to say, but one thing was certain: our lives, our paths had suddenly crossed, and the future now seemed full of endless possibilities.

When people say that love comes unexpectedly, they mean moments like this. There was a spark between us that couldn't be hidden or suppressed. Every glance we exchanged was filled with unspoken words, every smile was like a sweet melody of the heart.

We began meeting under any pretext – Rolando would bring me papers from the office, or he'd claim he needed my photo for some documents... There was always an excuse. We met more and more

often, and our tête-à-têtes gradually turned into increasingly passionate dates. The wind blew through my hair, and my heart played
a symphony of feelings. You could say that butterflies were dancing
in our souls. Although life isn't always simple and full of roses, there
were moments when I felt truly alive. And it was all thanks to Rolando. Even though I didn't know him completely yet, I knew he
would be an important part of my life.

In the heart of the city, among the winding streets and the whispers of the night, our two souls discovered each other anew, step by
step, touch by touch. It was like a dance between two people exploring uncharted territory – full of mysteries, uncertainties, but above
all, boundless joy. In the middle of the night, when the moonlight
filtered through the curtains, I could feel the warmth of his skin, the
gentle beat of his heart. Our gazes were like a promise of endless
moments of happiness. Then our lips met in the silence of a starless
night.

"You're like a song whose melody I didn't know, and now I can't
stop humming it," Rolando whispered, wrapping his arms around
me. His breath played on my neck like a musician on instruments,
and every touch was like a note in this song of love.

At night, we surrendered to each other in a passionate dance
where every movement, every glance was filled with desire and tenderness. It was a dance where longing was fueled by passion, and our
hearts beat in unison. His hands moved over my skin like a brush on
canvas, painting images full of love and warmth.

"You're like a dream I don't want to wake up from," I whispered,
pulling him closer. In response, Rolando kissed me with a passion
that was like a storm on a summer day – wild, unexpected, but at the
same time beautiful and overwhelming.

When dawn finally found us, we lay side by side in silence, immersed in a feeling that was stronger than anything else. I knew that what we had was unique, like that one moment when everything is perfect and right. Our passion was like a fire that burned brightly but didn't consume – it brought warmth and light in the darkness. To put it simply, we were crazy about each other!

If you've ever heard of the Twin Flame, yes, this was it.

One day, Rolando suggested something more than alcohol. With a dangerous glint in his eye, he pulled a mysterious package from his pocket.

Inside were small pills.

"Do you want to fly far away?" he asked, smiling intriguingly. Cautiously, I took one ecstasy pill. Indeed, I soared into different realms of consciousness.

Over time, we got more adventurous. We started experimenting with other substances. Magic mushrooms, though bitter in taste, promised a tempting journey. When amphetamines and cocaine joined our nighttime mix, everything began to speed up. My heart beat like a drum during a wild ritual.

In this way, our nights became even more intense. Colors became brighter, sounds more vibrant. At one point, amid the blurred lights and music, I felt as if Rolando and I were floating above the floor, looking at the world from a bird's-eye view. Everything seemed so real and yet so illusory.

"Do you feel it?" Rolando asked, grabbing my hand. His fingers pulsed with energy. "It's like flying into space, right?"

I smiled broadly.

"Yes, it's like a journey beyond this world," I shouted. "Like we're in a movie where the impossible becomes possible."

All of this triggered a powerful surge of emotions in us. We experienced a radiant life force that peaked high above our heads and then dissolved somewhere in the misty distance. Bathed in the dazzling glow of ecstasy, we forgot about the world around us.

But amid the euphoria and highs, there was also a shadow. The awareness that what was so fascinating could become a trap. The laughter and fun gave way to moments of reflection. When the drugs wore off, leaving us groggy, I felt something in our relationship beginning to change. What had started as endless fun was taking on darker tones.

But then, wrapped in moments of the impossible, we failed to see the warnings.

The air was thick with the scent of passion. The intensity between Rolando and me was so palpable that the outside world almost ceased to exist. We felt and absorbed each other, merging in an ineffable space, vibrating together in harmony. It was more than just music that we knew... His touch was like a flash of hellfire, the heat of which I felt in every cell of my body. His eyes, deep and mysterious, became my universe.

Despite our passion, shadows inevitably began to surround us. The white line on the table marked the beginning of each day, a line dividing sleep from reality. Even though I knew I was treading a dangerous path, teetering on the edge between who I was and who I was becoming, I couldn't resist the temptation.

"I miss you, even when you're right next to me," I confessed one day, looking into Rolando's eyes. I was as addicted to him as I was to the drugs.

Every time I traveled back to Poland, my mind was torn between the need to be with my family and the longing for Rolando and the craving for the next high. Buying drugs became a routine. Everything that had once been close to my heart began to fade in comparison to what now captivated me.

One rainy evening, sitting by the window in my family home, watching the raindrops dance on the glass, I realized something.

"I'm like a fly caught in a spider's web," I whispered to myself.

But instead of seeking a way out, I reached for another dose, trying to forget this sad truth. And then, for some reason, my mother's words, shouted at me years ago, thundered in my mind:

"Remember, everything has its price!"

I laughed sarcastically, snorting a line.

In the dazzling rainbow of emotions that swirled between Rolando and me, there was one color missing. One feeling that, although so strong and all-encompassing, didn't quite fit into my new reality. It was the feeling a mother has for her child. A feeling that, despite all the richness of moments with Rolando, still woke up in me every day with renewed strength. Throughout all those months in Holland, I missed Adam terribly. Every morning when I woke up next to Rolando, feeling the warmth of his body, I felt a cold wind of longing in my heart. In those moments, I would recall my son's small hands, his laughter, and how his eyes sparkled when he talked about something that fascinated him. And then I would start crying, unable to stop.

"Rolando," I said one evening, "Have you ever thought about having children?"

He smiled slightly, gazing into the distance.

"I never really thought about it before," he admitted. "But since you've been with me, the idea of a family doesn't seem so far-fetched anymore."

I swallowed hard.

"I want Adam to be here with us. I want him to experience a real family life, something he's never truly had," I declared with emotion.

Rolando looked at me with deep understanding in his eyes. He nodded and then kissed my forehead. He didn't need to say anything more.

Days passed, and my desire to bring Adam to Holland became obsessive. I imagined our days together – walking through parks, feeding ducks by the canal, teaching him to ride a bike on the cobblestone streets. I wanted him to have all of that.

But deep down, doubts gnawed at me. Could I provide him with a stable life, especially considering my recent decisions? Would Adam be able to adapt to a completely new environment? Would I be doing him harm by taking him away from what he knew?

However, I decided that since things were going so well with Rolando, I would bring my son to Holland. We would create the family he had never truly had. This became my goal, and I quickly set about making it happen.

CHAPTER 9

I must have been dreaming... But it felt so damn real that even today, it's hard for me to believe it was just a dream. No! It wasn't a dream!

The memory of that event hit me out of nowhere, sending shivers down my spine. My father visited me. It was a moment I will never forget. He visited me, even though he had been dead for a long time. His face was twisted with anger, his eyes shining with swirling accusations, filled with pain and rage. He must have heard me talking about him with mockery and disrespect the day before.

That's why he came... to punish me – I told myself, my words choking on bitterness and fear.

I don't know how we ended up in some old, abandoned school. The place seemed too terrifying to be real. A dilapidated ruin with walls dressed only in dirt and peeling paint. Rotten beams on the ceiling creaked, threatening to collapse, and the remnants of windows warned that even the sun was afraid to enter. Darkness cloaked the cobwebs hanging in the corners, casting shadows on my father's hate-twisted face. Emptiness and silence, mixed with the stench of musty air, surrounded us, and the atmosphere was so thick I could almost touch it. I wanted to get out of there, but he wouldn't let me.

"You can't escape," he said, his voice cutting through me like ice.

I tried to run, but with a mere wave of his hand, he shut all the doors. In an instant, I was trapped with my father in a place as dark and dangerous as the worst horror movie. Suddenly, he grabbed a pitchfork. His eyes flashed with fury as he pressed it against my throat. I felt the cold metal on my skin, and he pressed harder as if he wanted to drive it upwards, piercing my tongue.

"For what you said about me!" he screamed.

I started screaming and crying. I was utterly helpless. I tried to break free, but he held me tightly with those sharp prongs. I was terrified beyond belief.

"Please, Dad, don't do this!" I begged.

He just stared at me in silence. But that silence was loaded with anger, painted on his furrowed brow and in the hatred seething from his narrowed eyes and clenched teeth. He was terrifying and cruel, and I could feel the pitchfork digging into my skin.

I kept crying and screaming, but he remained unmoved. I knew I had to do something. Immediately! I tried to break free. I gathered all my strength and started to struggle. To no avail. His grip was like steel, and I was so weak, so devoid of hope...

The pitchfork pressed deeper, and I couldn't do anything. The thought pounded in my head, driving me to madness. Was this really happening? Was I really going to die here, impaled by my own father?

I realized then that my soul was trapped there. I couldn't return to my body, which lay sleeping on the bed. Something that was my identity, myself, was locked in that terrifying school with my father.

I don't know why I left my body in the first place. I suspect he yanked me out of it. My fear overwhelmed me like a flood, drowning everything I had ever known.

I cried. I screamed. My screams echoed off the empty walls of the school, creating an echo that deepened my terror. Eventually, those screams grew so loud that they woke Rolando. He woke up, but I couldn't escape from that dark nightmare my father had trapped me in.

Rolando tried to wake me, shaking me, shouting in my ear. For a good fifteen minutes, he couldn't reach me, and all I did was scream, cry, and thrash around.

"Wake up!" he pleaded, but I couldn't respond.

My body was with Rolando, but my soul was still trapped in that horrifying nightmare.

When I finally "returned," my body shook, and tears streamed down my face. My breath was shallow and uneven, and my heart pounded like a drum. Now I understand the saying, "It wants to jump out of your chest." My heart wanted to.

I was trembling all over and still scared! I feared it wasn't over, that I might fall asleep again and find myself back in that terrifying nightmare.

Seeing my fear, Rolando held me tight. He comforted me, telling me everything was fine, that it was just a dream. But I knew it wasn't just a dream. It was something more, something I would never forget.

At that moment, I was incredibly grateful to Rolando for not giving up and waking me until he managed to bring me back to reality. I knew he had fought for me, hadn't given up, even though I was already lost.

"Thank you, darling," I whispered with difficulty. "Thank you for not giving up."

Rolando smiled at me, but I saw fear in his eyes. He must have instinctively felt that what had happened wasn't just an ordinary nightmare. It was a battle! It was a battle between reality and the darkness that tried to swallow me whole.

That day, I understood that there is more to life than just our daily existence. There is something beyond our understanding, something that can change our lives forever. And the worst part is that it can happen without our consent.

I will never forget that night and that... thing. A dream? Another reality? I don't know, but I know Rolando saved me from the devil that night. And I realized I am not alone. Despite everything that had happened, I understood I could fight, I could survive.

I realized that even in the darkest moments, there is always a spark of hope. There has to be. There must be!

My body was still trembling as my mind struggled to process what had just happened. I had read about such things before. OOBE, out-of-body experience, astral projection. Is that what I just experienced? Did my soul get captured by my father? Was it lured to that dark side of the dream?

"Have you ever heard of OOBE, Rolando?" I asked, looking at him.

I no longer cared if he would laugh at me.

"OOBE?" He scratched his head thoughtfully. "Isn't that something from parapsychology? Like an out-of-body experience or something?"

"Yes. I've read about it," I replied, a bit uncertain. "Actually, I've read hundreds of books on the subject since I was fourteen. I know how it sounds... but I can't stop thinking that this is what I experienced. My soul seems to have been pulled out of my body."

I could see a mix of surprise and concern in his eyes. But he didn't deny it, didn't tell me I was crazy. He just sat beside me and listened.

"How is that possible?" he finally asked, looking at me with curiosity.

"I'm not sure," I shrugged. "But I know it was something different from a regular dream. Dreams always have a kind of hazy quality, something unreal. But this... this was so real, Rolando. So very real!"

I paused for a moment, searching for the right words. Then I continued:

"I've read that the soul can leave the body during sleep. Some people can control it; others... others can be drawn out, lured by someone. I suspect that it could have been my father."

Rolando looked at me, clearly frightened, but still silent. I could feel that he wanted to understand, that he wanted to help me. I was infinitely grateful to him for that. Unfortunately, he was as helpless in this as I was.

"We need to think this through," he finally spoke. "We need to understand what happened."

I nodded. I knew it was true. But at that moment, all I needed was the sense of security he gave me. The feeling that I wasn't alone in this uncertain world. Maybe it was crazy, maybe it was something I couldn't fully comprehend, but I felt that I had to face what had happened to me.

"That's why I'm so scared," I confessed, looking him straight in the eyes. "In that damn school, I felt so vulnerable, so powerless. Like I was just a puppet in my father's hands! And it was so real, Rolando. I felt the pain, the fear. I could even smell my father's sweat! You don't smell things in dreams!"

Rolando hugged me, trying to share some of his calm with me.

I could feel his warmth, his heartbeat. I knew I wasn't alone.

"We'll get through this together, okay?" he whispered.

His words were soothing, like balm on my open wounds. Though I was still trembling, I felt my confidence slowly returning.

We lay there, holding each other. I didn't sleep. I admit I dozed off a bit, but I wasn't ready to enter the world of dreams again. Rolando wasn't sleeping either. He held me close, one arm wrapped around me, the other gently stroking my hair. He held me tight, as if he was afraid something might pull me out of this reality, out of his world again. I didn't know what the future held, but for now, I had someone who would help me face this unexplained fear, this unknown.

And that was what mattered most at that moment.

That evening, with Rolando by my side, I realized that OOBE, astral projection, wasn't just an abstract concept in the books I had read. It was real; it was part of this world. And though I was still gripped by terror, I knew I had to understand what had happened to me, that I had to confront this invisible fear.

Eventually, Rolando fell asleep. I slipped out of bed as quietly as I could, trying not to wake him. For a moment, I watched him sleep so peacefully. I won't lie; I envied him that peace. To distract myself from the memory of that nightmare with my father, I grabbed Dante and buried myself in *The Divine Comedy*. But I couldn't focus.

My father had been dead for several years. Apparently, he wasn't dead enough. Maybe he wanted to come back and settle things with me?

To stop thinking about all of this, I dove deeper into Dante's work. I tried to concentrate on it as much as possible. As I pondered my father's death and the hell the protagonist of the book was going through, I noticed a certain similarity, an aspect that connected both contexts. I hated my father, who had left behind a lasting mark of pain and bitterness, but at the same time, after his death, a strange feeling of emptiness and loss appeared within me. It was a hatred full of contradictions, mixed with fear and reluctance, but also with a certain kind of sentiment. Just as Dante journeyed through the nine circles of hell, I felt that after my father's death, I too was traveling through my own kind of hell. Every confrontation, every word, every argument with him was like the circles of my own hell that I had to pass through to reach some form of reconciliation. Dante, who observed the punishment of souls in hell, saw it as the consequences of their actions on earth. Were my own hell, my struggles with anger and hatred toward my father, the consequences of his actions? Was this my hell that I had to survive to understand his influence on my life?

My father wasn't someone I would call a hero. But as I traveled through the circles of my own hell, I understood that even the worst demons, even those we hate the most, can teach us something. Just as Dante journeyed through hell to reach ultimate truth, so did I, going through my own hell, trying to understand the truth about my father, about myself, about our complicated relationship. My father's death was a confrontation with hell for me, but like Dante, it was also a journey toward understanding. Despite the hatred, despite the anger and pain, I realized that each circle of the hellish path I traversed was not only a punishment but also a lesson. I understood that even from the worst hatred, some value could be drawn.

Yes, those were difficult times. They were times when I felt like Dante, descending into hell. Unfortunately, the resentment and anger toward my father remained with me forever. I don't visit his grave; I don't bring flowers. All I can do is spit on his grave.

I closed Dante's book and sighed. Again, I thought about that dream, which might have been more than just a dream. And once again, a shiver of terror ran through me.

CHAPTER 10

The silence that evening was thick, like a curtain behind which my deepest desires were hidden. I sat staring out the window, watching the raindrops lazily slide down the glass. One thought dominated my mind – Adam. My little one. My son. His innocence and laughter were like balm on a wound that until now had seemed intangible. Yet, I was beginning to feel it more and more. So, I returned to the conversation I had started a few days earlier.

"Roland," I began quietly, almost in a whisper, as if this one decision required all the courage I could muster. "I want Adam to live with us. I want him to know what a real home, full of love and warmth, feels like."

Roland looked at me, and his eyes spoke more than a thousand words. He knew what it meant to me to have my little boy close. He nodded.

"We definitely need to make that happen," he said with satisfaction.

But deep inside, I knew that before I made such a move, I needed to make a promise. To myself, to him, and to Adam.

"When he's here with us, no more drugs!" I said, not taking my eyes off Roland's face. He nodded and then smiled.

"No! Seriously!" I insisted. "No drugs! Do you promise?"

"If that's the price for the home you want to give him, I'll pay it gladly," he declared and kissed me.

Yes, I knew the road ahead would not be easy. But in my heart, there was a certainty that I could move mountains for Adam. And I believed that Roland could too. Cutting ties with the demons of the past was a step I had to take for him. For us.

Why the change? Why could I no longer live in Holland without Adam? It was because of a sudden impulse I felt. Once again, I stood at the threshold of my family home, where I had left my heart. Adam, my dearest boy, stood beside me, his eyes full of tears. His birthday was approaching, and I was about to leave for Holland again, leaving him under the care of family once more. This time, something was different. My heart beat harder, and my soul was being torn to shreds.

When I hugged him, I felt the warmth of his body and the innocent beating of his heart. That's when the impulse came. The one that changed everything. I felt a powerful wave of emotion, unlike anything I had experienced before. In that embrace, in that moment, I realized that my life made no sense without him. Every departure, every separation, every goodbye – it all took on a different, tragic dimension.

Adam's tears rolled down his cheeks, and though I tried, I couldn't hold back my own. I whispered a promise to him:

"This is the last time, honey. I promise."

Although I had made that promise many times before, this time it carried a different weight. It was real. To the fullest extent. It wasn't an empty promise thrown out as a goodbye. I knew I had to change something. Adam, my sunshine, my everything, could no longer suffer because of my absence. I wanted to have him with me. I wanted, together with Roland, who had become my rock in Holland, to create a real, warm home for Adam.

There was one more issue to resolve. The moment I decided on a divorce, the air around me thickened, as if it was waiting for something momentous, something that would turn my life upside down. Anthony, though absent from my life, was still present on paper. I was still formally tied to the past. But I felt it was time to close that chapter. So I filed for divorce.

When the time came, Roland drove me to Poland for the divorce hearing in his car.

The sun was slowly setting on the highway, wrapping the world in copper tones of dusk. The road seemed like an endless ribbon of asphalt cutting through the heart of Europe, leading us into the unknown. At a speed only the highway could allow, we felt time become fluid. With each kilometer, I cut away pieces of the past to open up to new possibilities. The future seemed like something wonderful, still hidden beyond the horizon of what was to come.

Suddenly, Roland slowed down and then pulled into a parking lot. We stopped. The car fell into a deep silence, only the gentle hum of the engine breaking the almost sacred peace. It seemed as if everything around us had frozen in that one, concentrated moment. I looked at him questioningly. He smiled and caressed my cheek.

"When I look at you," he began unexpectedly, "I see an ocean full of mysteries and endless possibilities. Every moment with you is like a grain of sand that together makes up eternity."

His eyes, deep and inscrutable, reminded me of a mysterious lake where the sun was reflected. For a moment, I had the impression that I could see our future together in them.

"I want you to be my eternity," he continued, reaching into his pocket and pulling out a small box. He opened it slowly, as if he wanted every second to last forever. Inside lay a ring that sparkled like a star in the rays of the sun, like a great treasure.

"Will you be my compass, my guide through storms and calm days, my eternity?" His voice trembled, and his eyes glistened. "Will you marry me?"

For a moment, the world stopped. My heart was pounding so loudly that I had the impression it was beating for both of us. In that simple ring was contained the entire story of our love, all its ups and downs. His question was so unexpected that for a moment, I lost my breath. I knew I had a divorce hearing ahead of me, and behind me – so much pain and suffering. But Roland was like a lighthouse in the darkness, like the sun after a storm.

"I don't know what to say," I whispered.

"Just say 'yes.'"

"There are so many unknown roads in life, but with you, Roland, I want to travel them all. Yes, I want to be your eternity," I replied, opening my heart to a new chapter in our shared story. I looked into his eyes, searching for truth, love, and understanding. I found them.

In the grand, austere courthouse, there was an incredible calm. High ceilings seemed to separate people from their problems, and every step echoed among the great marble corridors. In such a place, it's easy to be reminded of the fleeting nature of human problems in the face of eternity.

Before entering the courtroom, anticipating the emotions that might await me there, I decided to take a moment and catch my breath. The past cannot be changed, but the future can always be written anew.

He emerged from around the corner. I stood face-to-face with Anthony. We hadn't seen each other for a long time, and yet, this moment was devoid of awkwardness. His eyes, though a bit tired, gleamed with old familiarity. His lips seemed ready to smile.

"It's been a while," he remarked, kissing my cheek in greeting.

"That's true," I replied with a hint of nostalgia in my voice, recalling everything that had been beautiful between us, although there wasn't much of it. "But life goes on, right?"

The surprise in his eyes turned into warm understanding.

"You always said that. Life is a river that flows, regardless of our decisions," he reminded me.

We laughed, recalling the old days and what used to amuse us. Even in that court hallway, where every corner shouted formality, we found a place for memories.

"It's a shame it all had to end this way," Anthony said, a bit more seriously.

I looked at him with a gentle smile.

"That's life," I muttered, giving him that cliché because nothing else came to mind. After a moment of silence, which seemed to last forever, we both added almost simultaneously:

"Thank you for everything."

We parted on good terms, and that was the most important thing. After all, we both knew it had no chance of lasting.

The evening was quiet, full of nostalgia and reflection. The sun was setting on the horizon, casting red, orange, and golden reflections on the facade of my family home. In those soft rays, Anthony appeared at the gate, holding a toy for our son. He crossed the threshold of the house and paused. He looked around as if trying to catch echoes of the old days. Our son ran up to him with a beaming face.

"Daddy!" he shouted, and Anthony crouched down, showing him the toy.

Suddenly, Roland appeared in the doorway, and I froze for a moment, unsure of how the situation would unfold. But the two men looked at each other with a kind of curiosity, not hostility.

I introduced them, and then we all sat down in the living room. It was an unusual situation, but despite the circumstances, the conversation was calm, respectful, and at times, even humorous. The tension that had appeared at the beginning of their meeting quickly dissipated. They looked at each other, and I saw a shadow of understanding in their eyes. Despite cultural and life differences, they both loved the same boy and wanted the best for him.

At least that's what I thought at the time.

After a longer conversation and a few beers, it was time to say goodbye. Anthony approached me and hugged me in farewell. Then he looked at Roland.

"Take care of her," he said and left.

"He's a good man," I said, watching through the window as he walked across the yard toward the gate. "He has a heart of gold, but our marriage was a disaster. Anthony was a good friend, but as a couple, we weren't meant for each other. That fiction had to end."

Roland put his arm around me.

"At least now you're all mine," he noted.

When the door closed behind Anthony, the warmth of the setting sun's rays slowly faded, giving way to the cooler evening air. Roland and I stood in the living room, gazing deeply into each other's eyes. He took my hand, and our hearts began to beat in unison. There was something electrifying in the way he looked at me. It was something that sparked intensely. Those sparks were invisible to the eye, but they were as real as possible in our hearts. This feeling was entirely different from what I had ever felt for Anthony.

"I wonder how it could be that you only found true love now?" Roland asked, and I could sense a certain passion in his voice.

"I have no idea," I laughed, thinking of Boris.

Roland moved closer to me. I felt the warmth of his body, and the scent of his skin brought back all our shared moments.

"I don't know what it was before," he whispered in my ear, "but now... this is true love."

His lips found mine in a hot, passionate kiss, and I lost myself in the moment, giving in to the waves of desire that engulfed us. Roland's touch made me feel as if we were one body, one spirit. Everything was intense, like fireworks on New Year's Eve. Breathing heavily, I pulled away from him for a moment, searching for words that could express what I was feeling.

"With Anthony... it was like walking through a clear, uneventful day. There was no storm, no sunshine. Everything was monotonous, colorless," I explained.

Roland pulled me close, and I felt safe in his arms.

"And now?" he asked.

I smiled, looking deep into his eyes.

"Now, it's the brightest star in the sky. Something out of this world."

In that moment, standing in my family home, I knew one thing – true love is worth the wait. Even if you have to wait a lifetime.

That day, after Anthony closed the door behind him and left us in Roland's care, he also closed the door to his life for Adam. His son saw him for the last time that day.

It wasn't just Anthony who withdrew from Adam's life; almost his entire family did.

I don't have the best memories of them. After my divorce from Anthony, I had to return wedding gifts to some of his family members! After six years! Laughable! Yes, I did it. But today, I would have done it differently, in my own style.

The one person from his family for whom I always have open doors and an open heart is Anthony's younger sister, Isabella. Our wonderful Bella. The only one who was there for Adam through all those years – when he was growing up, when he started school, when he lost his first tooth, or when he scored an important goal in soccer... They still keep in touch. She never turned her back on him and maintained contact despite the many miles between them. She always remembered him.

Of course, still present in Adam's life is also my Madeline, along with her husband, Ralph – Anthony's brother – and their beautiful daughter, Samantha.

The worst was Adam's grandmother, my ex-mother-in-law. Gertrude again! Damn it! She disowned my child. She said she no longer had a grandson! She did this right in front of young Adam. Well, fine! As you wish! One day you'll regret it!

Many years made me wait for that sweet moment. Luckily, I'm a very patient person. Very patient!

When Gertrude heard from Bella how much my Adam had grown, how wonderful and well-behaved he was, she suddenly wanted her grandson back. Oh, how I had waited for this!

"Go to hell! You don't have a grandson, remember?" I said to her with amusement. I turned on my heel and walked away with undisguised satisfaction. I didn't even try to stifle my laughter.

You weren't there for him all those years when I was raising him alone, so now Adam doesn't need you. He's all mine!

The only regret I have is that my son grew up without a father. He has his father's character and the same kind, sensitive heart.

Anthony supposedly wanted to reconnect with Adam once he turned eighteen... I don't understand why he waited... for the 18th birthday, for the weekend, for the weather, for the right moment...

The only thing we truly have is here and now. Tomorrow may never come.

For Anthony, it didn't...

Two weeks before Adam's fifteenth birthday, we received a sad phone call. Anthony had passed away.

CHAPTER 11

The sun rising over the Dutch horizon was undoubtedly different from the one in Poland. I had the feeling that the rays here were subtler, more muted, yet at the same time carried with them a certain hope. I liked watching how the world stretched out in the morning light and woke up to new challenges. With every step on Dutch soil, I felt the weight of the past lifting from my shoulders. I had become free, not only from the iron shackles of marriage but, most importantly, from myself and my addictions. It was like a miraculous morning. The morning of my future life. I had no inkling then just how wrong I was. How could I have known?

I already had my wonderful little son with me. My heart pulsed with the rhythm of his laughter, creating a melody full of love and hope.

I recalled the days when I would fall into the abyss of drugs.

When the sky turned dark, and the days were filled with grayness and a monotonous rhythm. It was true love, my motherhood, that became my lifeline. The thought of Adam reminded me of what was important.

"Mom, where are we?" Adam asked when he entered the Dutch apartment for the first time.

"We are home, sweetheart. In our new home," I replied with great joy.

My son's smile grew even wider. His joy was contagious and filled the entire space around us. I knew he was feeling the same things I was: relief, hope, and the joy of a new beginning.

In my new life abroad, there were many challenges, but nothing was more difficult than battling my own demons. Sarcasm was often my defense mechanism when I told myself:

"Surely, it's easier to pick yourself up after a fall in the Netherlands than in Poland."

I didn't know if that was true. The important thing was that I believed it.

In a sense, my life was like a river that flowed through mountains and valleys, creating beautiful landscapes but also bringing destructive floods. There were moments when I felt as if I were drowning in its depths, but there was always some kind of lifeline. This time, it was the love for my son and the desire to create a safe home for him.

So, here I was, in the land of tulips, windmills, and bicycles, with my head full of dreams, my heart full of hope, and my son, who was my greatest treasure. I was ready for a new chapter in the book of my life.

Adam was just as enchanted by the Netherlands as I had been when I first arrived. Our walks through the park, the smells and colors of the flowers in the fields, the bike rides – all of it brought us immense joy. And "swimming on the swimming," as Adam called the fountains in the middle of the canals, fascinated him. He loved watching them.

One day, when we returned from a city excursion, even before I opened the apartment door, I felt an odd sense of unease. The atmosphere was thick, heavy, like a storm gathering just before the lightning strikes. Although Adam didn't know what was happening, he instinctively gripped my hand tighter.

When we crossed the threshold, the scene before me felt like a punch to the heart. Rolando, with his nose to the table, was inhaling a white substance that gleamed like a devilish spark in the dim room.

"Adam, to your room! Now!" I yelled without looking at him.

My voice was filled with rage and determination. The boy obediently headed toward the door, casting a worried glance at Rolando. He knew something was wrong.

I closed the door behind Adam and turned to Rolando, who was now staring at the floor. A voice in my head screamed in disapproval, and my heart ached.

"How could you?" My words were icy, piercing.

"You know I'm weak... I need this," he whispered.

His response made me even angrier. "And you do this when my son is here?!" I shouted.

Rolando lifted his head. His eyes were red, full of sadness and pain, but also a desperate determination.

"You don't understand. This is my fight, my demons," he tried to explain.

"We had a deal!"

He grabbed my arm. His grip was strong. Very strong.

"Don't tell me what to do! You know what it feels like when your body screams for more, when you're standing so close to the edge!" he said angrily.

The edge! That's exactly how I felt, standing in that dark room with a man who was a shadow of his former self. The feeling of terror, pain, and disappointment hit me like a wave.

I pushed him away, shouting, "Adam hears everything! Do you know what you're doing to him?!"

Rolando collapsed to the floor, resting his head on his knees. It was clear he was broken. But this wasn't the time for pity. I thought about Adam, who was sitting in the other room, probably covering his ears with his little hands.

As I left the room, I left behind a man who didn't have the strength to fight his own weaknesses. But my determination was stronger than ever. I had to protect my son!

Adam's presence had changed my life abroad. For him, I had stopped taking drugs, which I had been addicted to for two years. I wanted to give him, despite everything, a normal life and family. Unfortunately, it seemed Rolando hadn't followed my path and hadn't stopped using. I had made it clear when my child arrived: no more drugs! But fate laughed at me once again.

In the half-darkness of Adam's room, wrapped in the scent of his childhood dreams, I lay there listening to my own heart. It drummed in my chest with a rhythm of pain, uncertainty, and loss, and each beat reminded me of the decisions I had to make.

The wind whispered through the slightly open window, carrying with it the sweet smell of blooming trees, which contrasted with the bitterness in my heart. In the distance, I could hear the nighttime sounds of the city, which now felt like an ironic commentary on my life, crumpled up like a piece of trash and thrown away.

No more drugs! I repeated to myself, trying to convince myself that it was the only right choice. One condition, Rolando. One!

In my mind's eye, I saw his face – full of pain, frustration, despair. Could I help him? Had I tried hard enough? But what about Adam? Didn't he deserve a better life, free from the demons of the past?

These thoughts, shaken by emotions, swirled in my head, creating a whirlwind of feelings in which I was nearly drowning. The moonlight cast a pale glow on the walls of the room, drawing shadows that danced like my uncertain thoughts. Longing, anger, sadness, determination – everything mixed into one overwhelming cauldron of emotions.

After hours of sleepless wandering through the labyrinth of my thoughts, I decided. When the first rays of morning began to appear outside the window, I got up and quietly packed Adam's and my things. Then we left, leaving the past behind and heading toward an uncertain future. Sadly, there was no place for Rolando in it.

I took my son to his grandmother, my mother. It was then that I decided to break up with Rolando. I wanted to do it in person, not over the phone. I thought he deserved that. I wanted to handle everything with dignity. That was the least I could give him at the end. So, I left my son in Poland and flew back to the Netherlands by plane.

On the way to the airport, I reflected on everything that had connected me with Rolando. Love, passion, but also pain and disappointment. As I waited for check-in, I found myself observing couples – young, old, and middle-aged. Each of them had their own story, their own ups and downs. Why was it that I wasn't given the chance again to be part of a relationship with a man I loved?

As the plane took off, the words "Personally, with dignity" buzzed in my head. They were meant to guide me in the difficult conversation I was about to have with Rolando. Even though I felt some fear in my heart, I knew my decision was the right one. He deserved honesty, the truth. And I deserved a new life, where my son could be happy and safe.

Rolando was waiting for me at the airport exit, holding a bouquet of tulips in one hand and an unmistakable glimmer of hope on his face. His eyes brightened when he saw me, as if, for a brief moment, he regained the certainty that everything would be alright. He wanted to embrace me, to pull me into the tangle of emotions. His lips sought mine with longing desire, but I turned my head, unwilling to succumb to that sweet temptation.

As we got into the car, the tension between us was palpable. It felt as though we were having an unspoken conversation, full of misunderstanding, pain, and yearning. When we arrived at the apartment, I didn't want to prolong things. Everything inside me screamed to end it as quickly as possible. Like a wound that couldn't heal as long as there was a foreign object lodged in it. I knew I had to do it. It had to be like ripping off a bandage – an intense moment of pain, followed by relief.

I stood face to face with Rolando, looking into his eyes, trying to find the man I had loved. Finally, I took off the ring. The same ring that was supposed to symbolize our intertwined fates, and I placed it in his hand. His fingers froze in shock, and his eyes widened in disbelief.

"But I love you!" he whispered, his voice full of despair, overwhelmed by what was happening. "You love me too!"

I didn't answer right away. I felt an inner pain, because the truth was more complicated than he thought.

"It's not about love, Rolando," I replied quietly, in a subdued voice.

I did love him. As deeply as one can love someone they've planned their whole life with. But sometimes, love isn't enough to fill all the voids and heal all the wounds.

Rolando looked at me, as if trying to pierce through the fog of my decision, searching my eyes for even a shadow of doubt.

"You can't do this," he pressed, his voice heavy with the weight of our shared memories. "We can't just end everything... after everything we've been through together."

"Do you think this is easy for me?" I replied, struggling to catch my breath. "Do you think this is a decision I made in a single moment?"

It was only then that he seemed to truly grasp that it was over. In one instant, the hope that had still flickered within him transformed into immense pain. The realization that there was no way back unleashed a beast in him. He screamed in fury and began to destroy everything around him. Each item he smashed on the floor carried memories of the moments we had once shared.

As he shattered the laptop, I recalled our evenings spent watching movies and laughing together. The printer he angrily knocked off the desk was the same one we had used to print photos from our trips. And when he grabbed our pictures, I felt my heart break into pieces. He tore them to shreds, as if he wanted to erase every trace of the feelings he had ever had for me.

But the most painful moment was when he took the engagement ring – the symbol of our love, our promise. For a moment, he stared at it with a mixture of pain and anger, and then he hurled it with all his strength into the trash.

In the end, Rolando's rage turned to despair. He began to cry uncontrollably.

As sorrow filled the room, and Rolando's tears flowed like rain on the darkest day, silence fell between us. I didn't know what to do. I wanted to cry myself.

"What will everything look like now?" Rolando finally choked out, his voice breaking with every word. "What will I tell our friends? The family that planned our wedding, the ones who believed in our future?"

I felt the weight of responsibility and pain pressing down on me. I shrugged, even though inside, I wanted to scream that this is what life is – full of unknowns, incomprehensible decisions, and unforeseen turns.

"I don't know, Rolando. My life is falling apart too," I replied, fighting back my own tears. "I know it hurts. But it's necessary."

The sense of hopelessness that consumed him was so overwhelming that for a moment, I forgot why I had come here.

Luckily, only for a moment, because I knew I couldn't change my decision. For Adam!

I hugged Rolando one last time. Then I rushed to the door, leaving behind the shattered world we had once built together. The only things I took with me were memories and feelings. My heart was filled with so much: love that I couldn't deny, sorrow that I didn't want to share, and pain that was too heavy to bear.

As I closed the door behind me, I felt the tears flowing down my face, marking each step. I walked away in sobs.

The first time I saw Rolando, everything around me faded, as if the world had disappeared, and I had fallen into the depths of his dark eyes. His hands were like songs I didn't hear, but I felt in every corner of my heart. I knew that he understood my deepest thoughts before I even spoke to them. His presence made me want to dance in the rain, even when it wasn't raining. Because nothing was impossible when I was with him.

Only a few are fortunate enough to experience such chemistry. That feeling that makes the world stop existing, where the universe revolves around just the two of you. Our love was like beautiful, but fragile porcelain in a world full of stones. That "something" that was meant to bind us together became the reason for our arguments, our pain. Despite that spark, that unimaginable chemistry, we couldn't survive the storms around us.

I returned to Poland, the country I had longed so much to leave behind. Conflicting emotions tore at me. On the one hand, there was joy in being close to my son, but on the other, a feeling of oppression and bitterness that accompanied every thought of returning to my homeland.

As I crossed the threshold of my family home, I could almost feel the shackles of the past on my skin. Everything here reminded me of what I had so desperately wanted to forget. The furniture, the photos on the wall, the people – these were all relics of a life I wanted to leave behind.

My son, glowing with light and innocence, ran toward me with open arms.

"Mommy! Mommy!" he called, and his smile was like a ray of sunshine in a dark room.

I hugged him tightly, feeling his little heart beating in rhythm with mine. Yet deep down, I knew we couldn't stay here. For him, for us, I had to find a better place where we could start anew.

In the evenings, when my son was already asleep, I stared at the ceiling, thinking about how to find a way out of this situation. I knew Poland wasn't the place for me, that my dreams and ambitions would never come to fruition here.

I wanted my son to grow up in a place that offered more opportunities, where he could thrive and blossom. A place where I could rediscover myself and find new hope.

"Wherever we go, Mom, we'll always be together," my son whispered, giving me a sweet kiss on the cheek.

I nodded because the emotion tightened my throat. Deep down, I knew that a true home isn't a place but a feeling you carry in your heart. And I was ready to search for that feeling anywhere in the world.

CHAPTER 12

The sky over Poland was like the gray days I spent here. There was undeniably something magical about watching a starry sky with my son, but this place, so intensely scented with childhood and nostalgia, couldn't fill the void that defied any dictionary. All the while, spending days with Adam, a landscape of longing etched itself into my soul. It was as if my heart had been imprisoned in some malevolent castle, its walls built from stones of resignation and the concrete of unfulfilled dreams.

We strolled together, hand in hand, through the alleys of my childhood town, which could have been described as charming if not for the longing in my heart. Every step we took felt like a distant echo of the steps I longed to take on the streets of Amsterdam, the place where everything began to revolve around my dreams. And those dreams even started to come true.

"Look, Mom! A bird!" Adam pulled me out of my reverie, pointing at a sparrow perched on a nearby tree.

"Beautiful, isn't it?" I remarked, trying to immerse myself in the moment, in his childlike joy that was like balm for my weary soul.

And so we wandered around the town, through the shops, eating ice cream and smiling as we went. Yet, beneath that mask of maternal care and joy lay the soul of a nomad, yearning for a horizon that, here in this country, seemed so faint.

"When will we go back to the Netherlands, Mom?" Adam looked at me expectantly, as if my answer would guide the direction of his own dreams.

"Soon, sweetheart, soon," I replied, although I knew that this promise was shaky and teetering on the edge of my own uncertainties.

Yes, I was happy beside Adam, but I felt that I couldn't let this fleeting joy become everything I could achieve. I didn't want to give up on myself, on my own "self" that longed for life in the Netherlands, for the life I had left behind there. No, I wasn't ready to give it up. Not now. Not here. Not in this stupid country. My entire life spent in Poland had been a constant struggle, and nothing good had come of it. I didn't want to stay here.

And then everything unfolded in a way I never expected. Oscar, an old friend from the past, from our old gang, who had been living in Germany for some time, came to visit.

The sun, frozen in the southern sky, bathed our faces in rays that seemed warmer in the company of old friends. Oscar, always one step ahead, always a word too much, now seemed much more mature. But was he really? Do people truly change, or do they just put on masks, hiding their true nature?

After a get-together that Oscar organized for us to recapture the specific vibe of our old gang, we sat together on the balcony, surrounded by cigarette smoke and the uncertainty of the future.

"I've been thinking about you a lot lately," Oscar began, glancing at me. I smiled uncertainly, not knowing what he meant. But Oscar continued, "Have you ever thought about trying with me?"

That question hung between us unexpectedly. No wonder a slightly awkward silence enveloped us. Finally, Oscar broke it.

"I've always liked you," he admitted. "And now that you're free… well, you know, I think it might be worth it…"

Surprised by his words, I didn't know what to say for a moment. I remembered him as the eternal joker, always casually flirting with every girl. Perhaps he was shy only with me, maybe because I was a bit older than him. But now? This was a different Oscar, more mature. But was he really?

My mind swirled with thoughts. I was a divorcée, with a heart still aching from the breakup with Rolando. Should I throw myself into another relationship? Or was this a chance for a new life? On the other hand, I knew Oscar. He seemed like a constant in this chaotic world.

"Oscar," I began hesitantly, "this is all so… unexpected. Honestly, I don't know what to say. Maybe this is the moment to put everything on the line and take a risk. I don't know. You surprised me."

Oscar smiled, but something changed in his face. His eyes gleamed as if the light in them started to refract differently. Or maybe I was imagining things?

"I won't promise it'll be easy," he declared. "But I want to try."

If someone had told me that after returning to Poland, I'd fall into another relationship, I wouldn't have believed it. But it could happen. In that moment, surprisingly, I didn't rule it out. Smiling, I stood next to a man I'd known for years and was perhaps ready to take another chance. In the background, somewhere far off, the sounds of the city, which had always seemed like a prison to me, could be heard. But now, with Oscar by my side, it could become a symbol of something new, a sign of a beginning. Were the doors to a new life opening for me then? Or perhaps to another trap? Time would tell.

However, I couldn't make a decision right away. Not after everything I had already been through in life.

The sun shone intensely through the window as I asked my brother for his opinion about my potential relationship with Oscar. The lullaby of the wind carried with it the whisper of trees and memories of the times when my brother, Oscar, and I were going to different teenage parties, dreaming about what the future would bring.

My brother's reaction surprised me.

"I think it's the best thing you can do," he stated. "Oscar has always dreamed of you. When he was 17, he told our mom that he loved you and would wait for you. And as you can see, he kept his word. Another thing is that Mom tried to talk Oscar out of having feelings for you. After all, you were with Anthony then and already had Adam. But now, you two should definitely be together. It's a good decision."

In principle, I agreed with him. Besides, I pretended to myself that my possible agreement to this relationship didn't hide anything inappropriate. But the truth was that I was a broken woman, desperately seeking a way out of the labyrinth of my life. Using Oscar was selfish, but deep down, I believed that somewhere in the background, true feelings might be hiding. Although, at that time, I couldn't find them in myself. That's the truth. This relationship probably started out of boredom and the desire to escape from here.

Fucking Poland! At that moment, I felt every reality of this country, every sound of the street, and the whispers of people at bus stops. All of it disgusted me! In my heart, there was no place for love for the land of my ancestors. Poland was like a toxic relationship for me – full of pain, disappointment, and bitter memories.

The following days passed quickly. Packing, planning, goodbyes. Leaving Poland became a metaphor for escaping myself, from my demons. I felt the wind under my wings, the freedom that brought with it a new life abroad. Oscar was supposed to be my guide in this new reality.

Again, I felt that life was beginning to take on color. But were they true colors, or just an illusion created by my desperation? Time would answer that question. But then, at that moment, the only thing that mattered was the fact that I had the chance to leave. I was escaping a country that suffocated me, alongside a man who offered me a new beginning.

I suggested to Oscar that we try, but not in Germany, rather in the Netherlands. There, I felt more at home. My proposal surprised Oscar. I could see a glint of curiosity mixed with uncertainty in his eyes.

"The Netherlands?" he repeated, as if trying to process what he had just heard. "Are you longing for the canals and tulips?"

I smiled, feeling that the Dutch soil was still a place where I could be free.

"There, I feel more… myself," I muttered. "It's a country full of contrasts and surprises, just like me. Maybe that's where we'll find our place on Earth."

He pondered for a moment, taking a deep breath.

"If you want to go there, let's go," he finally declared. "Even to the ends of the earth. Just for you."

I didn't expect that answer. There was something so beautifully naive, so youthful in it. Those words only reinforced my belief that this was another step towards finding myself.

The first weeks in the Netherlands were tough. Returning to that place brought back memories of Rolando, which I tried to avoid. Every street, every corner of Amsterdam reminded me of that love, which somehow didn't want to fully dissolve into the past. However, every new day with Oscar was an opportunity to lose myself in his arms, to forget the past, and to look to the future with hope.

One day, while sitting by the canal, Oscar asked, "Aren't you afraid that by returning here, you'll live only in the past? That you'll miss what was?"

I looked at him, surprised by his insight. Then I nodded.

"I am afraid," I admitted honestly. "But you know what's worse than returning to a place full of memories? It's much worse to stay where you feel like a stranger."

He smiled at me, reaching out to pull me close.

"We'll be here together. Through every tough moment. We'll build something new, something beautiful," he assured me.

I believed him. Or at least, I wanted to believe him. But there were moments when my soul wandered the streets of Amsterdam, returning to memories of times with Roland. In those moments, Oscar was my anchor, reminding me of the present, of what we had now. He would pull me from that turbulent ocean of memories and help me find solid ground in the present.

And so, among the tulips, canals, and old buildings, we wandered, trying to build our own little world. Even though the past still haunted me, I knew I had someone by my side who could help me overcome it. It wasn't easy. Really! All we had were heads full of dreams, a few clothes, an old tent, and my car, which, as it turned out, became our saving grace. We couldn't find a place to live in the Netherlands, so for a few weeks, we lived in the car, and when the weather was good, we pitched the tent somewhere by the river and stayed there for a few days.

Among the canals and old cobbled streets of Amsterdam, our life took on a routine. The days passed quietly, even though living in the car and dealing with daily challenges was far from comfortable. Over time, the car became not just a shelter but a symbol of survival and untamed freedom.

Oscar always had great ideas on how to make each evening unforgettable. One day, he found a picturesque spot by the river, where we set up the tent and stayed for a few nights. The sound of the water and the gentle breeze lulled us to sleep. The stars above our heads were like little lamps lighting up the darkness of the night.

"You know what's wonderful about our situation?" Oscar asked one evening, looking at Adam and me. "It's that despite everything we face, despite the difficulties, we're together. This river, these stars... it's all for us. We don't need luxuries to be happy. We have each other."

Adam, despite his young age, seemed to understand the gravity of the situation. Although there were moments when he missed having a permanent roof over his head, he was always brave. His innocent laughter was like a melody that brightened our days.

"Mom, look, a shooting star!" he shouted one evening, pointing at the sky.

That was when I realized how much we lose while chasing daily worries, missing the beauty that's right beside us. One morning, waking up in the car parked at a gas station, I wondered how much longer we would continue this nomadic lifestyle. I felt that we needed to change something for Adam's sake. But looking at Oscar, who was already preparing breakfast on a small gas stove, I felt calm. I knew everything would work out. I just knew it.

"Let's welcome the new day!" Oscar laughed, handing me a cup of hot coffee. "Every morning is a new chance. Who knows, maybe today we'll find our place? I feel it's going to be a wonderful day!"

Those words gave me strength, and they also reminded me that despite all the hardships, we had each other. Together, we overcame every obstacle. It was an opportunity for feelings to grow. After all, nothing brings people closer than shared adversity.

But every day was truly a challenge for us. Many times, the weather was our enemy. A rainy evening spent in the tent was like a test of character, and every meal we shared in the cramped car was a small celebration. Despite the difficulties, we were there for each other, like guardian angels in an unfriendly world.

I often listened to the sounds of the city during brisk mornings while Oscar searched for a place where we could wash up. The sound of car horns, the roar of engines, and the buzz of people reminded me that beyond our car, there was a world that wasn't always friendly but could also be fascinating.

"Oscar," I asked one morning, as the sun reflected off the river. "Do you think we'll ever return to normal life? Do you feel like we're like birds searching for a safe haven?"

He smiled warmly, looking at me with his shining eyes.

"You know, when birds search for shelter, that's when they most often find their way home," he said seriously. "We'll find our own sanctuary too because we have something many couples long for: we have each other and our love, which is stronger than any storm."

I wanted to believe him. The following days, however, showed that our path to finding a home, to finding our own place, might be more complicated than we thought. And it might not necessarily mean staying in the Netherlands.

Before the storm arrived, there was tension in the air. The night was dark, with thick, damp fog enveloping our campsite by the river. The sound of raindrops hitting the tent was like nature's way of telling us we weren't welcome here. Amidst the natural murmurs of the storm, another, more unsettling sound could be heard in the distance – footsteps and conversations in a language I wasn't unfamiliar with but didn't want to hear at that moment. It was the Dutch police.

"We're out of luck," Oscar whispered as the flashlight beams drew closer to us.

When I saw the shadows of the figures on the tent's canvas, my heart started to race. A voice spoke to us in Dutch and English, telling us to leave the campsite. Stepping outside, I saw two officers. Their faces, illuminated by the flashlights, looked like images from a surreal dream.

"You can't camp here," one of the officers said, wiping raindrops from his face.

"We're sorry, we didn't know..." I began, but Oscar interrupted me.

"We're sorry, but please understand. This is our last hope for shelter," he said with desperation in his voice.

The officer who hadn't spoken yet shrugged and stated, "We understand, but the rules are clear. This place is dangerous, especially during a storm." He bent down and looked into the tent. "Do you have a child in there?"

An alarm went off in my mind. The last thing I needed was for them to take Adam away from me. Instinctively, I blocked the entrance to the tent with my body.

We quickly thanked them for their understanding and started packing our things. Sitting in the car, I watched the distant lightning dance across the sky, and a realization began to take shape in my mind – that the Netherlands, a country known for its tulips and windmills, had turned into a battlefield for us. In a way, it was the irony of fate.

"Well," I said sarcastically, "It seems this beautiful Holland doesn't want us here. Maybe we should consider another option."

"There's always Germany," Oscar replied with a thoughtful expression. "We might have better luck there."

As we traveled to Germany, the rain stopped, and we silently admired the passing landscape. I was filled with a mix of hope and uncertainty. This was a new chapter in our story, a new page in my own *Divine Comedy*, still being written by fate. By a fate that was laughing at us.

What was I expecting from the place we were heading to? I wasn't sure. But it definitely wasn't what I found there. It quickly became clear that I would have to deal with Oscar's mother, Irene, and his sister, Veronica. It was exhausting and terrible. But his brother, Mark, was all right.

From the beginning, I felt like an intruder there. To put it bluntly, Irene had a good heart, but she wasn't the sharpest tool in the shed.

I'll tell you more about her soon. In any case, I didn't fit in with them at all! I felt it from the very start!

The shadows of Oscar's German home seeped into my soul every day, building a wall between me and his family. Even Irene and Veronica's style of dress reflected their conservative approach, with no room for my point of view. No wonder they often looked at me with disapproval. Whenever I tried to connect with them, I hit a wall of misunderstanding.

"You don't belong here!" – that thought was always present in their gazes. I was the outsider disrupting the peaceful rhythm of their daily life. I was altering the image of the perfect world they wanted to live in.

"Couldn't he find another girl?" I overheard Veronica say one day when she thought I wasn't around.

"I can't understand why Oscar brought her here," Irene replied.

Her kindness was just a facade. In reality, she was naive, unaware of the world outside her little corner, where her life was confined.

Why do people so often judge others, even when they don't really know them? I often wondered about this during that time. I felt like an alien from another planet, accidentally stranded on Earth by some divine mistake. Maybe it was a cosmic GPS error that landed me on this planet? Perhaps it was another mistake in the script of my life that placed me in the home of these people?

But I didn't want to be like them. I didn't want to judge based on appearances, especially since I hated being treated that way myself. I decided to give them time. Maybe they just couldn't cope with this new situation? Unfortunately, I soon realized that no amount of time would change them. Oscar's family was a conglomerate of prejudices.

I felt like a foreign organism trying to join an ecosystem, only to be constantly attacked by white blood cells. Luckily, Oscar cared about me, and I saw that. I felt it every day.

In this complicated maze of emotions and misunderstandings with Oscar's family, if there was one thing that calmed and enchanted me, it was the town of F., where we had settled. This place, nestled in the heart of North Rhine-Westphalia, was like a small corner of heaven on Earth.

When we first arrived in Finnentrop I was in awe. The rolling hills surrounded the town like caring guardians, covered in patches of green trees and colorful flowers.

In one of the squares, a church with a towering steeple stood proudly, looming over the area as if it was holding up the sky. The stained-glass windows of the church reflected the sunlight in such a way that the entire square was bathed in a colorful, mysterious glow. Walking by, it was hard not to feel that this building held the secrets of many generations of the town's residents.

Not far away, the Lenne River flowed lazily through the town, as if keeping watch over the area. Its quiet but firm murmur reminded us that not everything changes, that there are certain permanent, unchanging elements in this world. Like the river itself. It whispered its song day and night, flowing steadfastly for centuries. Locals strolled leisurely by its side, as if they knew how to tame time so it wouldn't slip away. There was always an atmosphere of calm, even a kind of stagnation. It was strange. In Poland, everyone seemed to be running around, angry and stressed, but here, there was such peace! Maybe the people of this town, or their ancestors, had already been through enough turmoil and had discovered that "everything's shit," as one famous Polish rock band sang in a song of the same name. After all, they had already undergone the transformation from a farming village to what it was today.

"You know," Oscar said one day during our walk, "There's something about this town that just calms you. Do you feel it?"

I nodded, leaning into him. Finnentrop really did have its charm.

Oscar smiled and kissed me on the forehead.

"Maybe this place will help us find peace in life," he said.

How very wrong he was!

Every day, despite the difficulties I encountered in Oscar's home, walking around Finnentrop helped me regain my balance. Although there were moments when I wanted to give up and return to Poland, the beauty of this place always reminded me why I had come here. Despite everything, Finnentrop became my small enclave of peace in a turbulent world.

Although Irene could be hard to bear, she was undoubtedly a woman of action. A few days after our arrival in Finnentrop, she helped us find an apartment. It was a small but charming place with a balcony overlooking the picturesque hills of the town. The roof, covered with red tiles, reminded me of the classic German houses I had seen on postcards.

"It's not a palace," Irene said, "But it's a solid German apartment. It'll be enough for you."

Her tone was a mix of pride and sarcasm, but it was one of those moments when I appreciated her straightforwardness.

The worst part was that the door to our new apartment opened directly across from Irene's door, and our windows faced Veronica's windows.

"Seriously?" I asked myself in horror. "Do you really want that much control over our lives?"

Despite everything, I didn't want to complain. I was just happy we had a place to stay.

Oscar returned to work, leaving me and Adam in our new home. During this time, my days were filled with the routine of caring for my son and trying to adapt to the new environment.

Although the days in Finnentrop had their steady, rhythmic pulse, mixed with monotonous chores and daily routines, there were also moments that shone like stars in the night sky – bright, pleasant, permanently etched in my memory.

Oscar was someone who knew how to suddenly introduce exciting disruptions into those days. I had grown used to his spontaneous gestures, which would make me burst out laughing or bring me to tears of uncontrollable emotion. He knew how to surprise me, and soon he took advantage of that.

One day, we were driving to Poland. The road was long, and it was gray and dreary outside. Just before the border, we stopped at a gas station.

"I'll be right back," Oscar said, grabbing his wallet.

Out of boredom and fatigue, I looked around, automatically registering the images around me – trucks, cars, people hurrying to fill their tanks and get back on the road. Amid this routine, Oscar returned to the car with one exceptionally large, blood-red rose in his hand. He opened the door on my side. Suddenly, he knelt on one knee, with a certain sparkle in his eyes.

"Will you marry me?" he asked, his voice trembling slightly. "For real this time. I mean, really for real," he began to stumble over his words.

Surprised, I burst out laughing. It took me a moment to realize that Oscar might take this the wrong way. I quickly took the rose from him. But he kept looking at me with that questioning gaze.

"What?" I feigned surprise, because who said a guy should have it easy?

"Well?" he almost whimpered.

"It's a beautiful flower," I said, smelling the rose. "Really wonderful."

"Please, have mercy…"

I smiled again.

"What do you think, you fool?" I asked him, and he looked more and more bewildered. "Of course, I'll marry you. But only if you promise that our whole life will be as crazy as this moment."

"Deal!" Oscar finally laughed, jumping back into the car.

Five months later, in front of a German civil servant at the Civil Registry Office, surrounded by Oscar's family and friends, we made vows... something along the lines of: until death do us part. I had no idea what exactly, because I didn't know a word of German. But do people even make these vows sincerely, or is it just a worn-out phrase recited automatically? Of course, I wasn't thinking about that at the time. The doubts came later.

The beating hearts of two people in sync had always been, for me, the essence of love. And even if the world around us were to go up in flames, that synchronized heartbeat gave a sense of security. But was that what I felt, standing next to Oscar on our wedding day?

"I've always said the best relationships are the ones that age like fine wine," I laughed one day, looking at Oscar with a sparkle in my eye.

He smiled, raising his eyebrows in his characteristic, slightly sarcastic way.

"Well, yeah, because our relationship is like a ten-year-old Bordeaux: deep, full of character, and... expensive to maintain?" he asked provocatively.

We dissolved into shared laughter.

I dreamed of having another child. This desire grew within me week by week, month by month. I felt ready for the next challenge of motherhood. One evening, sitting on the balcony of our apartment, I looked at Oscar.

"I'd like us to have another child," I confessed.

Oscar studied me in silence for a moment, then said, "If you're sure, then I want that too."

And so, less than a year later, in one of the German hospitals, we held a little Arthur in our arms. His skin was as soft as velvet, and each breath he took reminded me of a gentle breeze on my face on a summer day. His tiny fingers wrapped around mine, and in that moment, I felt like I needed nothing else.

"Look at him," Oscar whispered. "He's our little miracle."

We fell in love with Arthur at first sight. And even though we knew that life with two children would be full of challenges, we were ready for whatever adventure fate would bring us. At least I was ready.

The sun bathed the room in a golden glow as I held the small, lively bundle in my arms: Arthur – our little star, who brightened our days with his childlike laughter. His rosy cheeks, tiny nose, and little hands that grabbed everything within reach could melt anyone's heart. I fell head over heels in love with him, just as a bird falls in love with the morning, singing the first notes of a new day. I was as enchanted by him as I had been by my wonderful Adam. It was the same beautiful feeling.

I wasn't the only one smitten with this little one. Oscar, who had previously looked at Adam with care and kindness, now only had eyes for Arthur. Adam became like the moon in the daytime sky – always present but invisible in the sunlight. My heart broke at the thought that my older son felt overlooked.

"Mom, why doesn't Dad Oscar have time for me? Why does he spend his free time only with Arthur?" Adam eventually started asking questions, looking at me with his big, sad eyes.

I took him onto my lap, trying to find the right words.

"Adam, you know, Oscar really likes you," I began cautiously. "It's just that Arthur is little and needs a bit more attention. You're already independent. You can even help with Arthur."

Even though Adam hugged me, I knew my words hadn't fully convinced him. It broke my heart. I suspect everyone around noticed that Oscar was head over heels in love with his one son while the other was pushed aside. I watched it with sadness because it was truly painful. I tried in every possible way to make up for the love, both as a mother and a father, so that Adam would never feel unloved.

It was probably an impossible task, but I had to try.

My children became my whole world. I didn't notice that the years were passing and that my second marriage consisted not only of a husband and wife but also of a mother-in-law, a sister-in-law, a brother-in-law, and the rest of that family. We carried on like that for many years. But disaster was looming because it had to come. After all, this marriage was by no means an oasis of peace. Oh, it was not!

CHAPTER 13

There's something chilling about the routine that had become a poison in the daily life of Oscar's family. Their life was like an old, monotonous melody from a gramophone, where the needle constantly skipped over the same, all-too-familiar notes. Examples? Let me give you a few!

There was the morning sun, trying to break through the drawn blinds in the living room. In its glow, Oscar sat on the couch, holding a plate with breakfast remnants, and drowning in the sticky sauce of television. Next to him stood a beer bottle, its contents diminishing with each passing minute. This image of him glued to the screen, oblivious to the world around him, became my everyday view.

"Oscar, maybe we could go for a walk today? Maybe to the park?" I suggested that day, trying to pull him out of his apathy.

"My favorite show is on in a minute," he replied, without taking his eyes off the TV.

"And after that?"

"Then I'm playing on the console," he said with no emotion whatsoever.

In the middle of the day, when the sun was at its highest, Oscar's mother sat at the kitchen table with a cup of coffee. Her conversations with her daughter Veronica, which always revolved around the latest gossip, felt like an irritating drone attacking my head.

"Did you see the dress that tramp from down the street was wearing? She looked like a sack of potatoes!" Irena laughed. "And that forever red lipstick of hers!"

I couldn't listen to the constant insults thrown at that woman anymore. It was awful! What did they know about her? Nothing! All they could do was judge and mock people. Meanwhile, that woman turned out to be a truly wonderful person who had helped me greatly in life, for which I would always be grateful.

"And her husband? I heard he lost his job again. What a family!" Veronica shook her head, continuing their ritual of degrading others.

And that's how it always went. Life in Oscar's family consisted of sitting, eating, drinking, gossiping about others, and watching television. Nothing else. And this went on for years. It's enough to drive you mad! When I think about it, I get nauseous. Unfortunately, I had to participate in it, because they organized regular family gatherings, and Oscar would drag me along, despite my protests.

The days passed one after the other, and I felt as if life was moving in some strange, slow motion. As if each day was a copy of the last. Routine became our prison, and I felt like a convict sentenced to life, forced to serve it in this misery. Maybe this was the life Oscar wanted, but for me, it was hell on earth. Somewhere in this daily grind, I lost myself, and my dreams and desires turned to dust.

Within the golden bars of my life, even though the sun shone, I felt as if I were trapped in a perpetual shadow. It might have seemed like I was surrounded by financial stability and care, which should have made me happy, but my soul bled in solitude. Oscar didn't understand that my heart longed for freedom, that it yearned for real life. Every time I looked into his eyes, I saw a reflection of the same golden cage in which I was trapped. I wanted to scream that I needed a real life, real love, but the words often wouldn't leave my throat.

In the evenings, when everyone had already fallen asleep, I would sit by the window and gaze at the star-filled sky. I imagined myself as one of those shining points, free and independent, able to fly wherever I wished. But then I would remind myself of my reality, of the golden cage I was stuck in, and the tears would begin to creep down my cheeks.

With each passing day, I felt my life slipping through my fingers like sand in an hourglass. I felt that I was slowly losing myself, becoming a shadow, merely an echo of the woman I once was. I felt that I was slowly dying, suffocating in this prison.

Irene and Veronica. To the world, they appeared to be the perfect companions. But to me, they were just two monkeys in the same zoo, full of envy and intrigue.

My mother-in-law and her daughter, shallow and insincere, were masters of pretending to be friendly. First, they'd have coffee with me, smiling all the while, and then gossip behind my back, mocking my choices, my life, as if theirs were perfect.

I was stunned when I found out that the two of them had visited my family home in Finnentrop, along with my brother and his wife. All three vipers hissed and spat venom left and right. Without any restraint, they hurled slander at me and my husband. If it weren't for a kind-hearted person who overheard their filthy tirades through an open window, I might never have known what "honorable" people I had around me! And all of this happened in the presence of my brother. How could he allow it? His silence was louder than any scream. Had someone ensnared him like a mouse by a snake? Had someone's poison paralyzed his heart, and I had become a stranger to him? Eventually, he broke contact with me and then slowly cut himself off from the rest of the family. He didn't speak to our mother for years, and he hasn't spoken to me in over a decade. Of course,

I have my nominations for "Viper of the Year," but let's keep that a sweet secret.

Once, I stumbled upon some correspondence, and accidentally – though, in truth, intentionally and with full premeditation – I read a letter from my sister-in-law to Veronica. I was horrified by what I found. Nothing but vile insults directed at me! Calling me a whore, a slut, a tramp... The contempt, no, the sheer hatred toward me! I couldn't understand why. I had done nothing wrong to these people; in fact, I had welcomed them into my home with an open heart.

It's horrible how cruel one woman can be to another. I don't know what fueled this aversion toward me, but I knew for certain that I didn't want these two-faced, hypocritical people in my life. Though I missed my brother deeply, the fact was, if he didn't want me in his life, then I accepted his rejection with honor and stepped away, wishing them happiness.

With each passing day spent in the abyss of Oscar's family, my skin seemed to turn to stone. My heart, once pulsing with hope, became surrounded by walls so thick and high that daylight had no chance of penetrating into my soul. I became my own fortress – invisible to others, untouchable by human emotions. Each new shadow on my path added another brick to my wall, making it stronger and more impenetrable. My mind turned into a labyrinth of corridors, most of which led nowhere. Inside, my thoughts swirled endlessly, whispering of loneliness and pain. In this cathedral of alienation, my altar was self-sufficiency, and my prayers were my precious children.

Oh, how grand my fortress was! Anyone who tried to approach was met with the cold barrier of my walls, losing the will to make closer contact. I was like an island in a sea of people – unapproachable and unreachable. All around me, I heard the whispering wind, carrying the mocking laughter of a world that had realized my choice. In this way, I protected myself from external chaos, but the internal turmoil I carried was just as terrifying. With each passing day and night, my hatred for the world grew, along with my resentment toward those who dared to chase their dreams.

I became like eternal winter in the midst of summer – surrounded by sunlight, yet frozen inside. I owed it all to that wall I had built over the years. My body could be present among people, but my soul was like a bird trapped in a golden cage, screaming for freedom yet terrified of the open sky. In the boundless silence of my inner world, only hatred and anger comforted me. It was my way of defending myself in this mess of false people.

In my heart, an unsettled wind full of questions blew, vibrating with a note of melancholy. Perhaps if Oscar and I had allowed our wings to carry us far from his family, our story might have had a different ending. Perhaps there would have been fewer false notes, fewer grimaces on faces.

Oscar was a good guy, but maturity was foreign to him. Though a spark of love shone in his eyes, there were also shadows of neglect. He simply never grew up, never matured! Our marriage became a stage on which I played the mother of three children. On one side, our two wonderful kids, and on the other – Oscar, the eternal boy with a head full of dreams and thoughts as fleeting as falling autumn leaves.

"Honey, could you help me with the kids a little? You know, I'm not here alone," I tried to catch his attention one evening.

He looked at me with a vacant gaze, as though peering through the fog of his dreams.

"In a minute, just one more mission," he replied, gripping his controller without taking his eyes off the screen, where his soldiers followed virtual orders in the world of the video game *Battlefield*.

I wanted to scream, to yank him out of this world of dreams, to show him real life. Sometimes, I had the urge to treat him like a rebellious teenager – grab a belt and teach him a lesson. But how can you punish someone who looks at the world with such naivety?

His reality was confined to the pixels on the screen, the sounds, and the challenges posed by the virtual battlefields. I often asked myself: Where is my real husband? Had he truly gotten lost in those virtual forests, or was he hiding there from the responsibilities expected of him in the real world?

My heart bled as I looked at him – this boy trapped in the body of a grown man, unable to find his way to the real world, not the virtual one. Didn't I have the right to feel betrayed by fate, which had given me an eternal child as a husband?

I must admit, however, that my marriage with Oscar wasn't only an endless grayness. Despite the difficult moments in our shared symphony of life, there were also interludes filled with sunlight. In the kaleidoscope of memories that formed our shared history, there weren't just stormy clouds but also golden rays of joyful moments. When I reflected on our marriage, it was often these bright moments that came to the forefront, even if only for a little while.

When I think about our trips, my heart begins to beat in the rhythm of those journeys. Europe unfolded its mysterious map before us, and together we explored its corners. Oscar could be fully present during those times, his eyes filled with curiosity, and the hands that were so often lost in the virtual world would hold mine with the passion of a true explorer. We traveled many roads together – from the narrow streets of Rome to the majestic boulevards of Paris.

Europe became our private theater, where every scene was a different country, and every curtain separating the acts was a new border.

With each trip, with each place we visited, our hearts raced with the thrill of the adventure ahead. On these off-the-beaten paths of the continent, our children, like little butterflies, fluttered to the most beautiful flowers of culture, filling their wings with the colors of new experiences. Their proud tales in the school hallways echoed the joy of discovering the world. Our children, little nomads with backpacks full of adventures, had the chance to become tiny ambassadors of the world. And although their primary concern was their yard's ranking and boasting about the number of countries they had visited, for me, those trips were like medicine for the soul, briefly soothing the pain of everyday life.

If I were to evaluate the symphony of our marriage, I would say it sounded like a collection of contrasts – between the euphoria of travel and the sadness of everyday life. Even though our hearts beat next to each other for nearly twelve years, I often felt that in this duet, we lacked a constant note of appreciation and care for one another. When we returned from our travels, Oscar would immediately retreat into his shell, becoming inaccessible and immature. In this way, I was thrust back into the darkness of daily life.

Behind the curtain of those joyful travels, in the shadow of those golden moments, something more mundane and painful lurked. It was the lack of respect and stability, things that were as essential to me as air – vital for life. While Oscar could be a wonderful travel companion, at home he often seemed to forget those basic values.

I waited for them, like a desert waiting for rain, but they were like a mirage – unreal and unattainable. I waited for respect and a sense of security. Oscar did not give me that.

I do appreciate, however, that he always stood by my side in confrontations with Irene or Veronica. He defended me from his family, but at the same time, he unknowingly allowed me to change. With each passing day, I became stronger and more wild. Unintentionally, his entire family turned me into a "beast." They made me into someone full of power and strength, ready to fight. And I grew to love this fierce side of myself. When I looked in the mirror, I saw her – that wild spark in my eyes. And although there were moments when I feared this new "me," deep down, I knew I had become stronger. For that, I was grateful to Oscar.

However, there was also a time when I was very weak, and Oscar pulled me down. We both had a problem for some time...

Dancing demons of invisible despair, piercing images of chaos and emptiness, seemed to be our constant companions – a formless master of ceremonies leading us through every pain, every argument, and every bottle of vodka disappearing into the depths of our parched souls and throats. Even though Oscar and I threw ourselves into the whirlpool of chaos, escaping into the embrace of intoxicating alcohol, finding solace in it was as likely as finding peaceful sleep while falling into a deep abyss.

It wasn't an easy life, that's for sure. Like two souls dancing with hopelessness, we grabbed for alcohol like a lifeline on a raging sea. Days and nights passed by, and in our hearts, instead of warmth and closeness, there spread an ever-growing emptiness.

I was often submerged in that sea of bitter tears, soaked in red wine. I danced with Oscar on the edge of abandonment and alienation, where every drop of liquor was like metaphorical ripples in the water, pulling us deeper into that darkness with each moment.

But then came a time when life spoke to me in a different way. It was during that period, when I felt the desire to become a mother again, that I realized I had to break free from the addiction.

When I became pregnant with little Arthur, a new hope and a new love began to grow within me. But Oscar? Unfortunately, he didn't change his habits. His hands still clung to the glass, and his eyes lost their sparkle, becoming cold like steel. One night, after yet another dramatic argument, I felt such desperation that I nearly gave up. Thoughts of ending it all, of jumping off the balcony, began to close in on me with such force that it was hard to resist. As I stood on the balcony, ready for the final act of my desperation, I felt the gentle kicks of Arthur in my belly. It was a sign. Fate reminded me of the life I carried within me. That gentleness, that innocence, gave me strength. He was my little miracle that kept me alive.

One thing was certain: Arthur gave me a reason to fight, a reason to live.

In the darkness that Oscar and I created together, that small point of light became my guide. And I knew I had to protect him, no matter what.

In the dark corridors of my mind, where echoes of childhood memories intertwined with the present, the knife became a metaphor for my rebellion and desperation. I often felt the cold, steel touch of the blade in my hand, as if it were a silent witness to my inner drama. Would it serve as the tool to free me from my suffering, or perhaps as a tool of revenge against Oscar? These thoughts tangled in my head like thorns, constantly wounding my heart. Yes, many times I grasped the knife in an act of desperation. To this day, I don't know whether I wanted to use it to cut my wrists and end my torment in this marriage or to kill Oscar.

I was on the verge of a nervous breakdown.

Each new day in that toxic relationship felt like a sarcastic dance with fate, where risk and pain were constant companions. I wondered where my inexplicable patience to survive in such an environment came from. The answer lay deep in the past, in those early days filled with screams and tears that shaped my youth. I realized that my choices were driven by the demons of the past. I stayed in this suffering because I didn't know that I could live differently. That was how I was raised; it was what I brought from my family home. I didn't know any other life, any other way of being. That was my truth, brutal and painful. In the eyes of the world, we were the perfect couple, but in reality, I was a prisoner of my own mind. Deep down, I hated everyone for what they had done to me: my parents for their poor upbringing, Oscar for not being my support, and myself for accepting such a life.

But it was that same hatred that became my strength. It brought me to the point where I realized I had a choice. I could end this nightmare, break free from this cycle of pain and suffering. I came to understand that I was the master of my own fate, and only I could decide what my tomorrow would be like. And so, I chose to free myself. I knew that true happiness was within my reach; I just had to have the courage to grasp it. Unfortunately, it took time before I could do it, before I could break free.

Amid the daily intrusions of Irene, where every moment, every whisper became public property to my mother-in-law, my world turned into a small, claustrophobic theater. The morning sun filtered through delicate curtains gave me a headache. Instead of signaling a new day, it became a daily reminder that Irene would soon show up at my apartment again. We lived door to door, and apparently, she was bored at home. After I gave birth to her first grandchild, my mother-in-law started visiting us several times a day.

I understand, the first grandchild, the joy, and all that, but, for God's sake, woman, give us some space!

"Oscar, can you ask your mom to stop visiting so often?" I begged my husband, teetering on the edge of fury and murderous thoughts.

He looked at me with a hint of helplessness.

"You know how she is..." he shrugged. "She just wants to be close to her grandson."

"Being close is one thing, but what she's doing is paranoia!"

"Don't exaggerate," he replied, his voice trembling slightly. "She just wants to be part of our life."

"Oscar, this is not part of our life! This is a full-on invasion! If I wanted to see your mother this often, I would've married her, not you!" I exploded, unable to hide my fury any longer.

A flicker of irritation appeared in his eyes.

"She's only trying to be helpful," he waved it off.

That was the last straw! We had no privacy. She knew what we were doing, what we were eating, who we were talking to. I'm sure she even knew when we were having sex. It was awful! And exhausting!

Dark clouds gathered over our marriage, and each visit from my mother-in-law brought new storms.

Those first years of marriage, if you could even call it that, passed by like dance steps along the edge of a cliff. Somewhere in the distance, I could hear the echo of dreams and assurances that it would be different. But each day reminded me of the reality I was stuck in, clinging to illusions.

Oscar looked at me with love less and less frequently. Instead, I saw uncertainty and aggression in his eyes, born from the bottles he emptied, which replaced our future together. With each sip of vodka, our intimacy evaporated, and his gaze wandered more often toward the screen and the gaming console. The world of virtual characters and levels to be completed replaced real emotions and real conversations.

I couldn't understand why our love had transformed into such a dark spectacle. Instead of promising each other eternal support, we filled our days with grievances and accusations. Oscar, instead of caring about our shared well-being, drowned his frustration in alcohol, and though I tried to pull him back into reality, I felt like real life was slipping through my fingers.

The most painful part for me was that I couldn't understand what had caused this change in Oscar. Above all, his sick jealousy had no justification for me. The fact that he spent hours playing games instead of talking to me made it clear that our marriage had become a prison for him. It became a trap, from which he tried to escape through alcohol and video games.

My days passed in the sounds of empty bottles and the hum of the gaming console, as the meaning of our marriage slipped away. Although I tried to keep our relationship standing on those weak, unstable foundations, every day I saw another thread of understanding between my husband and me snap.

The sadness, the sense of failure, and the realization that the relationship I had built over the years was based on illusions became my daily companions. Oscar was no longer the man he once was, and

I was no longer the same wife. Our marriage ceased to serve its purpose, and our hearts, once full of love, had become a barren desert of emotions.

Yes, Oscar, my "knight in shining armor," had turned into the unbearable nightmare of my reality. He transformed into a scream of terror. The face I once loved had become the source of my fear, and the hands that once were my sanctuary had become instruments of pain.

Oscar's blows fell on me like rain in the dark of night – unexpected and overwhelming. With each hit, I felt a piece of the woman I once was – full of hope and love – die within me. Oscar abused me more and more frequently. My mental health deteriorated, and after those brutal moments, he would look at me as if nothing had happened, as if abusing the weaker was normal, as if his ego hadn't suffered any damage. His apathy was just as painful as the cruel words and blows he delivered. No empathy! No remorse!

The irony of my life was clear. I had become one of those shadows who endlessly repeated the phrase: "I'm doing it for the kids." I believed my sacrifice was for their good, that a family, even one as dysfunctional as ours, was better than no family. I was blind and deaf to their suffering. My children, witnesses to this grotesque theater, were learning to live in fear, while I disappeared in my marriage, succumbing to the violence.

I would hide in the corners of my house and cry whenever I had a moment. I pressed my face into a pillow to muffle the sound, praying the children wouldn't hear. But they knew. They saw my red eyes. They knew their mother was unhappy.

If I could go back in time and look my younger self in the eyes, I would tell her to stand up and dare to live. To escape this toxic relationship and give herself and the children a chance at a better life. But back then, I didn't have the strength to stand up to the monster my husband had become. I didn't know then. But now I know. I know that true love doesn't hurt, and a real family supports and cares for one another.

That day finally came when I regained enough strength to face my fate and start rebelling against the crushing reality that overwhelmed me. I knew my marriage was a mistake, a failure, a scream into the void. I wanted to end the hopeless symphony playing in the background of my life. I opened my heart to Irene. I thought she, of all people, would understand what I had been through, what our children had endured. After all, she too had experienced domestic violence in her own marriage.

"I need to leave him," I said, looking her straight in the eye, hoping to see even a glimmer of empathy.

She looked at me with a warmth that misled me.

"I understand," she replied, squeezing my hands. "I can see how he's changed. How your marriage has changed."

She hugged me then. Her scent reminded me of the perfume she wore when I first crossed her doorstep.

"Don't give up, don't let him win, don't back down from the divorce. You'll always be my daughter-in-law," she whispered in my ear.

Her words gave me courage. Maybe I finally had an ally, someone who understood my pain and could name it. I was hopeful. But once again, I let myself be deceived. I was a naive fool!

But Veronica grew closer to me. This time, I felt it was sincere. We spent a lot of time together. She stopped being mean and cruel. But that didn't change the fact that I remained cautious.

The room smelled of fresh leather and polished wood – a classic lawyer's office scent. I stood at the threshold, a mixture of anxiety and determination pulsing in my heart, the same as anyone else who walked into this place.

Klaus Hoffmann, the divorce attorney, was an elegant, well-dressed man with a calm gaze and a charming smile. I wasn't sure, however, if he had any real understanding of my situation.

"Please, have a seat," he invited, motioning to a leather sofa. I began cautiously, "I'm not sure if I want to go through with this, as I mentioned on the phone. I contacted you, but I think it was more to show my husband that I'm serious, that I'm ready to do whatever it takes."

My words sounded so helpless in that professional environment. Hoffmann raised an eyebrow.

"Do you want to give him another chance?" he asked, surprised. "Another one?"

I bit my lip.

"I wanted us to go to therapy," I said. "I thought it would help. Maybe if he saw that I was serious, he'd understand and start getting treatment."

"And if he doesn't?" The lawyer looked at me intently.

Over the next few weeks, I tried to prove Klaus Hoffmann wrong. Without success. I begged Oscar to go to therapy, to take some step toward saving our marriage.

"Oscar, let's try together. We loved each other once... Can we give this one more chance?" I asked, with less and less hope.

But his answer was always the same, firm and unyielding: "I don't need any therapy. I regret nothing."

Each time I heard those words, I felt something inside me break. I felt like a glass, where someone taps the edge every day, waiting for it to shatter.

By the second visit to the office, I was more confident. I knew what I wanted.

"To be honest, Mr. Hoffmann, I didn't decide on the end of our marriage. He did," I declared. "All this time, I've asked, begged him for us to try and fight together. But he refused."

It was time to act!

At that moment, I knew I was doing the right thing. Sometimes, we have to make the hardest decisions to save what matters most.

That day, when I officially filed for divorce, it felt like a heavy weight had been lifted from my heart. But the relief was fleeting. When Oscar found out about the divorce, he reacted with the full fury of a hurt and desperate man. His daily curses were like vultures tearing at my emotions, leaving wounds on my soul. His growing aggression felt like invisible hands choking me, shortening my breath, squeezing through the darkness that hung over our shared life.

He drove me into such a deep depression that I often thought about giving up, letting myself drift into the endless abyss. His hatred was like a toxic fog, each day blocking more of the sunlight from my life. Maybe it was his way of dealing with my decision, or perhaps it was his attempt to punish me, to make me feel worthless, to make me believe I needed him.

At some point, I realized that staying in this environment posed a threat not only to my mental health but also to my physical safety. I had to leave, to escape his toxic influence, taking the children with me. When I stood before him, ready to return the keys that symbolized our shared past, his eyes were filled with fury. If looks could kill, he would have pierced me through. But instead, he did something worse – he spat in my face. That mark on my skin burned like a branding iron, revealing his complete disdain for me.

"How could you?! After everything I gave you?!" I shouted, looking at him with a mixture of horror and anger.

Oscar laughed mockingly.

"You gave me a child, but at the same time, you took my life!" he spat back, his words laced with resentment.

I breathed deeply, trying to calm myself.

"I gave you everything I had," I said through clenched teeth. "But you, even with everything, chose destruction over building."

I turned away. I didn't want to look at him anymore. Although I was rushing toward a new life, the memories of what I had been through remained. I thought of Oscar's parents, of how his father treated his mother. How could Oscar have learned to love, respect, and appreciate? He was simply replicating the toxic patterns he had seen at home.

One thing was certain: I wasn't going to let Oscar define my worth any longer.

When I look back now, I see that despite all the pain and hatred that consumed us from the inside, I took away valuable lessons from that relationship. I learned what I want, what I need, and what I deserve. I couldn't regret that marriage. Those twelve years made me wiser, though I paid a high price for it. That's how the story of me and Oscar ended. I don't regret the relationship because it gave me a wonderful son whom I love deeply. My amazing Arthur!

Adam and Arthur – my two greatest treasures! I love you both!

CHAPTER 14

The year 2016 felt like a storm that tore down the old structure of my life, leaving only the foundation on which I could rebuild something new. It was a time when my personal worlds – family and emotional – spiraled into chaos, only to later be reborn from a completely different perspective.

In the same month that I filed for divorce, as if fate was mocking me, I also lost my job. Or more precisely, due to the lies of someone in a higher position, I was ruthlessly fired without a second thought. I'll never forget the shouting of my esteemed boss, who, using his authority, threw me into the deepest pits of my already crippling depression. Tears streamed down my face, not just from helplessness but from the fear and humiliation I received as a "thank you" for my many years of dedicated work.

It was a moment when the life I had been building for years collapsed like a house of cards. In one brutal instant, I lost not only my marriage but also my livelihood, my financial independence, and my trust in people. I was left alone with two children and the looming shadow of depression that began to cast itself over my days.

It was a time when each day felt like a battle for survival. I woke up in the morning with a weight pressing me into the bed, and I spent my evenings wondering how I would make it through another day. Losing my job felt like the final blow from fate, draining the last of my strength.

During this period, I felt like a shattered boat, tossed onto the rocky shore by a merciless storm. My days became an endless, gray desert of time, where every minute dragged on like an hour. At night, I would lie motionless, staring at the ceiling as if it were a map of my infinite fears and anxieties. Thoughts of the future, of how I would provide a safe and stable life for my children, swirled in my mind like swarms of dark butterflies, giving me no peace.

I struggled with the all-encompassing emptiness that spread in my heart like a black hole, swallowing everything that once brought me joy and color. The feeling was a weight that made it impossible to breathe. The future appeared in my thoughts as an endless, dark labyrinth with no way out.

Often, I asked myself what was truly important, what gave me the strength to keep fighting. In those moments of despair, I thought of my children – little sparks of light in the darkness. They were my anchor, holding me in a safe place as the treacherous currents of life threatened to sweep me away.

I clung to every glimmer of hope, like a drowning person grasping for anything within reach. I knew I had to be strong, that I had to survive for them. Yet, at the same time, I felt that each day drained more of my energy, that every night was a battle with the demons of uncertainty and fear.

I felt like a warrior, defeated but still forced to rise from my knees to fight again. In this war with reality, in this constant struggle to survive, I discovered a strength within me that I hadn't known before. I learned that sometimes life requires us to become warriors of our own destiny, to fight for every breath, every day, and every moment of joy that we can wrestle from the hands of an unpredictable fate.

I fought against the depression that became my daily companion, while my ex-husband ensured that I sank deeper into its jaws. Sometimes, collapsing to my knees in helplessness, I begged God for it all to finally end. But Oscar didn't give up; he tormented me, harassed me, and wore me down mentally for many months, and even years, after our separation.

Over time, though, I began to see that this painful marital catastrophe, which had just ended, was opening the door to a new world, to a new version of myself.

In the emptiness, I started to see endless possibilities, as if the universe itself was giving me a chance to redefine who I was and how I lived.

In my mind, I repainted every corner of my existence, adding color where there had once been only gray. It felt like creating a new painting, where each bold stroke of the brush was an expression of my inner strength, my courage to face the unknown. I learned to cherish every moment of peace, every smile from my children, every ray of sunshine that pierced the clouds of my everyday life.

Gradually, I began to rebuild myself on stronger, more solid foundations. It was a slow process, sometimes painful, but also filled with hope. I was like a phoenix rising from the ashes of my past life, from my mistakes and disappointments, soaring toward new challenges and new dreams.

In my new reality, I found the peace and harmony I had longed for.

Wading through those difficult times, I learned that sometimes life demands that we tear down everything we know so that we can build something new, something better. With each day, with every step I took, I felt myself gradually regaining control of my life.

I became stronger, more aware, and more resilient to the challenges life threw at me. I began to understand that true strength doesn't come from what we possess, but from who we are and how we handle the difficulties fate places in our path. I learned that life is a constant balance between joy and pain. Each day, each challenge, grounded me more deeply. I started to see that every difficulty, every obstacle, was a lesson leading me to a better understanding of myself.

With a courage born from the deepest corners of my despair, I decided to pursue a path that had once been only a hazy dream of my youth. I remembered my long-forgotten dream – driving large, powerful trucks, those mechanical giants that rule the highways. With a determination worthy of battling my own demons, I set out to earn my "CE" driver's license.

I remember the day I first sat behind the wheel of a truck. It was a moment when I felt not only the weight of responsibility but also an incredible sense of strength and freedom. The huge, loud engine under my control, the cabin surrounding me like a fortress, gave me the sense that I could face anything. Every kilometer I drove was like another step in my internal journey – from solitary struggle to triumph over my own limitations.

It wasn't an easy career choice, especially for a woman. The world of trucking was dominated by men who didn't always welcome me with open arms, though some were more than willing to do just that. But every skeptical look, every biting comment only strengthened my determination. I wanted to prove that I could be just as good a driver as any of them – maybe even better. Of course, there were always some who couldn't resist making advances.

"Hey, sweetheart, maybe we should go out sometime?" I heard that every day.

"NO!" I'd answer confidently. No more men! Of that, I was certain!

This new chapter in my life was like a journey through uncharted territory, full of challenges but also unexpected joys. On the road, in the solitude of the cabin, I found the peace I had been missing. The landscapes passing by the window were like living paintings, showing me an ever-changing gallery of the world's beauty.

With every kilometer I traveled, my confidence grew, as did my belief that nothing is impossible. This new job, though demanding and often exhausting, gave me more than just a means to live – it gave me a sense of purpose and freedom. I was like an explorer, rediscovering the world, and every bridge I crossed was another step toward finding myself.

I came to understand the importance of being authentic, of living in alignment with my own beliefs and dreams. I stopped being afraid of being myself; I stopped being afraid to express my feelings and desires.

So, 2016 became a year of transformation for me, a year in which I closed one chapter of my life to begin a new one. It was a time when I learned to appreciate moments of peace but also to accept and transform chaos. Through the storms and the calm, I reached the place where I am now – a place full of strength, wisdom, and readiness for new adventures.

CHAPTER 15

Through the labyrinth of life, which led me through storms and gales, through moments when loneliness was my only companion, I eventually crossed paths with M. We had known each other from my previous workplace. A young, shy guy, different from the swarm of flirtatious men around me. Sometimes he offered to help with the computer, other times with changing the tires on my car – just a colleague, nothing more. It never even crossed my mind to build anything beyond a simple acquaintance with him.

After all the disappointments I had gone through, after the storms in my heart, I was done with relationships. I just wanted peace. Only peace.

And M. gave me that peace. He didn't want anything, didn't expect anything, didn't push for anything... he simply *was*. We met up as friends. Shared workouts at the gym, walks, bike rides, conversations that lasted until dawn... sometimes, we'd simply lie in silence on freshly mown grass, breathing in its aromatic scent... other times, we wandered aimlessly in the rain. And for months, our relationship remained that way, never pushing us into anything more.

But over time, we began to see each other differently. M. was like a quiet wind, gently changing the direction of the sails, never pushing, never forcing. He was always there, with a warm smile and an openness I rarely encountered. His calmness was like a safe harbor amidst the storms of my life.

His jokes, his lightness of being, his intelligence, and the way he listened – all of it began to build a bridge over the chasm of my fears.

One day, during one of our walks, M. took my hand. His touch was gentle but meaningful. He looked at me with those captivating eyes and said:

"I don't know where we're heading, but I want to walk this path with you."

There was no pressure in his voice, just honesty. It was at that moment that I felt my heart begin to open.

With each passing day, with every shared moment, the walls I had so carefully built started to crumble.

M. brought peace and harmony into my life, the very things I had longed for. He taught me that you could be close to someone without losing yourself, that you could love and be loved without a shadow of fear.

I realized that M. wasn't just a stop on my journey – he had become a part of it. He was like a gentle melody that filled the spaces of my life. With him, I felt safe, as though my heart had found shelter from the storms of the past.

Isn't it amazing how life can surprise you? How, after the storms, comes a time for calm seas? It was then that I understood that happiness isn't just the quiet after the storm, but also the courage to let someone see our true selves and accept our scars. My heart, once an empty room, was now filled with light and warmth. It was still full of scars, but now each one told a story of survival and rebirth.

There had been men in my life, now mere echoes of the past. Each of them unknowingly reminded me of a world ruled by fear, pain, and injustice. It was as if fate continually tested me, sending people my way who confirmed my belief that love was a struggle, not peace.

But M. was different. He was like a light breaking through stormy clouds. With him, I learned that love didn't have to be painful, that it could be light, full of understanding and acceptance.

One evening, while sitting on the couch wrapped in his arms, I shared my thoughts with him.

"You know," I began, looking into his eyes, "with you, for the first time, I feel that love can be different. It doesn't have to be a fight; it can be a dance we share together."

M. smiled warmly and replied:

"For me, love is partnership, respect, mutual support, and the joy of being together. I want you to know that I will always be here for you, to support you and love you."

His words were like the sweetest music. I had always thought that in relationships, I had to fight, that I had to be strong and independent. But with M., I could just be myself, without the need to prove anything.

With him, I learned that a healthy relationship is one where both sides feel safe, where you can be yourself without the fear of rejection. Thanks to him, I began to believe that love could be beautiful, that it could heal wounds instead of causing more pain.

Every day with M. was like discovering a new world, where love wasn't a warrior battling against all odds but a peaceful guardian of our happiness.

When I first met M., I was struck by how different he was from the people I had known before. He came from a home where love and respect weren't just empty words, but a daily reality. He was raised in a family where emotions were expressed freely, not hidden behind a mask of indifference. In his home, childhood had the taste of joy and carefree moments, not constant fear and uncertainty.

The love of my father, as you know, was like a weak ray of sunlight on a cloudy day – rarely felt and even less often lasting. It was a conditional love, coming and going, leaving us in a state of uncertainty and longing for something stable and enduring. The moments when my father showed affection were like short breaths in a long marathon of survival.

Living in such a home was like constantly walking a tightrope over an abyss. The feeling of constant threat was my daily companion, and each day brought new challenges. Learning how to cope with those emotions, with that unpredictability, became part of my personality.

Yes, in my family home, emotions were like powerful forces of nature, untamed and unpredictable. And though I spent years trying to learn how to live with them, only now, in adulthood, have I started to understand how deeply they affected my psyche and how I perceived the world and relationships with others. My childhood shaped me into someone who was always waiting for the next storm, unable to experience peace without fearing what tomorrow might bring.

With M., it was different. His home was like a safe harbor, where emotional storms were a rarity.

His presence was like a warm, calm evening after a stormy day. His emotional stability and calmness were new to me, almost foreign.

Watching his relationships with his parents, I began to understand how much I had missed in my own childhood. M.'s parents were his support, his guides, not his tyrants. Their love was unconditional, not dependent on moods or behavior.

M. showed me that there was another way. That a family doesn't have to be a battlefield, that it should be a place of peace and love. That emotions can be expressed freely, without fear of consequences. Thanks to him, I learned that love doesn't have to be a fight; it can be a soothing balm for a wounded soul.

Through M., I discovered that there are different faces of love in life. That you can build relationships on respect and understanding, not fear and control. His family home was like a new world, giving me a chance at a new beginning, at the life I had always wanted but never believed was possible.

So let me tell you how the beginning of my wonderful relationship with M. unfolded.

CHAPTER 16

The moonlight danced on our faces when, for the first time, I noticed how his eyes sparkled like stars in a cloudless night. We had started dating seriously, and each of our dates felt like turning the page of a fairy tale that never wanted to end.

Our meetings were like walks through a garden full of roses, where every petal told a story and every shadow hid the promise of something new. Time spent together by candlelight, sipping wine that tasted like carefree summer days, was filled with intoxicating conversations. His voice was like a song that soothed my senses and calmed the storm in my heart.

M.! My M.!

One magical night, we sat on an old bridge, gazing at the calm river below. The water reflected the moon, casting golden flickers across its surface. Suddenly, M. took my hand, his touch as gentle as the flutter of a butterfly's wings.

"Is this it?" he asked, almost rhetorically, his voice a mix of hope and fear.

Is this it? I was silent for a moment, contemplating every word and every gesture that separated us from the past. We both already knew that what had woven itself between us was something far more than a fleeting infatuation. It was like the whisper of the wind bringing change, like the first smile of the sun after a storm.

Was this it?

Yes, it was the strongest bond, the kind two people, lost in the uncertainty of the world, dream of. It was.

Despite that certainty, the decision to introduce M. to my children wasn't easy. I had to be sure this would be a lasting and meaningful relationship. I had promised myself that if someone met my children, they would be a part of our lives forever.

One evening, when the stars shone brighter than ever, I made the decision.

"M., are you ready to become a part of our world?" I asked, looking deeply into his eyes.

His response was quiet but firm, full of determination and love.

That was the moment when our separate paths began to intertwine into one, leading toward a future filled with unknown but promising possibilities.

Finally, the day came. I was nervous but excited. It was the day my beloved little rascals would meet M.

The world outside seemed to hold its breath as Adam and Arthur came home, their joyful laughter echoing down the hallway, unaware of the tension that hung in the kitchen. There, by the island, on a bar stool, M. sat frozen, like a sculpture carved out of a mixture of fear and hope.

His face, usually confident, now clearly showed signs of tension. His pant legs trembled slightly, and his hands, typically so sure and steady, now fidgeted aimlessly, adjusting his perfectly knotted tie again and again. He sat motionless, except for the nervous bouncing of his leg, like a ticking clock counting down to the inevitable meeting.

His gaze, usually sharp and focused, as if he were crafting reality from the world around him, now wandered uncertainly around the room. He avoided my eyes, as if afraid that within them, he would find questions he wasn't ready to answer. The usual sparkle of humor and life in his eyes was now replaced with a blend of apprehension and hope, like sunlight struggling to break through heavy storm clouds.

His figure, typically so composed, like the sculpted form of a Greek god exuding strength and masculinity, now seemed hunched under the weight of unspoken questions. Every muscle, normally poised for action, trembled under an invisible burden. His back, which usually stood proudly straight, was now slightly hunched, as if trying to protect his heart from the upcoming challenge.

I realized that M. was simply scared. He was terrified. The thought even amused me a little. His eyes reflected the internal battle he was fighting, struggling with the hope for acceptance and the fear of rejection. Every blink seemed an act of courage, and his hands, once a source of strength and support, now twisted helplessly, unable to grasp the certainty we both needed.

At that moment, M. was a man standing on the edge of a new, unknown world, where every step could lead to either a new beginning or a painful fall. In his eyes, I saw a reflection of the same fears and hopes I had faced when I first took on the challenge of motherhood. His struggle with these emotions, so human and fragile, gave him a new dimension – he was no longer just the strong man I knew, but someone who dared to face the most intimate fears and, at the same time, my boys.

Arthur burst into the house, his small feet hitting the floor like thunder, but his gaze never lingered on M., who was nervously twisting in the middle of the kitchen. His young soul, full of mysteries and worries, directed itself straight to the stairs, which, at that moment, seemed like a mountain to conquer. Arthur's head was bowed, hidden beneath his hoodie like a treasure buried deep underground.

He ran up the stairs, which creaked under the weight of unspoken emotions. Each step was like a climb along the path of unexplained feelings, where every stair symbolized another layer of his inner world. This rush upward wasn't just an escape from the presence of a stranger but a fragment of his world, where each floor felt like another chapter in the book of his young life.

As he moved further away, his footsteps transformed into the echo of childhood struggling with the adult world, the echo of a heart beating in the rhythm of uncertainty. With every step Arthur took on the stairs, he dove deeper into his kingdom of solitude and secrets, leaving M. and me somewhere outside his world.

When he reached the top, he disappeared into his room, leaving behind a silence that fell upon us like a curtain after a dramatic act in the theater of life. His deliberate retreat was like an unspoken question hanging in the air, leaving M. and me searching for answers we didn't have.

M. looked at me, pale. I shrugged. What could I say? It was obvious to me that Arthur would have a negative attitude toward our relationship from the start. His young heart had been smothered by the smoke of words spoken by his father and the rest of the family in the past. Each word was like a needle piercing the delicate fabric of his soul. To him, M. was an intruder, a foreign bird trying to invade a nest that had already been abandoned once.

Yet M., in his remarkable wisdom and intuition, didn't force Arthur to accept him. He didn't linger impatiently like a gardener trying to force a bud to bloom. Instead, he was like a patient stream, slowly but steadily shaping the stone lying in its flow, without haste, without force – gently, almost imperceptibly.

The days passed, each like another drop of rain on a hot day – unassuming but essential. M. didn't push for any meetings, didn't impose his presence. He simply existed – quietly observing, ready to extend a hand when Arthur would be ready to take it.

One day, as autumn painted the world in shades of gold and crimson, Arthur asked M. if they could play a game together. M. looked at me, his eyes twinkling like stars in the darkness, and his smile was warm.

"Of course, I'd love to," he said, nodding.

And so it began. Game after game, conversation after conversation, Arthur's and M.'s laughter grew louder, and their relationship blossomed like a plant nurtured by shared moments. M. turned out to be a master of storytelling – captivating, intriguing – and Arthur listened, enthralled, as if every word was a spell.

Eventually, one evening, Arthur approached M. and, with the shyness typical of children, hugged him. It was a simple gesture but full of meaning. From that moment on, their bond deepened. Arthur didn't just like M., he started to treat him like someone close, someone he could trust. Their shared moments were like paintings by Leonid Afremov – vivid and full of life.

M., whose presence had initially been like a shadow among the light, had now become an integral part of our lives, like the sun that not only illuminates but also warms. I realized that sometimes what seems hardest to overcome is just a thin line that can be easily crossed when you have someone beside you to guide you through the darkness of uncertainty.

With Adam, the situation unfolded differently. My eldest treasure always saw himself as a guardian – both of my heart and of our home. His young shoulders carried a burden of responsibility that was far too heavy for a child. As the oldest man in the family, Adam had taken on the role of protector, though his only weapons were his young heart and determination.

Before, whenever I mentioned dating, Adam's brows would furrow like stormy waves, and his eyes would shine with worry.

"Mom, you don't need to go anywhere," he'd say with a determination that was both touching and terrifying. "I'll take care of us. You don't need anyone else."

His words were like a wall he was trying to build around me, trying to protect his mother from a world that had already hurt her so many times. Every "Don't go!" was like another brick in the wall of care and fear.

When M. entered our lives, Adam looked at him with a mixture of distrust and curiosity. His young eyes, full of questions, studied M. like a puzzle that needed to be solved.

M., always patient, responded to Adam's doubts with a smile. But Adam was like a gatekeeper – unyielding and vigilant. In his young mind, the responsibility for me and the fear of another disappointment were tangled into a complicated knot. But over time, as Adam watched how M. treated me – with respect, warmth, and above all, patience – he slowly began to untangle that knot. Day by day, his gaze grew less suspicious, and his words less sharp.

One evening, as we sat together for dinner, Adam suddenly asked:

"Do you really take care of my mom?"

His voice was soft but still filled with caution.

M. looked him straight in the eye, and his reply was simple and sincere:

"Yes, I take care of her more than anyone else in the world."

There was something in those words that finally reached Adam. Perhaps it was the first light that pierced through the wall of his distrust. From that moment, something softened in his demeanor, as if he understood that he no longer had to carry the weight of the world on his young shoulders.

Adam began to allow himself to be a child again, and M. became not only my partner but also an important figure in the lives of my sons – someone who brought joy and security, and who gave them moments of carefree childhood that they so deserved.

Life with M. felt like a rebirth after a long, harsh winter. His presence in my life became a light that dispelled the darkness of the depression into which my ex-husband had driven me. In his arms, I found not only refuge but also the strength to rediscover myself.

The depression that had engulfed me after the divorce was like a dark, impenetrable forest, where every tree was weighed down by memories of pain and betrayal. M., with infinite patience and understanding, became my guide through this thicket of sorrow, helping me find the path back to the light.

I'll never forget one evening when we sat in the park, gazing at the stars. The air was filled with the fragrance of blooming flowers, and the night's silence was like a balm to my frazzled nerves. M. turned to me and said, "You know, you're stronger than you think? I admire you every day for how you fight your demons."

His words were like rain falling on the scorched earth of my soul. At that moment, I realized that M. not only supported me but also showed me how to love myself again.

His love was like a gentle touch that calmed the storms in my heart. Each day, I felt myself growing stronger, beginning to enjoy life again. His presence was like an anchor that kept me safe in harbor when the waves of the past threatened to pull me under.

M. never tried to replace my ex-husband or erase the memories I had with him. Instead, he helped me build new, beautiful memories, ones that slowly began to overshadow the old, painful ones.

Even during the moments when my demons of depression tried to return, he stood by me like the most loyal guardian, like an angel.

"You're not alone in this," he would say, his voice full of determination and love. "I'm here for you. I'll always be here…"

With M., my life regained its color. His love helped me rediscover the joy I thought I had lost. Every day spent with him was another step on the road to healing, like a new note in the symphony of happiness that began to play in my heart.

A new harmony reigned in my life, like soft music playing in the background of a peaceful day. The work that once felt like a burden now became a boat that carried me on the waves of everyday life. My wonderful relationship with M. was like the light that illuminated each day, even the most overcast.

My children, who had come to love M., completed this picture. Their laughter and conversations with him were like explosions of happiness that filled every corner of our home. Adam, once so suspicious, now often sat down with M. for a game of chess, and their intellectual duels were like fascinating performances where every move carried weight. As for Arthur, once shy and withdrawn, he now sought M.'s support and companionship with confidence.

One evening, as we all sat together at dinner, I realized how much my life had changed.

"Look," I began, gazing at my sons and M., "how beautiful life can be when you open yourself to new possibilities!"

Adam, with a smile full of irony, responded, "Who would've thought we'd see Mom so happy again."

His words, though tinged with sarcasm, were filled with warmth and acceptance. M., taking my hand, said, "Your happiness is my happiness."

Yes, it may have sounded cliché, but it touched every part of my soul.

Each day felt like another step on the path to true happiness. The world, once full of uncertainty and pain, now resembled a garden filled with flowers and birdsong. With M., I rediscovered that happiness isn't just a fleeting emotion but a state that can be nurtured and grown.

In our home, once filled with silence and doubt, warmth and joy now prevailed. Every evening spent together felt like a small celebration, filled with gratitude for every moment shared. My life, which had once been a lost melody, now played a joyful symphony of happiness.

A year had passed like a short yet captivating song, filled with joyous chords and gentle, moving tones. M. and I found ourselves at a new juncture in our journey together. The decision to move in together wasn't just about transferring our belongings from one place to another. It was about intertwining our lives, like two rivers merging to form a powerful current.

One evening, as we sat bathed in candlelight, surrounded by a silence full of unspoken words, M. took my hand and asked, "Don't you think it's time we built a home together?"

His words were like a soft breeze on my skin. I paused for a moment, staring at the flickering candle flame that danced like a small spirit, signaling a new beginning.

"Yes, I think it is," I replied, my heart beating faster at the thought of this new chapter in our shared life.

That short but significant conversation led us to purchase a beautiful home. It wasn't just the fact that it was ours together; it truly felt like a scene from a dream. From its windows, we could see a breathtaking landscape, and every corner of the house seemed like a page from a fairy tale written just for us.

The process of moving in was like painting a shared canvas, where every item I brought in was a brushstroke on the canvas of our lives. Each vase, picture, or mug I placed on a shelf felt like adding another detail to that masterpiece. M., with his characteristic patience, carefully arranged my books on the shelves, treating each of my belongings with respect and care, like a sculptor delicately shaping his work.

Meanwhile, Adam and Arthur ran around, brimming with excitement. Their laughter and shouts energized us as we worked.

"Mom, look how big this garden is!" Arthur shouted, his eyes sparkling like stars.

Adam, though trying to maintain the seriousness of an older brother, couldn't hide his own excitement.

"Can I have the room upstairs?" he asked, pointing to the one with the best view.

When everything was finally in its place, I stood in the doorway of our new home and looked at M. His eyes were shining with happiness, and his smile was a promise of a beautiful future.

"It looks magical," I said, gazing at the shimmering light reflecting off the windows.

M. laughed. "Magical for us, my dear," he murmured. "This is our little paradise on Earth," he added, wrapping me in a warm embrace. "We're like a tree now – our separate roots have grown and intertwined, forming a strong, healthy trunk."

I loved that comparison. I realized that what had seemed like a simple step was, in fact, a giant leap into the unknown. But I knew we could handle it.

That evening, we sat together in the living room, surrounded by boxes and unpacked things. M. pulled out a bottle of wine he had saved for the occasion.

"I'd like to make a toast," he said, raising his glass. "To us, to our home, and to all the wonderful moments ahead of us." His toast was like a spell meant to protect our shared future in this place. We felt like we were embarking on a new chapter of life – one full of promises and hope.

"What more could we ask for?" I mused one evening, sitting on the terrace and gazing at the stars.

That's when M., his voice thoughtful, asked,

"What do you think about adding one more little member to our family?"

His words rippled through me like gentle waves on a calm lake. The thought of having a child together – a tiny, wonderful being that would unite all the pieces of our lives – was simply magical.

"You mean…" I began, my heart beating faster.

"Yes, that's exactly what I mean. I think we're ready for our love to grow into new life," M. said, and in his eyes, I saw the spark of excitement.

The idea of having a child together was like a new star in our sky – shining brightly, a hopeful light in the tunnel of life. Our conversations about expanding our family became more frequent. The vision of creating a life from the love we shared felt like a wonderful dream that could soon become reality.

There was just one more thing – talking to the boys. When I shared the idea of a new sibling with them, their reactions were mixed. Adam, always cautious, asked,

"Does that mean you'll have less time for us?"

"Of course not!" I shook my head. "It means we'll have more love and joy to share with one more person."

Arthur, with undisguised excitement, exclaimed,

"I'm going to have a little brother!"

"Or a sister," Adam added, with a hint of mischief.

In my mind, I could already see us welcoming this new life – our child, who would become the bridge that united us all even more.

When I found out I was pregnant, my world stood still for a moment, as if the scene had frozen in time. It was like a ray of sunshine breaking through the clouds, bringing with it new life and hope. In my heart, a garden of joy blossomed, and every thought of the baby growing inside me was like a delicate bud slowly blooming in the spring.

I knew I had to share the news with M. before the world found out about our little miracle. I placed a tiny pair of baby shoes on the pillow, waiting for his reaction as he woke up. When he lifted his head, his eyes lit up like stars in the night sky, and his smile illuminated the entire room.

"M., we're going to have a baby," I whispered, gazing deeply into his eyes.

He embraced me so tightly, as if trying to wrap his arms around the entire world.

"This is the best news I've ever heard," he said, his voice trembling with emotion.

A melody of hope and happiness began to play in my heart. Each day of the pregnancy was like another note in that song, telling the story of our love and the new life we were creating together. I felt like a flower slowly blooming, preparing to bring forth the fruit of true love.

Venice, a city where history intertwines with magic, became the setting for us to reveal our joyful news. St. Mark's Square, with its majestic basilica and towering campanile, served as the stage for our announcement.

Sitting at a café table, surrounded by the bustle of the crowd and the soft sounds of gondolas swaying in the canals, we knew the place was as spectacular as the news we were about to share.

The square felt like a grand stage – the pigeons danced through the air, and the sun bathed the ancient walls in a golden glow. Life around us continued in its eternal rhythm, like the city itself breathing gently over the water.

"Boys, we have something important to tell you," I began, looking at Adam and Artur, their faces full of curiosity. M. held my hand, giving me a silent boost of courage.

"I'm pregnant," I whispered, and it was as if the noise and movement in St. Mark's Square paused for a brief moment.

The boys' faces showed surprise, although they must have had an inkling. Adam, usually so composed, widened his eyes in disbelief.

"Really? We're going to have a sibling?" he finally stammered, his voice a mix of disbelief and excitement. "Well, congratulations then!" he added with a wide smile.

Artur, always more expressive in his emotions, leaped from his chair and rushed to hug us.

"That's awesome!" he shouted, grinning from ear to ear.

Their reactions were like two different chords in the same melody – one cautious and surprised, the other full of carefree joy. Both boys started asking questions, their voices overlapping in a harmony of curiosity and excitement.

"When? How? Will it be a boy or a girl?" The questions spilled out like pearls from a broken necklace. M. and I laughed as we tried to answer.

"All in good time," I said, looking at them with love.

That moment in St. Mark's Square became a symbol for us, not only of love and the joy of the coming baby, but also of our family's unity. In that magical place, among the historic buildings and bustling canals, our family took on a new dimension. It was the beginning of a wonderful new chapter in our shared story. Yet, it was also the beginning of something entirely different.

CHAPTER 17

When I became pregnant with Sarah, M. and I saw it as a sign of providence. In an instant, our lives took on a new, deeper meaning, as if every path we had walked led us to this very moment. It was the crowning of our love, its completion, as if Sarah were the missing piece that would make us whole.

The child I carried was a symbol of the purest, truest love that could exist between a man and a woman. Sarah was everything to us – she embodied our dreams, hopes, and desires. Every morning when I awoke, I could feel her presence like the fluttering of a butterfly's wings inside me. That feeling was like a warm ray of sunlight, penetrating me from within, filling me with joy and peace.

I knew that in the future, every time I looked into her eyes, I would see the confirmation that M. and I were destined for each other. Her gaze would reflect our love, our shared moments, and our dreams. I felt that every day, every moment when I could imagine her future, was a blessing. I envisioned what she would look like, how her hair would shine, what her smile would be like, and how her eyes would sparkle as she discovered the world.

The pregnancy was a time filled with excitement and anticipation. M. often placed his hand on my belly as if he wanted to feel our little girl's closeness, as if he already wanted to talk to her, to tell her about the world waiting for her. It was a feeling beyond words – a combination of hope, love, and impatience. Every day, I felt our love grow stronger, as Sarah, with each movement, each gentle kick, reminded us of the great joy that awaited us.

It was no coincidence that we announced my pregnancy to the boys in Venice. I wanted that moment to be special, and that city was the perfect place. The sight of their laughing faces, their sparkling eyes, and their endless questions about their little sister was our greatest reward. I knew that Sarah would have the best protectors in them, that they would stand by her every step of the way, loving and shielding her as fiercely as we would.

Our lives felt filled with magic and promise. We were the happiest people under the sun, as if the entire world had bent under the weight of our dreams. We lived in a world of vibrant colors, scents, and sounds, all creating a melody of our happiness. We prepared Sarah's room, laughing and dreaming of the future. Every purchase, every little addition to her room was like laying another brick in the world we were building. The colors, the fragrances, the textures – all of it formed a mosaic of our dreams. I didn't even need to close my eyes to imagine Sarah running around that room, her laughter echoing off the walls.

In the evenings, once the boys were asleep, M. and I would sit together on the couch, letting our thoughts drift toward dreams of our daughter's future. Those were magical moments, when our hearts beat in unison, and our minds painted images as vivid and colorful as the most beautiful dreams.

M. held me in his arms, and I felt his warmth seep into every part of me. His voice, gentle and full of tenderness, lulled me into a state of peaceful bliss. We dreamt of Sarah, of her future, of who she would become as she grew.

"Do you think she'll have your eyes?" I asked softly, looking at his profile, bathed in the soft light of the lamp.

"Maybe. But I'd rather she had your smile," he replied, gently brushing my cheek.

"No matter what her smile looks like, I'm sure it will always dispel the darkness," I said, closing my eyes and trying to picture the far-off future.

We often imagined what Sarah would look like, which traits she would inherit from us. I thought about her hair, wondering if it would resemble mine. I envisioned her tiny hands, her delicate fingers as she reached out to grasp the world.

"I wonder what her interests will be," M. mused, twirling a strand of my hair. "Maybe she'll love books as much as you do. Maybe she'll fall in love with Dante, like her mom."

"Or perhaps she'll be an artist, painting pictures full of colors and emotions," I added, my voice filled with excitement.

Those evening conversations felt like journeys into the future, full of hope and anticipation. We dreamt of Sarah's first steps, her first words, her first day at school. Each of these imaginings was like a jewel we added to the treasure chest of our hearts and dreams.

"Do you think she'll like music?" I asked once, hearing the distant sounds of our favorite song.

"Of course. She'll have your sensitivity to beauty," M. replied, holding me tighter.

Our dreams about Sarah's future were like a compass that guided the direction of our lives. Every vision, every thought was full of love and care. I imagined Sarah growing up, becoming a young woman full of passion and energy. I felt that her presence in our lives would be a blessing, making our family complete.

"I wonder what she'll become when she grows up," M. pondered, gazing into the distance.

"Maybe a doctor, helping people, or a scientist, uncovering the mysteries of the world," I replied, hope evident in my voice.

"Or maybe she'll be a poet, writing about beauty and love," I added, trying to hold back my emotions.

I felt that the future was full of promises and possibilities. Each day brought us closer to the moment when we would finally welcome our little girl into the world. We were incredibly impatient, and almost every evening, we wove new dreams, which for us were like the most beautiful melodies, carrying us through life and making the wait easier.

The due date was around M.'s thirtieth birthday. It felt like fate, giving our story an even deeper meaning. Sarah was going to be the most wonderful, perfect gift for M., as if his whole life had led him to this moment. I felt that it couldn't be a coincidence – every glance we shared, every thought, every smile guided us toward that day that would change everything.

For me, it was symbolic. I believed that nothing happened without reason, that fate wove our lives with the finest threads, intertwining them into a complex pattern full of meanings. Sarah's birth date and M.'s birthday seemed part of that pattern, a secret hidden in the heart of the universe, now about to be revealed. I imagined the joy I would see in M.'s eyes when he saw his daughter for the first time. I was sure that no better gift could exist, that this day would be magical and full of indescribable happiness. I had even bought a personalized outfit with birthday wishes for Daddy from Sarah, which the medical staff was supposed to dress our little girl in right after her birth.

I imagined M. holding her in his arms, his eyes lighting up with love and pride.

Every movement of Sarah in my belly was like the delicate brush of angel wings, reminding me of how close that special day was.

I felt we were on the brink of something great, something that would change us forever. Sarah was going to be our guiding star, the light that would lead us through life.

The due date approached relentlessly, and with each passing day, my joy and excitement grew. I knew it would be an extraordinary day, full of love and happiness. I was ready for everything the future held, with the belief that our love was stronger than ever. Sarah was going to be our most precious treasure, and her birth – the most beautiful gift we could have ever imagined. And she was M.'s birthday present. The best one!

Finally, the long-awaited day arrived – our due date. Early in the morning, I had my final appointment with my gynecologist. It was a day filled with anticipation, where joy and hope mixed with a slight unease, typical for any mother before the birth of her child. The world seemed brighter, and the air was thick with the scent of blooming flowers, as if all of nature was celebrating this special moment with us.

The atmosphere in the gynecologist's office was calm, as if it were a place detached from all worries and problems. I lay on the examination couch, looking at the screen where the last ultrasound of our Sarah before her birth was about to appear. I could feel my heart beating faster, filled with a mix of excitement and slight worry.

The gynecologist began the examination. Her face was focused, and her hands were sure and gentle. At first, everything seemed fine, but suddenly her expression changed. She froze for a moment, staring intently at the screen, then looked at me with terror in her eyes and whispered in shock:

"I'm sorry, the baby's heart has stopped beating."

Those words hit me with the force of a hurricane.

I felt my heart shatter into a million pieces. The world around me came to a halt, and I, dazed, couldn't believe what I had just heard. In my ears, the echo of those terrible words rang, robbing me of breath.

"How... how is that possible?" I managed to choke out, desperately gasping for air.

The doctor, clearly shaken, lowered her gaze, her voice trembling with helplessness as she replied:

"I don't know what could have happened. Everything seemed to be fine..."

Her confusion only deepened my despair.

Everything around me suddenly lost meaning, as if the entire world had gone dark, leaving me in the void. This was the worst day of my life. My thoughts were like shattered glass, a sharp and chaotic mess that pierced through me. It felt as if my whole body was trapped in an icy cage, and every attempt to move only intensified the pain.

The doctor's words echoed in my head, unreal, as if they came from another world. The baby's heart had stopped beating. I couldn't understand it, couldn't accept that our dreams and hopes had been destroyed in a single moment. Sarah, our beloved child, our miracle, was supposed to be here, and now it was all turned to dust? It couldn't be true!

I felt an emptiness, as if someone had torn my heart out and left a bleeding wound behind. My mind couldn't grasp that what was supposed to be the most beautiful event of our lives had turned into a nightmare. The pain was indescribable; it pierced me to the core, paralyzing every part of my body.

I sat in the doctor's office, devastated, unable to move. My world had crumbled, and I knew I would never be the same again. All the plans, all the dreams, everything we had built over those months had disappeared in a single moment.

I left the office in a trance, unaware of the world around me. The people passing me in the hallway were like shadows, their faces blurred in a world that no longer mattered. I was like a ghost, floating aimlessly in a void, without purpose or direction. Every step felt like an impossible effort, and every thought was filled with pain.

It took a moment for me to fully realize that Sarah was truly gone. That awareness hit me like a cyclone, knocking me to my knees right there in the hallway. Someone rushed over to me, saying something. In response, my body trembled, and tears streamed down my face as if they would never stop.

The day that was supposed to be the most wonderful of our lives had turned into a horror. Joy had been replaced with unspeakable pain, and our dreams were shattered. Sarah, our beloved daughter, who was supposed to bring light into our lives, was gone, leaving us in darkness.

How was I supposed to tell M. that his long-awaited, eagerly anticipated child had just died? How could I break such terrible news to him? My thoughts were like a broken mirror, reflecting fragments of our past, present, and future, now destroyed. I felt as if my entire world had turned to dust, and I stood in the midst of the ruins, not knowing how to gather the strength to tell M. the truth.

Dazed, barely conscious, I got into the car and drove to M., unable to bring myself to tell him over the phone. I wanted to be with him in that moment, though I had no idea how we would cope. Every kilometer that separated me from home felt like an eternity, and every passing minute was like a noose tightening around my heart.

To this day, I don't know how I made it to M. I was like an automaton, driving the car without any awareness of the world around me. The road was just a blurred background, and my thoughts churned in my mind, giving me no respite. I felt as though I were drifting in an endless ocean of despair, without a compass or any hope of finding the shore.

When I finally reached home, I saw M. waiting for me with a smile on his face. His joy was like a knife slowly sinking into my heart, reminding me of what we had lost. I felt as though I didn't have the strength to look him in the eye, to utter those dreadful words. His smile, full of hope and love, was a painful reminder of everything that was supposed to be, and everything that was now out of reach.

"What's wrong?" he asked, seeing my tears and the pain on my face.

With difficulty, I raised my eyes to him. My lips moved silently. I tried to find the words that could express my pain, our loss, but every word seemed so inadequate, so insufficient. Each word I wanted to say crumbled like ice.

"Sarah..." I stammered at last. "Sarah... is gone."

His face changed in an instant. It was overtaken by fear. He looked at me as if he couldn't comprehend what he had just heard. His eyes, which moments before had been full of joy and hope, were now empty, as if someone had extinguished the light in them.

"How... is she gone?" he whispered, his voice breaking under the weight of despair.

I couldn't find the words to explain, to describe what I was feeling. I was like a shattered shell, overflowing with tears and pain. I tried to move toward him, to hold him, but my legs felt like they were made of lead. I could only stand there, swaying.

"Her heart stopped beating," I stammered again, and my words were like a cold wind that swept through both of us.

M. doubled over as if he'd been punched straight in the stomach. His body trembled, and I saw tears streaming down his cheeks. I wanted to comfort him, but I didn't know how, didn't know what I could say to ease the pain.

We stood there, holding each other, trying to find some meaning, some solace in the chaos. But the pain was too immense, and our hearts too shattered to come together in that moment. We were like two drifting ships that had lost their anchors, floating aimlessly on waves of grief and despair.

I knew that this loss would change us forever, that our love, though strong, would have to face its greatest challenge.

We were trapped in a nightmare, unable to wake up. The despair that enveloped us was paralyzing. Losing a child we had longed for so deeply, for whom the room was already prepared, whose laughter we had already heard in our dreams, was a wound that could never heal.

I gave birth to our tiny, lifeless Sarah. Our beloved Sarah. It was like waking from the most beautiful dream into the worst nightmare, like falling from heaven straight into a dark abyss. The delivery room, which was meant to be a place of joy and new beginnings, had become the scene of unimaginable tragedy.

When the nurses left M. and me alone in the room with our little angel, time seemed to stop. We looked at Sarah, our tiny daughter, who looked so peaceful, as if she were merely sleeping, as if she would wake any moment and smile at us. Her tiny fingers were as delicate as flower petals, and her beautiful face was serene, without a trace of suffering.

It was the cruelest irony, to look at that little body, which was supposed to be full of life, now lying lifeless before our eyes. Our hearts were breaking, shattering into a million pieces, each one filled with sorrow and helplessness. The world had turned dark, everything around us seemed engulfed in shadow and sadness.

I didn't want to hold her in my arms, I knew it would destroy me. I was afraid that if I embraced her, my heart would break for good. M. held my hand. We both looked at Sarah, at our dreams and hopes that had now become mere shadows.

In that moment, I felt so empty, as if my entire being had been hollowed out and left without purpose. Darkness surrounded us, and every moment felt like an eternity filled with suffering. I knew we had to say goodbye, but how do you say goodbye to someone you loved more than life itself? How do you say goodbye to a part of yourself that was supposed to be your future?

Now, I regret not holding her. I regret not taking her in my arms then, if only for a moment, to feel her presence. It's something I will regret for the rest of my life.

I knew I would never forget that moment, that it would be a scar on my soul that would never heal. Sarah had been our star, extinguished before she could fully shine.

We wanted to say so much to her, but we couldn't. I regret that too. Later, I often composed words in my mind that I could have said to say goodbye to Sarah. What would I have told her? That I loved her, at the very least. That I so desperately wanted to wrap her in my love. That she deserved a beautiful life, but fate had betrayed her, the world had abandoned her...

I don't even know what the right words would have been in such a situation. Probably none. Perhaps silence is the only appropriate response...

The world around us had sunk into darkness. We were alone, immersed in our pain, holding on to each other, trying to find some shred of meaning in all the chaos. But there was no meaning.

They say time heals all wounds, but that's not true. Time doesn't heal wounds; it merely teaches us to live with the pain. From the moment we lost Sarah, I felt like I was living in the shadow of loss, that every breath, every step was marked by suffering that never ceased. It was like living in perpetual darkness, where the light of hope had been extinguished by the impenetrable gloom of despair. Time had no power to ease my pain; it only made the pain a part of me, an inseparable element of my existence.

When you stay in one state for long enough, it becomes your second nature. The pain of losing Sarah became embedded in me, it became an inseparable part of my life. It didn't disappear, it didn't soften; I just learned to live with it, like living with your own shadow.

Life after loss is never the same.

From then on, I woke up every day with a feeling of emptiness, with the heart-wrenching memory of our loss. It had nothing to do with healing. The pain was just as sharp, just as penetrating.

When you lose a child, the pain is beyond words. It's impossible to describe how deep the wound is, how boundless the suffering. It's like losing a piece of yourself, as if a part of your soul has been torn from your body.

However, I know that Sarah never truly left. Sometimes, I feel her presence beside me. Her presence, though intangible, comforts me, like a warm breeze on a chilly day. I believe that our love for her is eternal, that her soul will always be with us. This brings me a moment of solace in the midst of this never-ending torment.

Sarah will always remain with us. We will never forget her. Never. Darling, you were our dream... You are and always will be our love...

236

CHAPTER 18

A broken heart, a shattered soul, and a white rose in hand – that's how M. and I stood, beneath the gray clouds, next to the small white coffin. With every drop of rain that fell on our faces, tears also flowed, merging with the rain's curtain, hiding us from the rest of the world. Yes, even the sky was crying. Although our closest loved ones surrounded us, M. and I felt completely alone, surrounded by walls of despair built by the loss of our angel – our little Sarah.

The priest's voice, almost drowned by our sobs, carried words of comfort that collided with our grief, unable to penetrate it. The wind, moving the tree branches, seemed to be the only one that understood our pain, wailing a mournful melody of farewell.

At that moment, all I could think about was how fragile and unpredictable life is. How senseless it all felt. The only certainty was impermanence and the end of everything. The only reality was pain. The only truth was the loss that never should have happened. How cruel life can be, taking away the most precious treasures before we even get the chance to cherish them!

As we walked home from the funeral, every step felt unbearably heavy, as if the ground beneath us had turned into a swamp filled with sadness and despair. In our hearts, a fear loomed – a fear of the emptiness that now ruled our lives. Every corner of our home, which was supposed to be filled with Sarah's laughter and joy, now haunted us with a dreadful silence, screaming with the absence of happiness.

At night, when the world around us was plunged into quiet, and we were left alone with our thoughts, the pain became even more intense. In those dark hours, when despair seemed like our only companion, I sought comfort in M., who, despite his own grief, tried to be my support. Together, we sat in silence, trying to find a moment of relief from the unbearable suffering.

After Sarah's funeral, an even denser fog of pain and despair enveloped me, through which it was nearly impossible to see even the faintest ray of light. Each day, waking up to a new installment of the same nightmare, I was overwhelmed by the thought that I would never recover, that I had not only lost a part of myself but also all faith in the future.

Indeed, I am no longer the person I was before Sarah's death. This tragedy transformed me into someone I barely recognized, someone who carried within them the weight of unspeakable sorrow.

My world had turned upside down, and I found myself teetering on the edge of an abyss, staring into it each day, wondering if anything still made sense. The loss of Sarah felt impossible to bear. I felt as though I carried an enormous, unending void within me, swallowing every glimmer of light.

The world I once knew ceased to exist. I surrounded myself with walls of pain so high I couldn't see beyond their edges. My life had become a constant battle with trauma, an unending burden that I had to carry every day.

A perpetual winter settled in my heart. The landscape of my soul was covered in ice, and each breath brought pain. Sarah's death was a blow I couldn't understand or accept. I asked the question every mother in my position would scream: "Why my child?!" But I found no answers, only more questions, creating a labyrinth I couldn't escape. What I did realize was that the world is cruel. During this period of my life, each day felt like slow drowning. Despite the presence of loved ones, I felt invisible, lost in my own sorrow. I didn't know if I would ever rise again, if I would find my way back to the world I had left behind. My soul, soaked in grief, couldn't find solace, and I, curled up under the weight of indescribable pain, couldn't find the strength to fight for the person I used to be.

For M., it was also an incredibly difficult time. On his 30th birthday, his child died, and three months later, his father passed away. My beloved's heart was filled with losses of unimaginable weight. Yet he held on. Although I knew he was bleeding inside, he never complained, never lamented. He remained steadfast, like a rock in the midst of a storm, being a pillar of strength for all of us. He carried a maturity that many seasoned souls would envy. I believe it was from him that I learned what true strength is. Not the kind that fights with fists, but the kind that endures in silence, that survives the heaviest storms. M. was my guide through the wilderness of grief, showing me that even when the light seems farthest away, the road ahead still exists. More than once, I wanted to whisper in his ear:

"Thank you for being my strength."

But I couldn't. Something held me back. Boundless grief and a sense of injustice gripped me tightly in their claws.

Amid the gray days, in the abyss of nameless suffering, I found myself trapped in the labyrinth of my own soul. Depression, that uninvited companion, settled next to me like a shadow I couldn't shake off. The emptiness that engulfed me after Sarah's loss was like a black hole, swallowing all joy, hope, and light. I could no longer talk to anyone. Sometimes, I would timidly hold conversations with myself, silently uttering the words:

"How can I move forward when everything has fallen apart?"

"How can I breathe when my little angel no longer breathes?" I asked, teetering on the edge of my world, staring into nothingness.

"How can the world keep turning when there's no longer any hope for even a ray of sunshine?" I raged at everything that existed.

I felt like each day brought a new challenge, like every word, every glance required an effort I couldn't muster. My daily existence had become a series of mechanical movements, devoid of purpose and meaning. My relationships with those closest to me had turned gray, where there was nothing left to find but pain and sorrow.

In this journey through darkness, where each step seemed harder than the last, I searched for a guide to lead me back to the light. Where else could I look if not in my beloved *Divine Comedy*? Once again, I felt like I was traversing the dark corners of Hell in search of my own Paradise. And I had the sense that this Paradise was constantly slipping away from me. The road ahead seemed long and full of uncertainty, and at that time, I didn't even have faith that I would reach my destination. Everything was so hazy, so unclear! So, I returned to Dante's pages, hoping that I might find comfort there, something to give me the strength to keep fighting.

For two long years, time seemed to stand still. I couldn't leave the house, only the necessary visits to my therapist interrupted the monotony of days spent in my room. Each of those visits was like a journey to another world, where I could breathe a little more freely, even though returning home meant plunging back into the depths of despair. Therapy, though it provided only temporary relief, became a kind of bridge for me, an attempt to reconnect with reality, with a world from which I felt so painfully disconnected.

The constant presence of pain, suffering, reluctance to live, and, above all, the relentless question "why?" became my daily companions. I felt as though I was stuck in place, unable to move, while the rest of the world rushed forward relentlessly. The gap between me and "normal" life seemed impossible to bridge, yet deep down, I began to understand that I couldn't spend the rest of my days mired in this endless blackness. I had to find a way to learn to live again, even if every breath felt too much to bear.

The days passed, indistinguishable from one another, filled with emptiness and darkness. Only the visits to my therapist brought a flicker of change, a small spark of light in the engulfing darkness. In his office, I could briefly take off the mask of a strong woman and let words flow directly from my wounded heart.

"How are you feeling today?" the therapist always asked with the same warm tone in his voice, which made me feel a little safer.

"Like I'm spending yet another day in hell," I answered each time, my words vibrating with bitterness. "How am I supposed to live on?" I asked him repeatedly.

"Grief is a process," he replied calmly. "There's no magic solution or shortcut. Each day is a battle, but every day, even if you can't see it now, you're making a step forward."

In time, I learned to believe him. It took a long time, but something finally clicked inside me. Those sessions, though difficult, were like small rays of light in a tunnel, offering hope that maybe one day I would find my way to acceptance and peace. But even then, they were only temporary reliefs, unable to fill the vast space in my heart consumed by the sense of loss.

Life during that period felt like an endless march through a desert, where every step was a massive effort, and the hope of finding an oasis of peace seemed like an illusion. Apathy and tears were my only companions, and the days that once held joy and laughter had now transformed into boundless suffering.

Still, I clung to therapy because I had no other glimmer of hope.

During that difficult time, my younger sister, Lydia, was always by my side. From our earliest years, we were very close... and she was there for me then too. She cried with me... she sat in silence with me... She shared my pain, taking part of it onto her own shoulders so that I might suffer less.

"Together, we're stronger," she reminded me of our motto when the weight of daily life pushed me to my breaking point.

Yes, together we were stronger. We always repeated that to each other whenever one of us faced difficulties. Immediately, we found more strength within ourselves. It was like a spell. In those moments, we each remembered that we weren't alone, that we were always together. Always! Besides that mantra, we also had our song. It was a hit by the band Bajm, *Love and I*. It had been with us for as long as I could remember, almost the soundtrack of our lives. Whenever the first notes of that song filled the air, time seemed to slow down, and I would sink into the depths of emotions carried by the words sung by Beata Kozidrak. That song was like a bridge connecting me and Lydia, no matter the distance, no matter what separated us.

The song began softly, almost like a whisper, gradually spreading its wings into full emotional expression. Every verse, every line, every note felt as if it were about us – two sisters, two poles, bound by an unbreakable bond. "She and I, two sisters, two poles..." – those words always brought a smile to my face, evoking memories that tied us inseparably together.

"Her face, my face, the color of lips, the power of words..." – in those moments, the song seemed to tell the story of our lives, our joys, and our sorrows.

And when it reached the line, "How is it, I feel pain when she cries, when she cries," my heart clenched with both pain and love.

Because that's exactly how it was between us. Every one of Lydia's tears was also mine, every one of her sorrows was my sorrow. And my pain was her pain.

The music, flowing gently, carried by the singer's voice, slowly built tension, which exploded in the chorus, bringing both relief and an intensified desire for closeness. The chorus was like a confession, a declaration of the strength I drew from our sisterly bond.

"And so I share with her every sorrow and every mistake, and uncertainty, believing that her strength is with me..." – in those words was everything I wanted to whisper to Lydia, everything that went unspoken between us.

Every time I listened to that song, it felt like a journey into a world where only the two of us existed, where we could be ourselves, without any limitations. *Love and I* really meant Lydia and me. It was our song, our world, our story.

When things were at their worst after Sarah's death, Lydia would put that song on and say in a voice that brooked no argument:

"Listen! Open yourself to these sounds. Sink into the words. Don't think! Just flow with every note..."

And indeed, I listened. It gave me strength too. She knew how to reach me. I must admit, I've always admired Lydia. She's like a picture I wanted to paint. She's beautiful, with eyes like two blue lakes, deep and serene, in which one could lose oneself forever. Tall, well-groomed, always radiating an inner strength and calm that I often lacked. Though two years younger than me, she always seemed more mature, as if life had given her more balance and peace than it gave me.

Unlike my often chaotic existence, Lydia was always incredibly organized. In her world, everything had its place, and every day was meticulously planned. That was an extraordinary trait that added harmony to her life, a harmony I so often envied.

Lydia is a strong and independent woman of success. Her helping hand is always ready for action. In any situation, I could count on her. In her presence, problems seemed smaller, and sorrows temporary.

My little sister is loyal and devoted. Those are traits that are priceless in today's world. Having a friend like her is like hitting the jackpot in the lottery. When her heart loves, it does so completely. And when she hates, it's with equal intensity.

Sensitivity and empathy are second nature to her.

She was my anchor in moments when life became too difficult to bear. She was my guide through the darkest times, and her presence brought me solace. Perhaps I will never find the words to express how grateful I am for everything she has done for me. My sister – my greatest treasure. In our childhood and teenage years (before Madeline came along), we were inseparable, always together, hand in hand.

In the moment when the world collapsed under the weight of unspeakable grief, Lydia became my pillar. It wasn't a presence that forced comforting words, which would have sounded false in the face of such a great loss. No, Lydia was simply there – beside me, always ready to extend a hand when the darkness seemed impenetrable.

"Our Sarah," she would repeat, her voice infinitely gentle, as if afraid that any louder word might tear my heart into even smaller pieces. "Our Sarah..."

She still speaks about our little one to this day. Lydia was meant to be Sarah's godmother. Together, we spun dreams and fantasies about the days that would be filled with the laughter of our little girl.

Sarah's death was a loss for both of us, a part of ourselves and the dreams that faded with her last breath.

The shared anticipation of Sarah's birth was a time of hope for both me and Lydia, dreams of a future that would never come to be. We shared this pregnancy, every moment of it, from the first kick to the last breath that never came. When everything collapsed, when the world we had built with so much love for Sarah crumbled, Lydia was there where I needed her. She was there to help me rise from the ruins of our shared dream.

Our love for Sarah, even after her loss, never faded. Together, we walked through the darkness, holding on to each other like two grieving yet steadfast warriors. To me, Lydia was more than just a sister; she was a guardian angel guiding me through the storm. Thanks to her, even the darkest nights were bearable. Thanks to her, I didn't lose faith that after every night, dawn would come.

After Sarah's funeral, the world felt colorless to me, like a painting blurred by rain. Lydia became my shadow, my guardian, ensuring I didn't sink completely into the abyss of despair. Around me, a wall of sadness rose, an impenetrable fortress to which only she had access. We were like two ships in a stormy sea, holding on to each other to avoid crashing against the rocks.

"You don't have to speak," Lydia would whisper when tears filled my eyes again. "I'm here. I'll always be here. We can be silent together..."

Her presence kept me alive. I felt like my soul was a torn canvas, impossible to mend. And yet, Lydia's presence was like the gentle touch of a brush, trying to restore the lost colors of my soul.

Days passed, and Lydia and I existed as if in a parallel world, where only sorrow and memories of "Our Sarah" mattered. Sometimes I wondered how she did it. How could she be so strong when the world around us had fallen apart?

"Because I love you," she once answered to the unspoken question. "Because she was our Sarah, and I have to be strong for both of us."

She was my guide through the labyrinth of grief, my refuge when my thoughts became too dark. We were like two halves of one heart, which, though broken, still beat in sync with shared memories and the undying love for our little girl.

Without her, without the extraordinary bond that united us, without her unwavering presence, care, and love, I don't know if I would have ever found my way back to life. In her presence, I found tiny fragments of hope, like golden dust, slowly but surely rebuilding my shattered heart.

It was completely different with my older sister, Ursula. Life had dealt her a hard hand. I knew that well and didn't even hold it against her that she wasn't there for me during those dark days. Ursula had a kind heart, like a gentle ray of sunshine after a storm, but her mind was like a dark, restless cloud. Although I knew she cared for me deep down, her feelings were tangled like dense vines where love and resentment were inseparable. During the time of my loss, she once commented to Lydia:

"She got what she deserved."

Well, I accepted it with humility. She had the right to think that way – I hadn't always been the nicest to her.

In childhood, her jealousy had followed me like a shadow, trailing me no matter where I went. Even now, that shadow sometimes reappears unexpectedly, reminding me of its presence, though I try to live my own life, far from her turbulent emotions.

I've never been able to understand where her resentment came from.

Our relationship never resembled the traditional, ideal sisterly bond, full of shared secrets and endless support. Between us, there was always an insurmountable gap, filled with misunderstanding and lack of acceptance. My heart, though longing for her sisterly love, had learned to live without it, accepting that some bonds are too damaged to flourish.

The mistakes of our parents and the labyrinth of life shaped Ursula into who she is. Life threw too many challenges her way, hardening her heart and closing her mind to genuine feelings.

Sometimes, in moments of doubt, I ask myself whether it's even possible to repair what has been so deeply broken. Could our relationship ever become something more than just another story of two sisters who live side by side but are truly strangers to each other? Deep down, though, I know that there's no wound that can't heal; no bridges so burned they can't be rebuilt. I believe that one day, Ursula and I will stand on the same side of reality. I will wait...

Once, there was also my brother Walter. My little brother, the star of my childhood years, the ray of sunshine in our family home where shadows often darkened the walls. From the moment he was born, I enveloped him with all my heart, showering him with as much boundless love as I could.

My memories of him are like stained glass, through which light shines – colorful, vibrant, full of warmth. He was my companion not only in carefree play but also in the moments when our home was engulfed by storms. His smile was like a buoy, keeping me afloat when I was drowning in the sea of family tensions.

Walter and I were everything to each other – joy, comfort, safety. It was with him that I shared my secrets, my dreams; it was with him that I built sandcastles and made plans for the future. My love for him was like a rainbow after a storm breathtaking.

But life is an ongoing change, chapter after chapter. Suddenly, Walter and I drifted apart, and the space between us filled with silence, with words unsaid, with attempts to understand left unmade.

For over ten years, silence between us has solidified like concrete that once was fluid but now forms the foundation of a wall dividing our paths. Walter, once my beloved little brother, has now become like a ghost – present in my thoughts but elusive in the real world. He disappeared from my life, fading into the misty corners of the past, leaving behind only the echo of memories and the question, "Why?".

His silence became like an echo in an empty hall, returning to me with increasing pain, more incomprehensible with each passing day. He was the one who left, leaving a space where our mutual love and trust once existed. For years, I waited for him to reach out, to call, to hear a knock at the door of my soul, but there was only silence.

I never truly understood the reasons for our separation. A veil fell over our bond, leaving it in the darkness of misunderstandings and unspoken words. I had heard that it was Walter's wife, my sister-in-law, who persuaded him to cut ties with me. Once, there was love between Walter and me, but now only emptiness remains, reverberating with the silence of unspoken words, unanswered questions, and unforgiven emotions. All these years, the feeling of loss accompanied me daily, reminding me of the brother who became a stranger, closing the door to his life.

I wonder if he ever thinks of me? Has his life taken on new colors, where there's no longer room for me or our memories? Is it possible that our once unbreakable bond has simply been forgotten, pushed to the corners of memory like an insignificant detail of the past?

So many questions, and the answers could fit in a single glance, a single word. But the silence is a burden I carry alone, trying to find comfort in the thought that perhaps someday, in another life, our paths will cross again.

If all this truly was the result of my sister-in-law, over time, I began to understand her motives. The desire to be the only one, ir- replaceable, the center of the universe for the person you love – I know that feeling all too well. Over the years, I started to see her actions not as envy or malice but as a deep need for love, free from division and competition. Perhaps her soul, like mine, carried the scars of childhood, a longing for unconditional love that would be only hers, without having to share it with others.

Maybe her jealousy of my bond with Walter was simply the cry of her inner child, who, like mine, sought recognition and love. She couldn't understand our relationship, our inseparability, which wasn't born from competing for affection but from a deep sibling connection. In her eyes, perhaps, my presence was an obstacle to her complete happiness.

Though the pain of betrayal and rejection by my brother, who had once been so close, has not disappeared, I began to walk the path of forgiveness. I realized that we are all victims of our experiences, which shape our decisions and actions. Perhaps she, like me, was searching for a place where she could feel loved and safe. Maybe her actions, though they hurt me deeply, were just a naive attempt to pro- tect her own heart from rejection.

Understanding this, I started to see my sister-in-law in a different light. The hostility I once felt toward her was replaced by compassion and the understanding that love, although complicated and painful, is what defines us and paradoxically unites us all. I concluded that she took my brother from me not out of malice but because she didn't know how to do otherwise, because no one had taught her differently.

In the darkest days of my life, neither Ursula nor Walter was by my side. Nor was my mother... All the more, I appreciate that Lydia supported me every step of the way. Without her, my therapist, and my beloved M., I don't know how it would have ended.

I cannot forget the presence of certain guardian souls – Monika and her husband – whose subtle, unobtrusive, velvet-like support I felt the entire time. And I still feel it today...

In those dark moments, when the light of life fades before it has the chance to fully shine, when hope shatters like fragile ice beneath your feet before you can stand upon it, the journey through your personal hell begins. A journey like Dante's – filled with pain and despair, but also the search for a way out, a path to redemption and understanding.

Every day after the loss becomes another circle of personal hell. Thoughts spiral in an endless cycle of pain and sorrow, struggling with the question "why?" that echoes in the void, never finding an answer. This relentless fight against injustice, against a fate that turned so cruelly, strips every bit of hope from the heart, turning it into an unbearable weight.

Expressing what lies in the deepest corners of the soul feels like a task beyond strength. Words lose their meaning, becoming hollow, a mere faint echo of unending pain. And with each passing day, the burden grows heavier, becoming a cross harder and harder to bear.

Like Dante, journeying through the circles of hell in search of forgiveness, understanding, and love, I too sought my Beatrice – my solace. Through the darkness, Lydia guided me, showing me the path to light. She became my guide, my light in the tunnel I had to travel through.

Lydia, like Virgil to Dante, took my hand and led me through the deepest shadows of my sorrow, teaching me that even in the darkest night, a spark of light can be found, which can become the seed of a new day. In all this, our therapist supported us. He showed me that life, despite everything, continues, and though the loss will stay with me forever, I can learn to live with it and maybe even find joy again.

Over time, the steps on this path became a little lighter. The pain didn't disappear, but I learned to live with it. It took three years. For that long, depression suffocated me. I may have gotten back on my feet, but my heart will forever remain broken.

"I feel like I'm pieced back together, but a part could still fall off," I confessed to M. "A shattered mirror can be glued, and it may be whole again, but try looking into it..."

He didn't say anything. Instead of offering me empty words, he held me. Tightly. Just as I needed.

I've never pieced myself back together, returned to life, I smile... but I never laugh anymore.

Since that time, every year, I light candles for two people close to my heart. Some burn proudly on M.'s birthday cake, while others flicker with a sad flame on Sarah's grave.

And so it goes, year after year...

CHAPTER 19

When the world seemed like one giant cemetery of unfulfilled dreams and shattered hopes, fate suddenly spun me into the strangest dance and fulfilled our expectations. I became pregnant. And it was another girl. Lily. I named her that because it reminded me of a lily – a flower so delicate and fragile, just like every newborn spark of life after a great storm. I remember little of this pregnancy, as I was still submerged in sorrow over the loss of Sarah.

Life is a surprising director who never asks if we are ready for the next change. It moves forward, not waiting for us to dry our tears. Each day felt like turning the pages of an old, yellowed album full of images that would never regain their original colors. I felt as though my heart, torn so violently, could only beat to the rhythm of melancholy, and yet... it turned out that even a cruel fate can sometimes soften and fulfill a human dream. And that dream was undoubtedly a child.

Lily grew inside me, but I was still elsewhere. Each tiny kick, which should have been a reminder of life, initially brought a wave of panic. All I could think of was that every new life carried the risk of another tragedy. Would my heart endure if history decided to repeat itself? Was I ready for that? Most of the time, I wandered through the desert of my own sadness, where every grain of sand was, in reality, the ashes of a recent tragedy.

Life without Sarah was life in the silence after a great explosion – everything around me seemed only an echo of what was once melodic and full of color. Lily was like the promised land, though I wasn't sure if she was real or if she would become another mirage on my desert of grief. How could I prepare a room for new life when the previous one was still filled with the ghost of the past? How could I dream of the future when every dream felt like a replay of the worst nightmare?

But slowly, over time, like the first rays of sunlight cutting through the morning fog, I began to feel Lili's movements as music, an invitation to dance after a long night. I started to talk to her, whispering when no one could see, but hope was still suffocated by fear. I told her about Sarah, about the world waiting for her to discover, and about the pain that teaches us to cherish joy.

The pregnancy with Lily became a bridge between the past and the future, between loss and hope. Though every day was a battle between fear and the dream of a better tomorrow, with each passing week, I grew stronger, learning once again how to love life, which constantly reminds us of its fragility.

I rushed to Lydia as soon as I found out I was pregnant. I had to share the joyful news with her. I just had to!

I burst into her room like a storm. Lydia looked at me suspiciously, knowing I hadn't smiled in a long time. I wanted to shout my joy. But before I could, Lydia asked, narrowing her eyes:

"Are you pregnant?"

I nodded.

"Yes!" I almost screamed. "Isn't it wonderful?!"

Her face lit up for a moment, but then I saw confusion wash over her.

"I have something to tell you too," Lydia's voice was as soft as morning dew. "I'm pregnant too. Three months along. I was afraid of how you'd react because..."

"Because of Sarah..." I finished for her.

The room was once again filled with silence, broken only by our breathing.

"Yes, because of Sarah," Lydia nodded.

I rushed to her and hugged her as tightly as I could.

"This is wonderful news," I whispered through tears.

For a moment, Lydia gazed into my eyes, as if making sure I wasn't angry with her. I gently stroked her cheek. "I think this could be beautiful too, you know? Our children growing up together," my beloved sister whispered.

There was hope in her words, and I felt it was true. I began to believe that the new lives we carried would bring healing to our wounded souls.

"We'll be their shield," I said, my voice firm, full of determination. "We won't let anything bad happen to our little ones."

"Yes, they'll have us. And each other." Lydia squeezed my hand tighter as if she wanted to share some of her strength.

It felt like a vow we made before the invisible court of fate. I promised myself that although the world around us might be full of uncertainties and storms, I would stand ready each day to protect the small, new life already growing within us. Maybe we couldn't fully free ourselves from the past, but we could create a better future for those who would come after us.

Happiness surrounded me like a bright aura, yet fear wove itself between its rays like a shadow, refusing to let me forget the darkness of the past. This pregnancy was wrapped in both hope and anxiety, a dance between light and darkness, with steps that were uncertain but full of determination.

Within my womb, new life flickered – a precious spark of existence, whose desire equaled the intensity of pain. Every kick, every movement was both a comfort and a warning. The fear of losing this fragile being was as strong as the joy of her presence.

In moments of doubt, when cold waves of anxiety flooded the shores of my heart, I sought solace in literature. I immersed myself in Dante's words, finding echoes of my own journey through shadow and light in his *Divine Comedy*. Dante, lost in a dark forest, found a guide in Virgil. I too needed a guide – sometimes it was M., sometimes Lydia, and at times, my therapist.

As I traversed the realms of paradise, hell, and purgatory with the Italian poet, I learned to accept my own fears and to find hope where it seemed there was none. Every line of Dante's reminded me that my journey, though full of obstacles, could also lead to a place filled with light.

Pregnancy, this delicate thread connecting me to the unborn child, became a symbol of fighting for each new day, for every breath of the future. Each morning, I reminded myself that I had to be strong, not only for myself but for this tiny being who had yet to taste the world.

I was like a plant in winter, hiding beneath the snow the promise of spring. My growing belly, rounder with each week, was like the earth concealing a seed. Sometimes the sun of my joy would break through the clouds of fear, shining on that seed with boundless love.

It wasn't easy, but every small victory, every day survived without tears, became a milestone on this winding path. Each moment of peace was another step toward the paradise I was fighting so hard to reach.

In every uncertain moment, my concern for the future turned into fear, and that fear into a frenzy of actions. There were nights when, leaving the warmth of home, I would race through the sleeping city in my car, heading to the hospital just to hear the rhythm of my baby's heart. That sound, pulsating in the sterile white walls of the hospital, was the melody of life to me. I needed it. There were moments when I couldn't go on without hearing it. I had to be sure that Lily was okay.

"Please, let's check again if everything is alright," I would ask the doctors on night duty, my voice trembling.

At first, they might have protested a little, but over time, it became clear to them that I would come again on some other night. I think they got used to it. They understood that I needed reassurance.

They would simply reply,

"Of course, we'll do a checkup right away. Please calm down, everything will be fine."

But I could never stop the waves of anxiety until I heard the beating of my child's heart.

The examination room always felt like a mysterious space filled with humming machines that whispered to each other, discussing my fate. The medical equipment was like a magical window into another world, where on the small black-and-white screen, I could see what was most precious. The heart of my unborn daughter beat rhythmically, breaking the silence of the room, bringing me relief. Until the next time.

As I drove home afterward, for a moment, the world seemed beautiful and kind again. Through the car window, I stared at the empty streets, breathing steadily. But that peace never lasted long.

Anxiety was my shadow, following me step by step, regardless of the hour or the changing traffic lights.

I took care of myself as best as I could. I ate properly, rested whenever possible, and tried not to worry, though that was a battle with windmills. I couldn't escape the grip of fear. The care for this tiny being, whom I didn't yet know but already loved so deeply, was like a wild garden – full of beautiful flowers of love and thorns of fear. I felt each day brought new challenges but also new worries. I was the gardener of my fate, trying to nurture every petal of hope, plucking every weed of doubt, so my child could bloom fully in this world.

Immersed in fragile hope, I offered daily prayers from the depths of my soul, like raindrops on the cracked soil of my heart. My prayers, filled with both desperation and hope, floated toward the heavens like delicate flower petals carried by the wind.

"Oh, Mother who holds your Son in your arms, understand the heart of a mother who longs to hear her child's first cry. Have mercy on this little heart that beats uncertainly in my womb, like a butterfly's wings just after emerging into the world. Let its flight not end before it even begins," I pleaded.

"Blessed Mother, allow me to welcome this life, not bid it farewell before it is born. Let me not walk through the valley of tears again, for I cannot bear it a second time. Restore my faith in tomorrow, which should bring joy, not another goodbye," I whispered, believing that my words were not in vain.

Each prayer was like the earth breathing deeply in anticipation of rain, like the echo of a mountain valley crying out for mercy.

"Do not let fear be greater than my faith. May every worry dissolve in the rays of hope you send each day, lighting up the shadows of doubt. Let every beat of my heart be a prayer, filled with both pleading and gratitude for each day I get to live with this child," I asked.

"Grant me the strength to protect this fragile life from the storms that will inevitably come! Let my body be a safe haven, and my love a shield, protecting from the misfortunes of this world!"

My days and nights were filled with prayers and vigilance, watching over every movement in my womb, every sign that might indicate life or danger. Living in this suspended state, between fear and hope, was like constantly balancing on a tightrope stretched over an unimaginable abyss.

Each prayer was like a stone cast into the void. The echo that returned to me brought either silence or a whisper of hope. My life, intertwined with prayer, became a reality woven from pain, hope, fear, and the wait for a miracle.

The worst were the nightmares that descended like vultures whenever I tried to sleep. The night hours blurred the line between dream and reality, turning my bed into the shores of a dark ocean, where waves of merciless nightmares crashed against the rocks of reality. In one of them, the most harrowing and full of dread, I stood on the edge of an abyss, where the valley – like the one described by Dante – seemed to whisper my name, calling me into its dark embrace. I looked down into the land of shadows, where the reflections of the lost Sarah danced among burning ruins. Her face, veiled by some mist, transformed into a thousand terrifying masks; each one was a reflection of my deepest pain and fear. These faces uttered the most painful words a mother could ever hear: "Why didn't you protect me, mommy?"

The echo of her words reverberated against the soulless walls of that bleak place, each repetition a new blow to my bleeding heart. My feet, as if welded to the edge of that invisible chasm, refused to move, and I, helpless, could only watch as this vision devoured what remained of my soul.

From afar, as if from the deepest depths of Dante's hell, I heard the cries of children, cries I could not quiet no matter how hard I tried. Each cry was like a bell tolling my failures, my guilt, my own personal damnation.

In this nightmare, between light and darkness, the figure of my unborn daughter, Lili, slowly began to materialize. Her image, as if pulled from the fog of my fear, became more and more clear. I felt a mixture of hope and terror. Was it possible for light to be born out of such deep darkness?

When I woke, drenched in sweat, my heart pounding out of my chest, every beam of light that streamed into my room in the morning seemed like a promise of something better. In those moments, I most wanted to believe that one day life could be different, less soaked in pain. But those nightmares returned nearly every night, bringing with them the fear of facing yet another evening.

During the final weeks of my pregnancy, therapy became my lifeline, something to cling to in the depths of my fears. Each session with my therapist was like a precious breath of air, allowing me to surface from the darkness, even if only for a moment. My visits became more frequent, like desperate stops where I tried to catch my breath, resisting the current that was pulling me down.

"I can't stop being afraid," I confessed to my therapist, clinging to the hope that he would find a way to save me.

"It's normal to feel fear," he replied calmly. "But remember, fear is just an emotion. It doesn't define you or what's going to happen."

His words, and his warm, soothing voice, were a comfort to me, though I didn't always believe that my reality could be any different. Each hour of therapy was a battle, an attempt to find the strength within me to face my deepest fears.

In my mind, the question kept hammering away: could I survive another loss? Could my heart endure being torn apart again? I recalled every word from my therapist, trying to build armor out of them, something that could protect me from the worst.

"You have to allow yourself to hope," he said. "Just as a plant needs water, so does your soul need hope to grow and break through this pain."

As the due date approached, my heart was a storm of conflicting emotions. Joy intertwined with terror, and hope was constantly shredded by the sharp edges of pain. I knew that what was coming would be one of the greatest challenges of my life. I had to face my past, whose shadows still haunted my present, and I had to confront a future that was as uncertain as ever.

The day of the birth. I remember every second, every heartbeat, every sharp breath. The delivery room became an arena where every movement, every word carried immense weight. And in the midst of it all was me – terrified beyond the limits of human possibility.

"Breathe deeply!" the doctor instructed, but his words dissolved into the air like smoke.

M. held my hand tightly. His presence was my anchor in the chaos.

"Focus on me, just on me," he whispered into my ear.

"On you," I muttered, as another wave of pain overtook my body.

The midwife approached with more instructions, but her words were like the whispering of the wind to me.

"Push, please! You need to cooperate," she repeated.

M. squeezed my hand harder, signaling that everything was under control.

"You know you can do this. Do it for us," he encouraged me, and his words carried more strength than all the medical orders being thrown around the room.

The doctor intervened again, trying to restore order.

"Push!" he commanded.

But I didn't hear anyone else in that crowded room except for M. Only his words reached me. He whispered every instruction from the medical staff to me, guiding me through the noise.

M., my rock, never let go of my hand, continuing to speak to me through the commotion:

"Focus on me; everything will be okay."

And I truly believed him. Only him.

"Just think how quickly this will be over," M. said as the next contraction hit.

"Over?" I looked at him, searching for the truth in his eyes. He stroked my cheek gently.

"Focus on me, forget about the rest," he asked again.

"Your 'forget about the rest' always works like a spell," I muttered, trying to catch my breath between contractions. I knew it was time to focus on M.'s words.

"Every breath brings us closer to our daughter," he spoke again, his voice like a soothing balm on my frayed nerves.

A final, intense effort, a brief moment of tension, and then everything made sense when I heard the first cry of our baby girl. In that instant, all the frustration and anger melted into the air, leaving behind nothing but pure joy.

"We did it, together," M. said, and despite my exhaustion, I smiled through my tears.

At last, the most important thing was here with us. Or was it?

When the last scream of pain faded into the air of the delivery room, silence fell, broken only by my quickened breath and the sound of my heart, which seemed to be the only noise filling the space. In that silence, suspended between pain and hope, my thoughts wandered into uncertainty.

"Is she alive?! Please, tell me she's alive!" The words tumbled out of my throat, one by one, as if they had a life of their own, pulsating with desperation.

M. still held my hand, his eyes full of concern and love, searching for mine.

"Everything is fine, sweetheart. Our little girl is alive. She's healthy," he said, wrapping me in the calm I hadn't felt in so long.

But deep inside, where the wounds of my previous loss were still fresh, the embers of uncertainty continued to burn. My heart pounded like a bell, its echo carrying through the corners of my memory, awakening the not-so-distant past when death had been closer than breath.

"But are you sure everything is okay?" my words were a soft whisper, barely audible. "Please, let me see her. I need to see her."

M. nodded, his hands still holding mine, transferring his peace to me. A moment later, the midwife gently placed that tiny, fragile being on my chest. Only then did the fear and doubts begin to recede. I looked into her little face and saw more than just life – I saw the future, hope, a new beginning.

"She's our new light, M.," I whispered, feeling tears of joy welling up in my eyes.

My heart, so long trapped in grief, began to beat once more to the rhythm of life.

M. smiled at me and at our daughter, and in his eyes, I saw a reflection of my own feelings – a mix of joy, relief, and endless love.

In that moment, as they placed my newborn daughter on my chest, time seemed to stop, and the world around us dissolved, leaving just the two of us, connected by an invisible thread of love and life. Her small, delicate body lay on me, so light and yet so immensely significant. I held her close, and her warmth seeped through the layers of my exhaustion, fear, and sorrow, igniting a spark of hope deep within my heart.

The tears that streamed down my cheeks were salty witnesses to my love, my pain, my relief. Each drop reflected the depths of emotions that had surged within me during these months of storm and calm, of despair and hope. Holding her so close, I felt as if each of her sighs, every tiny breath, was a balm for my wounded soul.

I didn't want to let her go; I didn't want to give up that precious treasure I had waited so long for. When the nurse came to take Lily for her tests, my heart filled with despair. I didn't want to give her up! Never in my life!

It took a long time before, despite my heart's protests, I finally allowed the nurse to take Lili. Every moment of separation from my daughter, even for a brief time, felt like a goodbye. I watched as Lily disappeared behind the doors in the nurse's arms, and I stifled the scream of anguish that wanted to escape from my lips. The silence that followed was thick with tension, anticipation, and prayers that everything would be all right, that fate would be kind this time.

The moment I saw Lily again, my heart suddenly began to beat with renewed strength. The love that awoke within me was so powerful that it felt as though it could bring even the flowers in the frost back to life. Lili was like the first rays of sunlight after a long, dark night, breaking gently but persistently through the clouds.

I felt my broken heart begin to heal with each of her breaths, with every small movement she made. This little, fragile being filled the emptiness that had once gnawed at me from within. Every cry, every laugh was like a symphony that carried hope and healing. I was not alone in this magical moment of rediscovering motherhood. Lydia, my dear sister, was also experiencing this wonderful, life-changing journey. Our paths, though entwined with challenges and pain, led us both to this same beautiful place – motherhood. Together, we were starting a new chapter filled with love, a chapter that was rebuilding what had once been destroyed.

With each day, Lily grew, and I grew stronger alongside her. Watching her sleep peacefully, seeing her look around with curiosity, I felt all my previous fears and anxieties slowly fade away, making room only for boundless love and gratitude.

When I looked at Lili, I didn't just see a child; I saw a promise of a better tomorrow, proof that life, despite its unimaginable challenges, could also offer moments of pure, unwavering joy. Lily was my personal miracle, my angel who had come to teach me an important life lesson – that even the deepest pain can be transformed into something beautiful, that every ending can also be a beginning. This lesson was invaluable, though it could never fully erase the pain of losing Sarah.

The first two years of Lily's life were like an endless journey through a misty landscape full of contradictions. Each night brought with it a mixture of joyful dreams and nightmares of fear. A quiet, peaceful night could suddenly become the stage for my worst fears when I would drift off to sleep and no longer hear the rhythmic sound of my daughter's breathing. I watched over her as often as I could, sometimes with my eyes closed but always ready to react to her every movement, every sigh. In those moments, my heart danced on the edge of fear and hope. The joy of her presence was constantly intertwined with the fear that this delicate thread of life could snap at any moment.

Everything in me was on high alert, like a night watchman by the light of the moon – always vigilant, always on guard. My unconditional love for Lily was my greatest blessing, but it was also the source of an unspeakable fear that gnawed at me, feeding my deepest anxieties.

Each morning, her smile was my rebirth, confirmation that another night had passed successfully. Each shout of joy was like a balm for my weary soul, giving me a brief moment of forgetting the dark thoughts that so often stole my peace.

I was like a gardener, shielding my most precious flowers from even the slightest cold breeze, guarding every second of her existence, every breath she took. And so it went on for over two years.

In this strange balance between fear and happiness, every day was a challenge, and every night a trial. The mix of pain and delight painted my days in the most intense colors of life, teaching me that true love is not only the warmth of sunny days but also perseverance through the darkest nights.

With Lily's arrival, our lives became fuller. Every moment spent with her was like gentle kisses of sunlight on my cheeks. My heart, which for so long had fed only on sorrow and grief, began to beat to a happier rhythm once more.

"May this music never stop playing," I whispered softly, watching as Lili, our little one, smiled at me with eyes full of pure, innocent joy.

Adam and Arthur became Lily's guardians of carefree days. I often saw them playing with her, filling the room with happiness. Their laughter was like the sweetest melody, constantly playing, rocking us to the rhythm of love.

Lili's presence was like a breath of fresh, spring air that dispelled any lingering remnants of sadness. My sons, gifted with great sensitivity, understood how much their presence and involvement helped me navigate this new reality.

All these shared moments were weaving our lives anew. Lili, our little ray of light, was like a jewel that captured every gaze and every heart in our home.

"I think Lily has magic in her," I said one evening to M., as we both watched our daughter fall asleep. "There's no other explanation for how much she's changed our lives."

"That's true," M. replied, hugging me gently. "Every day with her is like another page in the most beautiful book we could ever read."

Thanks to Lili, I learned that life, despite all its uneven paths, always finds a way to surprise us and bless us with something beautiful. This feeling was like sweet nectar, something we wanted to savor every day.

On Lili's first birthday, I organized a trip as a gift for M. and me to celebrate our fifth anniversary together. In secret, I planned a trip that culminated in a cruise over the blue waters of the Aegean Sea. We sailed, surrounded by the magnificent views of scattered islands. In those moments, it felt as though we were reclaiming every lost note of our shared melody of love.

The ship we traveled on cut through the waves with the grace of an ancient mariner discovering new lands. Our journey felt like sailing through the different circles of life's experiences, reminding me of my own journey from darkness to light, much like Dante navigating his challenges. The sea around us stretched out like an endless expanse of possibilities, and the horizon seemed to promise an infinite tomorrow. The ship, gently swaying on the waves, became our safe haven.

The wind lightly ruffled the water's surface, and while Lili, our little treasure, slept soundly in her stroller, M. and I watched her, feeling the purity of her innocence and joy in existence.

On that special anniversary, as the sun slowly set, painting the sky with shades of orange and pink, I felt a deep sense of peace. My earlier fears and worries slowly melted away in the warm rays of the setting sun. Every minute of that journey taught me anew how to cherish what we have, how to live life fully, without looking back with regret.

That day, filled with reflection and personal thoughts, became a symbol of a new beginning. I realized that despite the darkness that had once enveloped my life, there is always room for new light, for new hope. And in that hope, wrapped in the love of those closest to me, I found the strength to keep moving forward. I owed it to both Lily and Sarah.

HEAVEN

CHRISTMAS EVE IN HEAVEN

Right after baby Jesus was born, I smiled. It was a pure, selfless smile, one that hadn't graced my face in a long time. The light from the shining star that guided the Wise Men to the manger illuminated every corner of my heart, revealing hidden desires and longings.

With each moment of Christmas, with every tiny twinkle of the lights on the tree, I felt like Beatrice from Dante's vision, gazing down from Heaven, full of love and understanding. A paradise was blooming in my soul. The world seemed perfect, and every step led to that long-desired garden of humanity where there was no pain or sorrow. At that time, my soul, lifted by the wings of angels, touched silver clouds and wandered among the stars, each one telling a story of fulfilled dreams. All of this thanks to the man who loved me.

When M. and I started dating, we knew immediately that this was it. We were like two odd puzzle pieces that suddenly realized they fit perfectly together. His presence in my life was like a beam of light cutting through the darkness, illuminating every step I took. His hand in mine was the confirmation that I was loved, that I mattered.

The joy on my children's faces was living proof that love in our family was real, that it was worth believing in goodness and that miracles do happen. Their laughter was the most beautiful melody to me, filling the house with warmth and happiness. I knew I was the happiest mother in the world.

Finally, Christmas became a celebration of family love for me, but also a rediscovery of myself, my inner Beatrice, who had spent her life searching for her paradise. That Christmas night, I felt like I had finally reached my Heaven, full of love, warmth, and acceptance.

Although fate often threw challenges my way, during that special time, I could see only beauty and harmony. The world took on deeper colors, and the heart beating in my chest sang a hymn of joy. I knew this was just the beginning of my journey toward fulfillment, but I was certain I was walking the right path, guided by the light of the Star of Bethlehem.

The preparations for Christmas Eve in the heart of Germany were something special, magical. Snow covered the streets and rooftops, painting the town in a pleasant white. Smoke rising from chimneys created colorful patches against the blue sky. M., with his characteristic smile, stood at the table slicing beets for the borscht. Arthur enthusiastically helped me make the dough, laughing at the cheerful gingerbread men decorated by Adam and Lily.

The kitchen was filled with the incredible aroma of spices and dishes that permeated every corner of the house. These wonderful smells mixed with warmth and love. The Christmas tree in the living room, decorated with bright lights and ornaments, twinkled and seemed to dance to the carols. I felt like the whole world had stopped, that time ceased to exist, and we, my family, were suspended in this one, perfect moment.

However, behind this idyllic scene, I began to feel a shadow of unease. I sat on the couch, looking at my treasures, and thought about how easily this moment could be lost. A sudden fear gripped me, almost crushing me – the fear that all this was only temporary, that such perfection could crumble in an instant.

I asked myself if this wasn't too beautiful to be real. Were we living in an illusion that could pop like a soap bubble? Or maybe I was just too skeptical, too sensitive about the future to enjoy the present? After all, these thoughts are normal, right? Doesn't everyone fear losing something that is most precious to them?

Curled up on that couch, I thought that most people probably fear loss when something truly good happens in their lives. It's the paradox of our nature: when life is good, we fear it will end, and when life is bad, we dream of better days. So how do we enjoy moments of happiness when they are constantly pulled by the fear of losing what's good? How?

I didn't want my fears to spoil this magical evening. I stood up and walked to the window. I watched the snow slowly, yet steadily, cover the streets, creating a soft, white carpet. At that moment, I thought that, despite everything, it was worth enjoying every moment because these moments are what make up our lives.

Nevertheless, the worries remained. I knew I had to face them, but not now, not tonight. Tonight, I wanted to enjoy the time with my family in the warmth of our home. I wanted to forget my fears and live fully in the present.

In that Christmas atmosphere, amidst the twinkling lights and the warmth of the hearth, the sound of the phone ringing brought a slight disruption to my peaceful world. The name "Lydia" smiled at me from the screen of my smartphone. My heart beat faster. My beloved sister, my personal lighthouse, illuminating the darkness even in the darkest night.

I answered the call and, as always, heard her cheerful voice.

"We're on our way, we'll be there by the time the first star appears," she informed me with enthusiasm.

"Drive carefully," I asked.

We laughed together, recalling childhood memories, both funny and touching.

Lydia was like a mirror for me, reflecting my own feelings, my thoughts. At the end of the conversation, there was a certain shyness in her voice, an unusual seriousness, as if she had suddenly reached the threshold of a great revelation.

"I love you very much, more than anything in the world," she said, and something inside my heart broke.

Those simple words felt like magic, like a balm for all the wounds life had inflicted upon me. I knew it was a huge step for her. She had never dared to express those feelings before. She couldn't say them, even though she had many opportunities. No one had taught us how. I still don't know how to say them. Yes, I can manage an impersonal "love," but the more personal "I love you" is something I still can't say. I'm still learning, and maybe one day I'll find the courage to say a true, heartfelt "I love you." But can I even feel that? I don't know.

In recent years, I hadn't felt much love for anyone in the family, except for Lydia, but she earned that herself – it wasn't always that way. It was her years of effort after our long separation that brought us back together. There was a time when I thought of her as a cruel woman. But back then, she wasn't herself. Influenced by someone else, she acted like a stranger. After such a trial of sisterly love, it wasn't easy to rebuild what had been lost. It was Lydia's hard work that led us to this new, strong bond.

It's no wonder. Our lives hadn't been easy. We'd been through many storms and tempests over the years.

And on Christmas Eve, such a surprise! Another level of Heaven! Sunlight in Paradise!

As I listened to her confession, my eyes filled with tears. Her words were like rain on a hot day, like a ray of sunlight breaking through the clouds. Maybe one day, I too will find the courage to say those same words. Maybe one day I'll confess my love to those who are waiting for it.

"Thank you," I replied after a moment of silence, knowing it wasn't enough.

I was ashamed of my own restraint, but at the same time, Lydia's words filled me with indescribable joy and emotion. Yes, that night, God was truly being born!

Christmas took on a new meaning for me ever since I met M. In that festive atmosphere, full of magic, light, and warmth, the past no longer suffocated me. With each day spent by his side, I felt myself shedding the weight of the past, a burden full of bitterness, anger, and misunderstanding.

There's a reason people say love has the power to heal. M. was the cure for the wounds of my soul that hadn't healed for years. He showed me how a touch full of passion and trust can be, how a warm and tender kiss can become the source of true, pure emotion. Sex, which had once been something dirty, filled with pain and shame, became something beautiful with him – something that connected us on the deepest level.

I remember how, in my past, I had desperately searched for attention and love, how I chased blindly after negative emotions that shaped my identity. I begged for love on my knees, but those pitiful pleas reached the wrong people. That's why, looking back at these holidays, I felt that every moment was a blessing.

Had I ever truly appreciated love before? Before meeting M., I thought real love was just a fleeting second of happiness that would disappear as quickly as it came. But now, having a man by my side who cradled my wounded heart and taught me to trust again, everything became clear. He showed me that love is more than just physical closeness – it's a feeling that gives strength, hope, and, above all, peace. Thanks to him, my life began to take on colors that had once seemed out of reach.

During this sacred time, looking at the baby Jesus, I felt grateful to have someone like M. in my life. For giving me what I had longed for – true, enduring love.

It was M. who soothed my emotions, who cradled my inner child, and poured love and peace into my cold heart. That's what I thanked Jesus for, the one who had just been born.

Thanks to M., I underwent a process of awakening, a kind of rebirth. I realized that happiness isn't a mountain you climb just once. It's like a river, a current you must follow constantly, picking up bits of silver and gold along the way. Every ray of sunshine, every glance, every smile, and every warm touch were pearls of that river, combining into one magnificent whole.

I was filled with gratitude for M.'s presence in my life. He brought out the best in me and taught me to cherish the moments that together made up happiness. Our days were full of those extraordinary moments – from early mornings spent in each other's arms, to afternoon walks in the park, to evening conversations by the fireplace. My children, who brought me so much joy, noticed the change. They saw the love that radiated from both of us – from me and from M.

But life, as everyone knows, is full of ups and downs. With that knowledge, I often thought about the balance between happiness and misfortune. Even though I was given the chance to experience Paradise by M.'s side, deep in my heart, the thought that a storm of misfortunes could arrive unexpectedly, like a black cloud in a clear sky, troubled me.

I couldn't help but think of Dante's story, in which his love for Beatrice was so intense and pure that it seemed to transcend all human limits. In *The Divine Comedy*, the lovers met in Paradise, a place where time and space didn't matter, where love was eternal and unbroken. Yet even there, in that idyllic space, there was always the shadow of something that could tear them apart. So, is that how it is in Heaven? Even there, the breath of uncertainty never fully disappears?

Although the joy of being with M. filled my days, I knew I had to be vigilant and appreciate every moment. Because, in truth, nothing in life is guaranteed forever, and heavenly moments are intertwined with moments of sorrow. That's why, with each passing day, I strove to weave my happiness, treasuring our shared moments and understanding that true fulfillment comes from being present, here and now.

But this was still my Heaven.

MIDNIGHT MASS

The night was cold, and the snow crunched under our boots as we walked home from the midnight mass. We held hands, as if searching for warmth in each other, the kind that was missing in the winter air. The icy wind brushed against our faces, and with each passing second, memories floated around us like shadows dancing in the night.

"What are you thinking about?" M. broke the silence, his voice warm, like a gentle flame in a fireplace on a cold winter evening.

I paused for a moment, gazing at the distant stars twinkling above us, as if to remind me that even in the darkest of nights, there's always a light of hope. My thoughts drifted to Christmas Eves from my childhood – those filled with pain and sorrow, when every moment was overshadowed by the past.

"I'm thinking about what was. About all those awful Christmases I had to endure in the past," I answered, a little somber. "Those that never turned out the way I imagined they would."

M. squeezed my hand tighter, as if his touch could chase away all my sadness. His presence was like a lighthouse in the stormy sea of memories that refused to leave me.

"Christmas has always been a hard time for me," I admitted. "But now, with you, I feel like I love Christmas Eve, Christmas itself, and everything that comes with it."

M. looked at me with tenderness, in the way only he knew how.

"I think there are still plenty of surprises ahead for you," he said mysteriously.

I looked at him suspiciously. He pretended not to notice, but he was always terrible at hiding things. That was something I loved about him.

We continued walking in silence, each lost in our own thoughts. Soon, we arrived at our home. The lights in the windows twinkled, promising warmth and safety.

When we opened the door, the warmth inside embraced us like a blanket, gently thawing our chilled bodies. I hurried to shut the door behind us. The snow clinging to our boots melted, leaving wet patches on the doormat. I took off my winter coat and carefully hung it on the hook, feeling a sense of relief as the cold slipped away.

M. was watching me again with that suspicious look. It was starting to make me nervous. Just as I opened my mouth to ask him about his strange behavior, he turned away and began taking off his coat. His movements were smooth and deliberate, as if the everyday routine held new, intimate meaning on this special night.

"I'll make us some tea," I said, shaking off my confusion. "We'll warm up."

I went into the kitchen and glanced around, feeling strangely out of place, as if I were seeing it for the first time. Where was this sense of being lost coming from? Should I be worried about M.'s behavior? Life had already battered me so much that I always assumed the worst.

Not wanting to dwell on it, I took two cups from the cupboard, their porcelain gleaming in the light, creating an illusion of warmth. Then I grabbed the kettle, filled it with water, and turned it on.

What's M. up to? I could already tell something was going on.

"I'll light the fireplace," his voice called from the hallway, pulling me out of my thoughts.

I peeked out of the kitchen. Sure enough, M. was busy by the fireplace.

I must be losing my mind, I thought, rubbing my increasingly aching temples.

I needed to escape all those dark thoughts!

I returned to making the tea. Soon, its aroma filled the kitchen, and in that moment, I felt like the demons of my past were losing their grip on me.

I knew immediately when M. entered the kitchen. I could always sense him when he was near. Always. Maybe it was because the bond between us was so strong?

"Come join me by the fire," he said with a smile. "The best place to be in December! We'll warm up soon."

I smiled back and nodded.

Carrying the tea into the room with the fireplace, I heard the familiar tune of "Silent Night" filling the air. M. knew exactly what to play. That carol always moved me.

Sitting in front of the fireplace, I felt its warmth seeping through my skin, reaching the deepest corners of my soul. The fire danced in the hearth, casting flickering shadows on the walls, reminding me of the past – still present, but now softened by time and forgiveness.

As I gazed into the flames, my thoughts began to drift back to years gone by, to memories filled with sorrow, anger, and pain. Every moment, every painful experience replayed in my mind, but without the intensity they once held. It was all like a distant echo, fading as time passed.

The reverie was broken when M. gently caressed my cheek. We hugged tightly, the warmth of the fire and the soft glow of the candles completing the magic of the moment.

Suddenly, M. straightened up. He looked at me intently for a moment, as if trying to understand my deepest thoughts.

"I wanted to do this in this special moment," he finally said quietly, his voice trembling with emotion. "All my life, I've been searching for someone to be my refuge, my warmth on cold days. I found that in you. I love you and I want to spend the rest of my life with you."

Tears welled up in my eyes. All the painful memories, all the fears and doubts vanished in that single moment. They disappeared like mist dissolving under the sun. I felt my entire world centering around this one moment.

M. knelt on one knee. His face was adorned with a smile, though tinged with a hint of nervousness. My heart began to race, and time seemed to stand still. My beloved reached out his hand toward me. In it, he held a small velvet box with a ring.

"Will you marry me?"

THE END

Memories flowed through my consciousness like a river, restless and dark. They reminded me of all those years when anger and pain were my companions, when every thought and action was marked by the shadow of suffering and disappointment. I recalled those nights filled with tears, when loneliness was my only companion, and my heart felt too heavy to bear another wound.

Then I thought, perhaps it had to be this way. Without all of it, I wouldn't be where I am now. I wouldn't be who I am today. Writing this book turned out to be more than just an escape into the world of literature. It became my therapy. Each word I wrote was a step towards liberation, towards forgiving myself and others. Every page brought relief, as if transferring these memories onto paper was cleansing my soul. Through writing, I began to understand that my life had been a journey through hell, purgatory, and heaven – much like Dante's *Divine Comedy*, which had accompanied me since childhood.

Hell was the time when I carried anger and bitterness, when the wounds were fresh and painful, and I couldn't find peace. Purgatory was the writing process, the time when I processed my experiences, learning to forgive and understand. Each sentence was like a stone I slowly removed from my heart, until eventually, I felt lighter. And now, sitting in front of the fireplace beside M., I had reached my heaven. It was a place where I felt peace, love, and acceptance. A place where the past no longer had any power over me.

The fire in the hearth reminded me of the power of transformation. Just like wood burning to give warmth, my experiences, though painful, were necessary to bring me to this moment. I felt gratitude for the journey, for every step that had led me here. I knew there would still be challenges ahead, but now I was ready to face them, with a heart full of love and hope.

My life had been full of contrasts – darkness and light, pain and joy, anger and forgiveness. Now, in this silence, in the warmth of the fireplace, I could finally accept everything I had been through and everything I had become. The fire danced, and I looked at it with a sense of fulfillment, knowing that the past was behind me and the future was open, full of possibilities.

This moment was my rebirth. I was ready to start anew, leaving behind all the demons of the past. I was ready for a new, better life by the side of the man I loved.

I had endured so much, but now, looking back, I saw that it was precisely those difficult events that shaped me into the person I am today. I realized that my scars were like seals of the experiences that had shaped my soul, teaching me resilience and perseverance. I was proud of myself, for with each passing day, I grew stronger, more resilient to life's storms.

My life was like a river flowing through rocky gorges, creating meanders full of challenges and surprises. The water, which once seemed murky and unclear, was now gradually becoming clear. What once seemed like unimaginable suffering now appeared as valuable lessons that taught me how to be stronger and more self-aware.

I learned that my past doesn't define me as a person; it is a distant echo of memories that help me shape my future. Every fall was an opportunity to learn to walk with more confidence. Every wound made my heart more resilient, and every disappointment taught me to appreciate true happiness.

Every day, when I look in the mirror, I see someone who survived the storms, someone who fought and continues to fight to be a better person. Determination and inner strength are my greatest achievements. These qualities have become my compass, guiding me through life, which is sometimes like a turbulent sea and at other times like a peaceful stream.

Now, standing firmly on the ground, I know that my experiences, though painful, have given me strength and courage I didn't have before. They taught me how to appreciate peace and joy in the simplest things. They made me realize that true strength lies in self-acceptance and in the ability to turn pain into power. Today, I look to the future with hope, knowing that I am strong, not just for myself but for my children, who are my greatest inspiration to be a better version of myself every day.

On my life's journey, I encountered many false people. Their presence in my life was like shadows sliding across walls in the twilight – not entirely visible, yet always there. These individuals were like weeds in the garden of my life. They grew secretly, rooting themselves in the soil of my experiences, trying to take control of my inner self. I knew I had to uproot them to make space for the true, noble plants that could bloom and grow in harmony with my soul.

Over time, I learned to recognize these toxic personalities. Their words were like sweet nectar that drew you in, but in reality, it was poison. Their promises were like empty shells that crumbled under the weight of reality. Their presence in my life was like darkness trying to obscure the light of my truth.

During this period of my life, I realized that the most important thing was to surround myself with people who were real, who had the courage to look at the world and themselves without deceit. People who could love unconditionally, who understood the value of honesty and trust. Those who weren't afraid to speak the truth, even if it was painful, became true treasures on this difficult road of life.

Each person I met along the way, both the false and the genuine, taught me something important. They helped me understand who I truly wanted to be and who I didn't. Because of this, I could continue walking my path – stronger, wiser, and more aware of what truly matters to me. And most importantly, I was no longer walking this path alone. With my wonderful M. by my side, I could go anywhere I dreamed of. Today, I know this for sure, though at the beginning of our relationship, I was only starting to feel it. Back then, I didn't fully understand it.

Throughout my life, I had to fight for everything! It was like walking across an endless desert, where every step was a struggle against the burning sand, the scorching sun, and an eternally dry throat. No one ever gave me anything; every success, every bit of space to breathe was the result of my determination, my strength. I had to break through the rocks of adversity to extract the drops of possibility.

Today, looking at my life, I see how beautiful the home is that I've built from all those hard-earned stones. A home filled with light, love, and warmth. A home where the laughter of my children resonates like the most beautiful melody. A wonderful family that is like a safe haven in the stormy sea of life! Now I have this. Healthy, wonderful children who are like rays of sunshine illuminating every darkness. An amazing partner who is like a lighthouse guiding me through the darkest night. My sister – my soulmate, and good people around me. I have everything one could wish for. Finally!

Each element of my life is like a precious stone in the mosaic of happiness. Sometimes, looking back, I'm amazed at how I managed to create such harmony out of chaos and pain. How, from the torn fragments of the past, I was able to arrange such a beautiful whole! It wasn't an easy journey. There were moments when I felt my strength slipping away and waves of doubt trying to drown me. But I always reminded myself in time of my inner strength, of that unbreakable will to survive, which was my greatest ally.

My life, although sometimes resembling a turbulent journey through dark forests and dangerous paths, consistently led me to the place I now stand. Today, I know without a doubt that this is exactly how it was meant to be.

I've arrived at a place where I can enjoy every breath, every smile of my loved ones, every warm touch. Now, when I look at my life, I see not only the struggle and pain but also the beauty and love that have become my reward at the end of this difficult road.

I have arrived... I have reached my Heaven...

FROM ME

My whole life, I carried resentment, anger, rage, and pain. And now? Now, I forgive all of you. I forgive everyone who has ever hurt me.

There is no more anger or hatred within me. Writing this book, I've come to understand one very important thing: when walking through hell, it's essential not to become the devil yourself.

On the tears of the past, I have built who I am today…
On the wings of the present, I soar towards a better
tomorrow...

The quoted excerpts are from the book *The Divine Comedy* by Dante Alighieri, translated by Julian Korsak, 1860, Poland, published by S. Orgelbrand Bookseller and Typographer.

9 788397 392601